Seeing Like a Smuggler

'This conceptually vivid book refreshes our vision. We can see how vulnerable people combine, innovate, and revise what they do to make geography from below. There, at the margins, is life in rehearsal.'
—Ruth Wilson Gilmore, author of *Abolition Geography: Essays Towards Liberation*

'At last, an urgent and brilliant collection of histories "from below", about the people and goods transgressing the borders of global capitalism. Thanks to Shahram Khosravi, Mahmoud Keshavarz, and their fellow contributors, the world economy will never look quite the same.'
—Marcus Rediker, co-author of *The Many-Headed Hydra: The Hidden History of the Revolutionary Atlantic*

'*Seeing Like a Smuggler* inverts *Seeing Like a State* and for good reasons. With views and presentations from various sites and angles, it tells amazing stories from the ground of how people negotiate with borders, states, local officials and carry on lives in the midst of everyday border violence and the precarity of borderland existence. There is no morality play here. Migration, clandestine existence, and illegal activities like smuggling – these are not acts to be found in some independent criminal universe. These are part of society's subterranean life. Mahmoud Keshavarz and Shahram Khosravi have done a remarkable job of interrogating the received sense of state, law and order, protection, and morals.'
—Ranabir Samaddar, Distinguished Chair in Migration and Forced Migration Studies, Mahanirban Calcutta Research Group

T0307981

Anthropology, Culture and Society

Series Editors:
Jamie Cross, University of Edinburgh,
Holly High, Deakin University
and
Joshua O. Reno, Binghamton University

Recent titles:

Seeing Like a Smuggler

Borders from Below

Edited by
Mahmoud Keshavarz and Shahram Khosravi

PLUTO  PRESS

First published 2022 by Pluto Press
New Wing, Somerset House, Strand, London WC2R 1LA

www.plutobooks.com

British Library Cataloguing in Publication Data
A catalogue record for this book is available from the British Library

ISBN   978 0 7453 4160 6   Hardback
ISBN   978 0 7453 4161 3   Paperback
ISBN   978 1 786808 37 0   PDF
ISBN   978 1 786808 38 7   EPUB

This book is printed on paper suitable for recycling and made from fully
managed and sustained forest sources. Logging, pulping and manufacturing
processes are expected to conform to the environmental standards of the
country of origin.

Typeset by Stanford DTP Services, Northampton, England

Simultaneously printed in the United Kingdom and United States of America

Contents

Series Preface

As people around the world confront the inequality and injustice of new forms of oppression, as well as the impacts of human life on planetary ecosystems, this book series asks what anthropology can contribute to the crises and challenges of the twenty-first century. Our goal is to establish a distinctive anthropological contribution to debates and discussions that are often dominated by politics and economics. What is sorely lacking, and what anthropological methods can provide, is an appreciation of the human condition.

We publish works that draw inspiration from traditions of ethnographic research and anthropological analysis to address power and social change while keeping the struggles and stories of human beings' centre stage. We welcome books that set out to make anthropology matter, bringing classic anthropological concerns with exchange, difference, belief, kinship and the material world into engagement with contemporary environmental change, capitalist economy and forms of inequality. We publish work from all traditions of anthropology, combining theoretical debate with empirical evidence to demonstrate the unique contribution anthropology can make to understanding the contemporary world.

Jamie Cross, Holly High and Joshua O. Reno

Acknowledgements

Borderland communities, border transgressors and smugglers, those who have been forced to live and work with borders and bordering have taught us a great deal on how to think about borders and nation-states differently. This book was mainly initiated based on the lessons learnt from them and we are grateful for that.

We are deeply indebted to the contributors for sharing their work in this book. This collection of essays stems from the symposium 'Seeing Like a Smuggler: Ethnographic, Ethical and Material Perspectives' held at Uppsala University in October 2018 and financed by the Engaging Vulnerability Research Program and CEMFOR (the Center for Multidisciplinary Research on Racism) both at Uppsala University.

We are also grateful to Jamie Cross, one of the editors of the Anthropology, Culture and Society book series, and David Castle, editorial director at Pluto Press, who helped us as we made the final push to get this book done.

The chapter 'The Border Merchant' by Aliyeh Ataei is translated by Salar Abdoh and was first published in the online magazine *Guernica* in November 2019.

About the Cover Image

Border Door

Site Specific Installation/Intervention Performance

Wooden door painted gold, nails, keys, doorknobs, blue wooden frame and hinges.

Free standing workable door installed on the Mexico/U.S.A. border ¼ mile east of the Rodriguez International Airport. The performance extended to the neighborhood where the artist grew up in Tijuana. Where he handed out over 250 keys inviting the residents of La Colonia Roma and Altamira to use his Border Door. Border Door destroyed two days later by unknown vandals.

Artist: Richard A. Lou
Photo Credit: James Elliott 1988

'Lou has situated his work, both physically and discursively, within the border region because he possesses a heightened consciousness about the violent and contested history of this charged site. The work questions the very existence of this border and the extreme inequities that it has ushered in, yet it underscores and celebrates the cultural hybridity that emanates from it. The site-specific and mixed media installation reclaims the hyper-colonized space of the border on behalf of its marginalized citizens: the undocumented immigrants who cross it every day, the residents of the nearby colonias and the impoverished neighborhoods, the subordinated laborers of the maquiladoras (assembly factory) industry, and the like.'

Guisela Latorre 'Public Interventions and Social Disruptions' in Scott L. Baugh and Victor A. Sorrell (eds) Born of Resistance: Cara a Cara Encounters with Chicana/o Visual Culture (The University of Arizona Press, 2015).

Introduction:
To See Like a Smuggler

Mahmoud Keshavarz and Shahram Khosravi

On 22 February 2021 a lethal incident along the Iran-Pakistan border became huge news in the region. In the Askan area, near the city of Saravan, Iranian border guards opened fire on a group of Baluch gasoline carriers (*sokhtbar*) resulting in several deaths. The incident took place in the Sistan-Baluch-istan Province in south-eastern Iran, the poorest province of the country and home of the Baluch ethnic group. The higher price of gasoline over the previous two decades in Pakistan has opened a tiny window of income for local people. Although cross-border trade has a long history in the region, it tends to increase during crises, such as the Covid-19 pandemic that resulted in soaring unemployment. In the official language this cross-border trade has been presented as criminal act of smuggling, while local people call it *sokhtbari* (lit. 'fuel carrying'). The terminology poses an epistemological problem with ethical and political implications. While *sokhtbari* demands urgent supportive policy responses and accountability from the state, *smuggling* grants the state authority to police and punish. Local unrest followed the incident. People stormed the police station and other official buildings. Soon the protests spread to other cities in the province, growing into widespread ethnic unrest against government authorities. Unofficial sources report dozens of deaths and hundreds of arrests.

Like the cases discussed throughout this book, *sokhtbari* is principally about protracted poverty and social marginalisation. Throughout the period of unrest, a slogan was circulated in the social media: 'If we are going to die foaming at the mouth [from hunger], then it is better to die while bleeding at the mouth.' Smuggling makes the precarity of the borderlands visible. As a response to the condition of precariousness, smuggling can no longer be seen merely as a criminal act, as the state authorities would claim, but becomes part of social protest against different oppressions: economic inequality, differential access to welfare and nation-state hegemony over borders and borderland communities. These events show how smuggling merges into a political movement, which demands social justice. It intertwines with class struggle, ethnic revolts, and anti- (domestic) colonial rule. Acts of smuggling such as *sokhtbari* are well anchored in the local social structures, not only economically but also socially and culturally. The so-called smugglers are admired and regarded as local heroes who jeopardise their lives to support their families. There are countless popular ballads praising them. This makes smuggling 'social', meaning it is historically and socially articulated.

In line with Eric Hobsbawm's concept of 'social banditry',[1] we approach smuggling as a widespread social phenomenon, which takes place along many borders across the globe. Either praised as local heroes or pursued as criminals, the position of smugglers in the sociality of borderlands cannot be overlooked. Similarly, smuggling – as a situated activity that is enmeshed within the historical and geopolitical conditions of borderlands – cannot merely be approached through the detached, simplified and centralised gaze of the state.

To avoid the state-centric approach, this book recognises the so-called smuggling activities in the context of their histories and localities, and from the subject position of those who find smuggling necessary in order to survive. To see like a smuggler is a tactical move that involves reading the mobility of people and things in ways that unsettle state-centric perspectives.

The state perspective reduces all practices outside the law to a single and simplified criminal action, such as smuggling or banditry. Such a perspective is based on a series of dichotomies such as law/outlaw, legal/illegal, or trade/smuggling. It externalises social forces, processes, and actors that do not fit in the state narrative. For example historical accounts show banditry as a form of anti-colonial resistance in Algeria.[2] Banditry has also played a central role in the emergence of nationalist myths of the modern Greek state during the independence struggles.[3] In some cases outlaws have turned into official local governors, such as in twentieth-century Iran and nineteenth-century Morocco.[4] In the case of piracy, Jatin Dua argues that rather than being an anachronism or aberration, modern maritime piracy in the Indian ocean, is deeply entangled with global capitalism and trade.[5] Aligned with these works, *Seeing Like a Smuggler* puts forward the argument that outlaw practices, banditry, maritime piracy, and smuggling are immanent features of modern nation-states.

From below

Seeing Like a Smuggler follows a tradition of history-from-below approaches. This book applies the ideas of C.L.R. James, E.P. Thompson, Peter Linebaugh and Marcus Rediker, and Hay et al., to the issues of borders and border transgression.[6] This book is built on a from-below approach for several reasons. First, it counters the regimes of visibility imposed by the state. Put in other words, it addresses *how* subjects, subjectivities, and activities have been made visible from above. Much academic and policy research has studied and analysed smuggling from a state-centric perspective, as an economic, social or political 'problem' that needs to be diagnosed and solved. Smuggling is posed as a problem because it undermines the state's authority over the mobility of people and commodities, and its assumed position as the sole organiser of social, economic and political life. By approaching the heterogeneous, complex, messy, decentralised, ad-hoc set of activities called smuggling, we aim to offer the perspective of those who are labelled – and criminalised – as smugglers. By refusing to follow the state's legal definition of smuggling, 'seeing like a smuggler' repositions these complex activities within a wider context of increasing social, political and economic bordering practices across the world.

Second, in contrast to the seeing-from-above approach which is based on externalising irregularity, this book aims to identify contradictions and inconsistencies within the system of the nation-state. In conditions of sustained crisis, through which improvised modes of living emerge according to the local, geographical and material conditions, things no longer exist without parallel. Every piece of legislation is accompanied by techniques to circumvent it, which ultimately neutralises and inverts it.[7] This parallel, subversive system comes with its own rules, rituals, ethics and protocols which, as Stuart Hall argues using his concept of decoding, is 'a mixture of adaptive and oppositional elements'.[8] In his book *Seeing Like a State*, James Scott argues that the state needs to see individuals in order to control them. It uses identification, registration and promotion of the language of law in order to tax people and maintain a welfare state, and create legibility in relation to people.[9] Visibility and legibility go hand in hand in order for the state to operate. Scott shows that movement and mobility had to be contained, regulated and constrained because they posed a challenge to the visibility-legibility framework and the authority of state governance. He asks us to follow that way of seeing in order to analyse the monolithic nature of the state but also to develop sensitivities to see the everyday resistance to that hegemony.

Scott, however, neglects to address the fact that the state is not necessarily the origin of phenomena such as borders, citizenship and taxation. In other words, the state as one homogeneous entity does not impose control but is itself a product of contestations around the control over mobile bodies, things, practices and ideas. In this sense, smuggling is both a consequence, and constitutive, of borders and bordering practices. By disclosing the contradictions within the nation-state system that are concealed by the official narratives there is – in Walter Benjamin's terms – a potential to opening up history[10] to include narratives of the illegalised, the outcast, the undocumented, the bandit, and the smuggler.

Third, to see like a smuggler is a methodological standpoint, taken in order to avoid the risks of reproducing state-centric concepts of smuggling. Some scholars have already shown that the use of terms such as 'smuggler' can reproduce criminalisation, reinforced by states through using specific language in research and policy documents; such scholars have suggested the use of other terms, such as broker and facilitator. The change of terminology in order to decriminalise or criminalise is evident on the part of state organisations too. For instance, in one of its latest attempts to criminalise the facilitation of the movement of travellers without the 'right' papers, the European Union has moved towards the use of other terms, such as trafficking, which mobilises harsher legal and political actions.

As each chapter of this book shows, there are many different forms of individual and collective knowledge, shared and negotiated between many actors during the process of a journey or the movement of goods, which depend on gender, class, ethnic background, and age, as well as the context of time and place. It is these collective and heterogeneous forms of sharing knowledge that explain why many travellers without the 'right' papers often do not see themselves as 'smuggled', with its implication of victimhood, but 'as actively staking claims to reciprocity and obligation from people they knew to access passage'.[11] This is why different communities in this book use different words to refer to those who facilitate the illicit movement of things and people, such as intermediator, handler, friend, *rahbalad* (guide), *dalal* (middleman), *lekami* (picker) and *semsar* (broker).

Nonetheless in this book we have taken the approach of reclaiming the word 'smuggler', and showing its complex positions in order to counter its dominant usage. By deploying and developing 'seeing like a smuggler', this book provides a collection of chapters on everyday informal activities around borders as forms of tactical livelihood or 'insurgent citizenship', where such activities operate through partially licit and illicit practices simultaneously.[12]

Coloniality

Many chapters in this book point to the complex relationships between states and smuggling in today's world. However the history of smuggling goes beyond the formation of the late modern states. This relationship is a continuation of smuggling's long-standing uneasy and contingent position within the colonial formation of the world. Colonial powers were themselves involved in smuggling (see Nichola Khan, Chapter 2), for example British merchants smuggled opium into China from Hong Kong in the nineteenth century. In other cases, there have been contests between local merchants who developed smuggling enterprises in response to the strict mercantilist policies of England in the seventeenth century.[13]

Conflict between the Crown and the colonists in New England over the monopoly of trade and customs escalated in the eighteenth century. Illicit traders and smugglers were punished as pirates under the English law. The British anti-smuggling policies helped spark the spirit of revolt. Conflicts over smuggling played a crucial role in the development of the American Revolution, to the degree that Peter Andreas dubbed the United States as a Smuggler Nation.[14] During this period smuggling came to be praised as well as condemned by liberal ideologies. For example, Adam Smith advocated for smugglers as 'excellent citizens' who, rather than violating natural justice, instead violate the 'unnatural' legislation that restricted free trade.[15] At the same time, the prohibition of importation of slaves in 1807 in the United States, and the Slavery Abolition Act in 1883, led to increasing border surveillance in order to fight slave smuggling. These smuggling operations were organised by capital owners, and usually detached from local communities and class struggles. Although some were against the colonial domination of states, they were not socially subversive, as they did not aim to challenge the class structure of the time but rather exploit it and secure profits.

The chapters in this book depict different stories. Many of the smuggling practices discussed here belong to the tradition of proletarian struggle against the oppressive economic order. What's more, smuggling as a social practice often evolves from the struggle between the central state and the people of the borderland. Smuggling is practised spatially 'remotely' from the centre and often by ethnic minorities who disregard the interference of central authority (see Amin Parsa, Chapter 5).

If we examine border transgression from below, then smuggling appears to be a response to the political and social precariousness people in the borderlands are exposed to through the internal colonisation carried out by the central power. In this context, local communities do not associate smuggling with crime but rather see it as necessary for survival. Smugglers remain part of the local society and their activities contribute to resilience of the communities, whether through financial smuggling in order to support local resistance against the central power, or through facilitating the movement of the persecuted and oppressed (see Aliyah Ataei, Chapter 3).

In the late Ottoman Empire, the Régie, a French company had a monopoly over tobacco production. Peasant cultivators started successful smuggling operations to resist both the French company's monopoly and governmental taxes.[16] Similarly, smugglers were key players in the formation of the seventeenth- and eighteenth-century movement of Jacobitism in England.[17] Other examples include Buddhist monks who facilitate the escape to India of Tibetans from China's colonial oppression,[18] the smugglers of the Gaza tunnels, and a former Kurdish freedom fighter who became a professional migration facilitator in the 1980s, who sees his work as an anti-colonial project:

> The rich world steal from the poor world. When people have tried to make a change in politics and change the ruling regimes, the superpowers have intervened and stopped the democratic movements.... This is our situation. As long as there are plunderers the plundered ones [i.e. refugees and migrants] will want to come and see where their wealth has ended up. And I help them.[19]

If we understand the current border regime to be a colonial infrastructure, that guarantees the freedom of movement of certain people and things in a way that maintains and increases the hegemony, wealth and security of former colonial powers, then these local as well as transnational acts of border transgression can be thought of as ways to challenge the current coloniality of the world order – as long as these transgressions work in the support of the survival and livelihood of the oppressed.

Visuality and materiality

To see like a smuggler also provides insights into the materialities and visuality of smuggling practices. While the dominant focus in smuggling studies tends to be on policy and discourse analysis, or on providing ethnographies of people who use smugglers' services (such as in the studies of human smuggling), this collection will provide a lens to examine the vehicles, infrastructures and objects involved in the processes of smuggling, not simply as supporting instruments but as productive agents which determine the scale, speed and forms that smuggling practices take. Kennedy Chikerema (Chapter 8) specifically focuses on this aspect of smuggling. Moreover, as we read in the chapters of Javier Guerrero-C (Chapter 6), Debdatta Chowdhury (Chapter 7) and Craig Martin (Chapter 9), the materialities of smuggled commodities determine the form of the smuggling. Sometimes, materiality can manifest alternatives to state authority. As Rebecca B. Galemba (Chapter 4) explains in her study of the Mexico-Guatemala border, by placing a *cadena* (chain) somewhere other than the legal location of the border, a new border is declared, giving rise to new rituals of taxation organised by the surrounding communities. This in turn generates an identification effect by uniting the communities that depend on this 'new' border, regardless of their nationality.

Smuggling both reveals and appropriates the materialities involved in states' bordering practices. In this sense, smuggling goes beyond the representative or utilitarian capacities of materialities that are so crucial in state policy, such as the use of imagery and technologies in bordering. Smuggling instead realises the potential of materials for creating numerous new possibilities of reassembling,[20] for example by turning everyday objects that may pass through borders unnoticed into containers of illicit things, or making unauthorised bodies look like normative, legalised bodies on the move.

This is also a matter of visuality and sensory awareness. Smuggling often works through the manipulation and reconfiguration of the senses of what is an accepted, legal and authorised moving person or object. However, it is the border that establishes this in the first place. Borders govern the senses as a way to regulate social processes and relationships. Borders do not have any essential qualities, but rather are shape-shifting and create fluid relations that can be reassembled to produce different perceptions for different bodies. In this sense borders work more like magic than protocols.[21] Magic changes our perception of the real: something turns into something else. Like magic, borders engender new perceptions. Borders turn neighbours into enemies. A short distance suddenly becomes farther. The skin of people on the other side becomes darker. Nomadic tribes become illegal border crossers. Cousins from the next village become illegal transgressors. Traders become smugglers. The value of commodities increases and decreases at the moment they cross the border. In this sense, borders try to control what a spectator sees. If borders function like magic, then smuggling works as counter-magic. Smugglers, for instance, work by changing the perceptions of border guards: they make an Iranian be seen as Greek; an Afghan as Korean. Smuggling consists of a range of techniques, from creating and forging specific papers, passports and supporting documents, to using and repurposing vehicles, and infrastructures of travel. Smugglers teach us that the magic of the border is actually a series of techniques and tactics that can be countered through the same means. To see like a smuggler is to shift the attention from the spectacle of walls and fences to the details, techniques, and operations of borders. As a counter-magic, smuggling both affirms the normative imagery of border crossing by identifying what is seen as licit and legal and adhering to it, but also unsettles assumptions about authenticity linked to legalised bodies and commodities. Smuggling shows that authenticity is only meaningful in relation to a specific border, body, or commodity, time and geography, and is always subjective and contingent on different materialities.

The mainstream regime of visibility and media aims to depict smuggling through externalising it. For instance, this is done by presenting the images of masculine – and in many cases racialised – bodies of smugglers, confiscated goods and the vehicles used to smuggle, as a threat to ethical and aesthetic norms, as well as to the well-being of the society. Externalisation – that is, hiding contradictions and gaps – also takes place in the form of regular public shows in many countries, in which confiscated smuggled goods are destroyed. The shows are often spectacular. Goods are burnt or smashed by military vehicles. The more expensive the goods that are destroyed (such as luxury cars), the more spectacular the shows become. The public show is a 'message', targeting consumers more than the smugglers. These rituals visualise smuggled goods as external phenomena penetrating the social body, and therefore in need of annihilation.

This externalisation however is not new. In the nineteenth century, smuggling was a recurrent theme in European literature and visual art. From the opera *Carmen* by Georges Bizet from 1875, to G.P.R. James's *The Smuggler: A Tale* from 1845 and also in the painting of *The Smugglers Return*, by Philippe Jacques de Loutherbourg from 1801. The smuggler appears as lonely figure who heroically stands up against the rulers. In G.P.R. James's novel smugglers are presented as 'men who break boldly through an unjust and barbarous system, which denies to our land the goods of another, and who … insist at the peril of their lives, on man's inherent right to trade with his neighbors'.[22] The figure of smuggler appeared as much in the literature of political economy as in tales and fictions. Perhaps it has its explanation in the Janus face of smugglers, who either were condemned as anti-social profit seekers and a threat to the national interest, or as heroes who ensured the survival of so-called free trade.

Today the defenders of 'free trade' are large-scale corporations which are often closely related to states. Accordingly, smugglers are included and excluded simultaneously, but always represented as external actors who unsettle, blur, transgress and breach the nationalised boundary between legal and illegal commodities and residents. Smuggling puts a mirror in front of this externalisation by engaging with bordering practices materially, visually, socially and economically. In doing so, as many chapters in this book demonstrate, smuggling emerges from the internal contradictions and gaps within the nation-state system and, as such, provides other imageries and imaginations about the position of smuggling and its relation to the everyday life of many communities and individuals.

Ethics

This collection focuses on smuggling as a productive endeavour, which is not merely an economic service but demands that we engage with the question of borders ethically and politically. One way in which smuggling is externalised is through overexposing smugglers' violence, while simultaneously hiding state violence towards the people in need of the services of smugglers, such as migrants or borderland communities. In contrast to the from-above practice of externalisation, this collection shows that the ethics of smuggling reside precisely in its relationship to individuals and communities as a form of negotiable protection from below when states fail to provide, or ignore or actively restrict the rights of certain groups to mobility, wealth and safety.

As Dawood Amiri – who has been convicted for human smuggling, and at the time of writing in May 2021, is currently serving his seven-year prison sentence in Indonesia – puts it:

> the people-smugglers were the real saviours of [the] asylum-seekers. We offered them survival and peace of mind for only $4,000 … on the other hand, if they were patient and prepared to work through the long-term legal processes of the UNHCR and IOM [International Organization for Migration] there was a chance of peace and survival for about 5 per cent of the people of their fourth generation – after 200 years. In the minds and hearts of the asylum-seekers, this slim chance never looked fair against the prospect of riding boats to Australia.[23]

Many borderland communities involved in informal cross-border trade have argued for the 'right to smuggling' to survive, as shown in Galemba's and Guerrero-C's chapters. In such a context, smuggling can be seen as an ethical endeavour. For example, Tekalign Ayalew Mengiste in this volume shows succinctly how the existing legal channels for the domestic workers programme between Ethiopia and Saudi Arabia take a long time, and are costly and selective, as only Muslim women are desired by employers. Moreover, these legal channels are controlled by the state and legal private agents, which leaves no space for negotiating the choice of employer or wage rates. In contrast, smuggling can provide workers with a higher degree of negotiating power. While the negotiations which result from smuggling can be temporary, fragile and vulnerable, nonetheless there is some level of control given to those who choose smuggling services. As Harvey (Chapter 10) argues, while 'seeing like a smuggler' identifies something affirmative in the strategies of circumvention and improvisation, and a reimagined kind of ethics through its creation of loosely bound communities, smuggling simultaneously teaches us about the partiality of any ethical framework.

Hobsbawm's thesis of social banditry, which has inspired this book to some degree, has been criticised as being Eurocentric, because of the absence of non-European concepts, ethics, techniques, and histories. We should therefore pay attention to how experiences of smuggling are formed by relations, religions, and moral economies other than Western ones. Studies of smuggling in the Middle East and Africa show, for instance, that local moral perceptions and religious conceptions, and not criminal law, regulate smuggling practices. Local communities engaged in smuggling in

North Africa make a distinction between licit and illicit goods based on the Islamic concepts of *'halal'* (permitted) and *'haram'* (forbidden).[24] By approaching smuggling through ethical frameworks other than Western ones, we may overcome some of the ethical and political challenges posed by the from-below position that this book takes.

Engaging with smuggling from below has its own methodological challenges too. Studying smuggling usually means encounters with archival materials which are produced through the lens of the states. Seeing smuggling from above is built upon judicial records or police reports. Similarly archives, and a large part of the available knowledge about smuggling are mainly produced by the official authorities or the organisations which represent the nation-state system. Therefore, in studies of smuggling discrepancies between *theoretical* claims of a critical approach on the one hand, and *empirical* data which are uncritically collected from official sources on the other, become difficult to avoid. Faced with such contested knowledge, which is tied to the state violence, the question is how should we study smuggling? Repositioning in order to look from below aims to build up new relations to knowledges and concepts that are not otherwise articulated in the processes of knowledge production. It is an attempt to liberate the field of smuggling studies from its state-centric structure.[25]

However, the question of what specific epistemologies are revealed and ignored by 'seeing like a smuggler' is indirectly addressed but remains unanswered in this book. How much should one reveal about the activities that sustain the lives of precarious and vulnerable populations, whether on the move or residing at borderlands? How much of the knowledge about activities such as smuggling should be kept within the communities who need these strategies in a time of harsher border controls, and how much can we share in order to decriminalise and politicise smuggling practices? While these are complex questions, we have tried to show sensitivity towards smugglers' fundamental right to opacity, that is, not *everything* should be seen, explained, understood and documented.

Furthermore, to see like a smuggler runs the risk of romanticising a practice that can involve exploitation, violence and coercion. Hobsbawm has been criticised for having a romanticised image of bandits, for instance by feminist scholars who believe that it reproduces a romantic view of masculine violence.[26] To write about smuggling is challenging, politically as well as ethically. How can we see like a smuggler and at the same time write in an academically honest and ethically responsible way about smuggling? How should we write about the gendered and racialised oppression which is embedded in some forms of smuggling, without reproducing the dominant, criminalised image of smugglers? How much do we risk romanticising the survival strategies specific to a location, time and community as generalised political acts?

The structure

The chapters of this book are selected and edited so as to present our understanding of smuggling as open-ended. Following traces of fragmented archives and histories, this volume is an attempt to show connection between bodies, geographies, materialities, images and economies. Different chapters provide nuanced accounts of the nuts and bolts of smuggling practices and together they offer a constellation of how fragmented parts intersect and how smuggling is constituted. We will see through the texts and images that smuggling is by no means exclusively a liberating practice and may produce new, or reproduce existing, structures of patriarchy, race and class. The chapters present a wide spectrum in terms of content, geography, style and empirical material, and offer dialogues across many fields including anthropology, geography, design studies, science and technology studies, law, and literary theory.

By tracing the illegalised movement of people and goods across borders, this volume shows smuggling as an immanent contradiction within the totality of social relations generated by the nation-state system. In this volume, we bring together a range of approaches, from personal reflections and ethnographies to historical accounts and visual representations of smuggling. The chapters span the globe from Colombia to Ethiopia, from Singapore to Guatemala, from Afghanistan to Zimbabwe, from Kurdistan to Bangladesh. The chapters collected in this book contribute to creating a more multifaceted picture of smuggling. They also add novel theoretical and empirical approaches to the field of border studies and studies of smuggling. The empirically based chapters create a space for discussing smuggling in relation to other social and political processes. They raise questions on ethics, materialities, histories, colonial power relations, and visual representations of the practice of smuggling, and together offer a distinct contribution to the public debate, as well as to the body of knowledge about borders and smuggling.

Tekalign Ayalew Mengiste (Chapter 1) offers a thick description of the emerging human smuggling route and migration facilitation between Ethiopia and Saudi Arabia based on long-term ethnographic fieldwork.

Tekalign takes the reader on a journey along the route from Wollo in northern Ethiopia through Djibouti and across the Red Sea to Saudi Arabia. During the journey Tekalign introduces various smuggling practices which involve particular strategies, plans and techniques. He shows how smuggling is a socially embedded collective practice and functions through local community supports and collaborative and trust relations between migrants and smugglers. The author concludes that state policies and the smuggling structures that mediate migration are complementary and co-constitutive processes.

Nichola Khan (Chapter 2) tells us the story of gold smuggling to India and South Asia and its role in Singapore's economic expansion and urban growth. Mainly based on archival research, the chapter shows state complicity in a number of illegal trades, and how colonial infrastructures facilitated the lucrative gold smuggling. Khan depicts social networks, trading routes, and international monetary politics that enabled high mobility of licit and illicit money to traverse from Singapore through Asia to Europe in particular periods. Various actors, such as dealers, brokers, money-changers and trafficking agents were involved in processes which have shaped Singapore's urban fabric and the city's variegated relation to other cities along trafficking routes. Khan points out the significance of pre-existing land and maritime routes in the trading movements of gold across Asia to illustrate state complicity in illicit trades, and the role of smuggling in the process of state formation.

Aliyeh Ataei (Chapter 3) takes the reader to the border between Iran and Afghanistan. Calling herself 'the writer of borders', Ataei usually writes fiction. Her piece is based on her observation of unauthorised border crossing with the help of a so-called 'human smuggler', called Mohammad Osman Yusefzai. The narrative, which is structured around her conversation with him, presents the complexity of migrant facilitators, who are reduced to a single undifferentiated criminal figure by the law. Ataei illustrates a landscape where border subjectivities are engendered. Mohammad Osman Yusefzai, in Ataei´s words, is a merchant who sells the border.

In Chapter 4, Rebecca Galemba examines the case of small-scale smugglers along the Mexico-Guatemala border to demonstrate the ways in which illegal practices discursively, materially and subjectively reproduce the state as structural effect. She shows how residents discursively understand the border and their relation to state authority, and how smugglers certify smuggled goods in collusion with state officials. Based on the rich ethnographic materials she has gathered, Galemba argues that smuggling practices do not simply subvert state control but, rather, can produce state effects of legibility, isolation, spatialisation and identification from subaltern locations.

A similar argument is presented by Amin Parsa (Chapter 5). Analysing the case of *Kolbari*, which is a form of smuggling of everyday goods carried on by marginalised Kurds across the border between Iran and Iraq, Parsa argues that smuggling has become a way for the Iranian state to circumvent international sanctions while punishing the smugglers at will when necessary. A scholar in critical legal studies, Parsa shows how borders become a lawless space where *kolbars* can be humiliated, discriminated against and easily killed while such spaces are heavily monitored through national law that is justified by international regulations on smuggling. The chapter is accompanied by a map made by Lucie Bacon. The map depicts *kolbari* practices in the maze of relations of borders while questioning the conventional maps by challenging the nationalist representation of regional borders and borderland communities.

Chapter 6, by Javier Guerrero-C, takes us to La Guajira in northern Colombia where illicit and illegal activities play a central role in the lives of the people. There is a long history of smuggling in the region, from alcohol and cigarettes to marijuana and, later on, cocaine. Drawing from ethnographic data and archival documents, this chapter provides an overview of the long history of technology and infrastructures of smuggling in La Guajira. The same infrastructure, that is, the knowledge of traditional maritime and land routes, has been mobilised for transportation of drugs and contraband. Guerrero-C argues that the illegal flows have been possible thanks to a continuous readjustment of old and new techniques, materialities and practices.

Similar to Galemba and Parsa, Debdatta Chowdhury (Chapter 7) argues that smugglers make the unofficial a part of the official. Geographically, the chapter is about the border between India and Bangladesh, where a long history of trade networks across the large territory of Bengal has been disrupted by colonial interventions and the newly formed border between India and East Pakistan (later Bangladesh) after the Partition of 1947. Based on studies of these cross-border practices in the India-Bangladesh borderland, this chapter provides ways to understand how 'seeing like a state' is just one side of it. It shows how understanding smuggling practices in these areas gives a sense of how the *past* affects, evolves into, and changes form to become what we understand as the *present*.

Chapter 8, a visual essay by Kennedy Chikerema, focuses on infrastructures of smuggling across South Africa and Zimbabwe. Long-distance buses in different bus stations in Johannesburg are loaded with luggage and goods such as furniture and boxes of cooking oil to be transported to Harare or Bulawayo in Zimbabwe. Chikerema visualises the smuggling routes and logistics in the form of an architecture that is patchy and bottom-up, and at the same time entangled with formal and informal economies, laws and practices generated by urban development, unstable political and economic situations, and bordering.

Craig Martin's contribution (Chapter 9) focuses on the tactics used by smugglers to conceal illegal narcotics in the form of legally sanctioned consumer goods that demonstrates a form of illicit design thinking and innovation. He explores illicit and non-expert designer approaches to 'problem solving' in the context of drug smuggling. To reflect the globalised nature of drug trafficking, the chapter employs a range of case studies primarily from the USA, but also from Europe, Australasia and Asia. These include: the adaptation of consumer goods, both as tourist luggage and in larger-scale freight shipments; the disguise of drugs as other perceptibly normal legal artefacts; and the use of hidden compartments in imported automobiles. Building on these examples, a primary focus of the chapter is the micro-geographies of these practices – this is the awareness of the illicit potential of everyday consumer goods to smugglers as 'objectiles'.

In Chapter 10, Simon Harvey argues that smuggling is either presented to us as something entirely hidden or else it is overly evident, *transparent*, documented by the police or news agencies. He wonders if these simplistic images of a diverse and changeable circulation like smuggling really offer us a sensible approach to the subject. Harvey explores the shortcomings of transparency as a socio-political ideal in relation to smuggling and brings in *partial visibilities* of smuggling, for instance its practice in plain sight that nevertheless withholds something. Harvey asks us to shift our perspective to what we might learn from smuggling with its only *partial offerings* when demands are made upon it, and on us, to yield all to scrutiny.

The volume concludes with an afterword by Nandita Sharma, who asserts that anti-smuggling discourses and policies are techniques to reproduce racial and class hierarchies. Nation-state borders are not only racial borders but also borders against the world's poor. She sees the local and practical knowledge of smugglers as an alternative route to resist global injustices. Sharma recognises the potentialities of the practical skills and knowledge of – and created by – smuggling, and looks ahead towards fundamental social changes through the rejection of the state and class rule. In her powerful afterword, she suggests re-politicising, and thereby making visible, what nation-states' anti-smuggling efforts are meant to conceal: that smuggling is a structural feature of the international order and not an 'external threat'. As Sharma puts it, what 'we should be opposing is not smuggling per se but the criminalisation of mobility and the commodification of life'.

By refusing the state-centric approach, which tends to read smuggling in terms of lack (of law and order), defects (irregularities), and as anomaly (through externalisation), *Seeing Like a Smuggler* takes a different position and asks the reader to see smuggling practices in wider historical, social and cultural contexts. Rather than placing smuggling outside nation-state rationality, *Seeing Like a Smuggler* puts smuggling practices in a dialectical relation with the national order of things. Along with the contributors, we invite you to see like a smuggler.

Notes

1. Eric Hobsbawm, *Bandits* (London: Weidenfeld and Nicolson, 2000 [1969]).
2. Antonin Plarier, 'Rural banditry in Colonial Algeria', in Stephanie Cronin (ed.) *Crime, Poverty and Survival in the Middle East and North Africa: The 'Dangerous Classes' since 1800* (London: I.B. Tauris, 2020), pp. 105–16.
3. Sappho Xenakis, 'Trouble with the outlaws: Bandits, the state, and politcal legitimacy in Greece over the longue durée', *Journal of Historical Sociology* 34(3), 2021, pp. 504–16.
4. Stephanie Cronin, 'Noble robbers, avengers and entrepreneurs', in Stephanie Cronin (ed.) *Crime, Poverty and Survival in the Middle East and North Africa: The 'Dangerous Classes' since 1800* (London: I.B. Tauris, 2020), pp. 101–2; David Hart, *Banditry in Islam: Case Studies in Morocco, Algeria and the Pakistan North West Frontier* (Wisbech: Middle East and North African Studies Press, 1987), pp. 19–26.
5. Jatin Dua, *Captured at Sea* (Oakland: University of California Press, 2019).
6. C.L.R. James, *The Black Jacobins: Toussaint L'Ouverture and the San Domingo Revolution* (London: Penguin, 2001 [1938]); E.P. Thompson, *The Making of the English Working Class* (New York: Pantheon Press, 1976); Peter Linebaugh and Marcus Rediker, *The Many-headed Hydra: Sailors, Slaves, Commoners, and the Hidden History of the Revolutionary Atlantic* (Boston, MA: Beacon Press, 2000); Douglas Hay, Peter Linebaugh, John G. Rule, E.P. Thompson and Cal Winslow (eds) *Albion's Fatal Tree: Crime and Society in Eighteenth-century England* (London: Allen Lane, 1979).

7.   Achille Mbembe and Janet Roitman, 'Figures of the subject in times of crisis', *Public Culture* 7(2), 1995, pp. 323–52.

8.   Stuart Hall, 'Encoding, decoding', in Simon During (ed.) *The Cultural Studies Reader*, 2nd edn (New York: Routledge, 1993), p. 516.

9.   James C. Scott, *Seeing Like a State: How Certain Schemes to Improve the Human Condition Have Failed* (New Haven, CT: Yale University Press, 1988).

10. See 'Theses on the philosophy of history', in Walter Benjamin, *Illuminations* (New York: Schocken Books, 1969).

11. Stephanie Maher, 'Out of West Africa: Human smuggling as a social enterprise', *Annals of the American Academy of Political and Social Science* 676(1), 2018, p. 39.

12. James Holston, *Insurgent Citizenship – Disjunctions of Democracy and Modernity in Brazil*, (Berkeley: University of California Press, 2009).

13. Amar Farooqi, *Smuggling as Subversion: Colonialism, Indian Merchants, and the Politics of Opium, 1790–1843* (Lanham, MD: Lexington Books, 2005).

14. Joshua M. Smith, *Borderland Smuggling: Patriots, Loyalists, and Illicit Trade in the Northeast 1783–1820* (Gainesville: University Press of Florida, 2006), p. 2; Peter Andreas, *Smuggler Nation: How Illicit Trade Made America* (Oxford: Oxford: University Press, 2014).

15. Smith, *Borderland Smuggling*, p. 2.

16. Cronin, 'Noble robbers, avengers and entrepreneurs', p. 95.

17. Paul Monod, 'Dangerous merchandise: Smuggling, Jacobitism, and commercial culture in southeast England, 1690–1760', *Journal of British Studies* 30(2), 1991, pp. 150–82.

18. Bodean Hedwards, 'The Buddhist people smuggler', April 2016, https://allegralaboratory.net/hedwards-the-buddhist-people-smuggler/ (accessed 26 April 2021).

19. Shahram Khosravi, *'Illegal' Traveller: An Auto-ethnography of Borders* (Basingstoke: Palgrave Macmillan, 2010).

20. Mahmoud Keshavarz, *The Design Politics of the Passport: Materiality, Immobility, and Dissent* (London: Bloomsbury, 2019).

21. Mahmoud Keshavarz and Shahram Khosravi, 'The magic of borders', *e-flux Architecture*, May 2020, https://www.e-flux.com/architecture/at-the-border/325755/the-magic-of-borders/ (accessed 26 April 2021).

22. G.P.R. James, *The Smuggler: A Tale* (Leipzig: Berhard Tauchnitz, 1845), p. 34, quoted in Ayse Celikkol, *Romances of Free Trade: British Literature, Laissez-faire, and the Global Nineteenth Century* (New York: Oxford University Press, 2011), p. 41.

23. Dawood Amiri, *Confession of a People-smuggler* (Melbourne: Scribe, 2014), p. 63.

24. Max Gallien, *Smugglers and States: Illegal Trade in the Political Settlements of North Africa*, PhD thesis, London School of Economics and Political Science, 2020, p. 146; Judith Scheele, *Smugglers and Saints of the Sahara:*

Regional Connectivity in the Twentieth Century (New York: Cambridge University Press, 2015), p. 96.

25. Saidiya Hartman's response to the dearth of information about lived experiences of abjection, exclusion, and racism in the archive of slavery has been creating spaces for imagining and speculations in order to rebuild histories of black women from fragments which still remain. See Saidiya Hartman, *Wayward Lives, Beautiful Experiments: Intimate Histories of Social Upheaval* (New York: W.W. Norton, 2019).
26. Donald Crummey (ed.) *Banditry, Rebellion and Social Protest in Africa* (London: James Currey, 1986), p. 12.

1

Smuggling as a Collective Enterprise: Ethiopian/Wollo Migration to Saudi Arabia

Tekalign Ayalew Mengiste

This chapter will focus on the emerging route of human smuggling and irregular migration facilitation between Ethiopia and Saudi Arabia. It is based on the argument that smuggling is a sociocultural practice and is founded on knowledge of the operations of states and border control activities. More specifically the chapter discusses the emerging facilitation of infrastructures that support and sustain Ethiopians' migratory mobility towards Saudi Arabia through the practice of smuggling.

Ethiopia has deep-rooted historical relations with Saudi Arabia through trade, religious pilgrimage and, following the rise of the oil economies in the 1980s, labour mobility.[1] For instance, between 2009 and 2014 nearly half a million Ethiopian labour migrants entered Gulf Cooperation Council countries – most commonly Saudi Arabia and the UAE (United Arab Emirates) – of whom more than 90 per cent were women, mainly less educated, unmarried, and Muslim.[2] Currently Saudi Arabia hosts an estimated 1 million Ethiopian migrants.[3] The majority of these migrants are thought to have used smuggling services from Wollo, a predominantly Muslim area in northern Ethiopia, in order to enter Saudi Arabia.

Despite Saudi Arabian deportations of 170,000 Ethiopian migrants between 2013 and 2015, the vast majority of deportees re-migrated to Saudi Arabia using the services of smuggling networks.[4] There is a well-established overland migrant smuggling route that links Wollo and Saudi Arabia: the route starts in northern Ethiopia and passes through the Afar region in eastern Ethiopia, it exits through Djibouti, crosses the Red Sea and proceeds to Saudi Arabia via Yemen. The route passes through towns such as Kombolcha, Gerba, Degan and Bati in Wollo then proceeds to

Djibouti via the towns of Mille, Logiya, Semera, Whalimat, Desheto and Galafi in the deserts of Afar region, and Tajora and Hayu in Djibouti.

During the 2010s, the Ethiopian government expanded control infrastructures and introduced tough regulations and policies to stem clandestine migration. This was mainly due to pressure from receiving countries. However, smuggling has increased since then and complex forms of clandestine international border crossing have emerged. Smugglers provide their services to migrants by generating and using certain knowledge about borders, states and labour markets in destination countries. Contrary to the popular assumption that it is an isolated criminal activity, smuggling is socially embedded and is part of the everyday lives of the local residents in origin countries and migration routes. Family networks, traders, religious leaders, pastoralists in border areas, ordinary people and local officials are all involved in smuggling activities.

This chapter considers migration, the smuggling structures that mediate it, and border control as complementary and co-constitutive processes which produce one other. It is based on extensive ethnographic fieldwork conducted between 2018 and 2019 in various departure and transit locations in Ethiopia such as Wollo, Addis Ababa, and Afar Regional State, as well as along the Ethiopian-Djibouti border.[5] Interlocutors included smugglers, potential migrants, returnees, deportees and government personnel involved in migration, facilitation and control processes.

In the next sections I will first elaborate on smuggling organisations and pathways. Next, the knowledge and networks of smugglers, the sociocultural and community dimensions of smuggling, and its ethical and political implications will be discussed. Finally, I will reflect on the logics, practices and functions of smuggling, and its relationship to larger structural issues.

The vitality of smuggling pathways

In the face of challenging socioeconomic and political conditions that deprive young people of life chances, compounded by limited legal migration paths, many Ethiopians – mainly young men and women – opt for overland exits. These journeys involve long and dangerous trails across deserts, difficult terrains and seas until they arrive in Europe, the Middle East, the Republic of South Africa (RSA) or other destinations.[6] Three major overland routes of irregular migration from Ethiopia have emerged: the eastern route leading to the Middle East and the Gulf states through Djibouti and Somalia and then via Yemen (which is the focus of this chapter); the southern route towards South Africa via eastern and southern African countries; and the north-western route leading to Italy/ Europe via Sudan and Libya.

Wollo is a predominantly Muslim region in northern Ethiopia and has deep-rooted historical ties with Saudi Arabia. Historically there have been movements of enslaved people, soldiers, merchants, traders, labourers, tourists, pilgrims and scholars, accompanied by commodities, money, language, ideas, and religion via a caravan trade route that links the two locations.[7] During the early 2000s a well-established smuggling network emerged along the Wollo-Afar-Djibouti-Middle East trade route, capitalising on the geographical, historical, religious, sociocultural and economic relations that have developed between Wollo and the Middle East.[8] More recently, labour migration has become one of the most prominent features of the relationship between Ethiopia and the Middle East, and the Arabian Peninsula in particular,[9] often using smuggling services along the stated routes.

Wollo migrants often prefer to use smuggling services along the land routes to move to Saudi Arabia rather than the services of formal Private Employment Agencies[10] (PEAs) that recruit and deploy Ethiopian labour migrants in Gulf countries. This is for three major reasons: first, these migrants claim that if they use the services of PEAs and Kafala system sponsorship,[11] it would bind them to specific employers with a fixed salary and contract period. Using irregular land routes and smuggling services gives migrants some level of freedom in terms of negotiating types of employment, wages, and other conditions with employers in Saudi Arabia.

Second, there is the issue of gender selectivity of domestic workers in Saudi Arabia. While PEAs commonly recruit and deploy women migrants as domestic workers in Gulf Cooperation Council – or GCC – countries, there are limited options for young men to find employment in these countries through PEAs. Therefore, male migrants often use irregular routes to move to the Middle East and frequently end up as construction workers, shepherds, guards and daily labourers in factories. Third, according to the latest state regulations, formal recruitment agencies must have the requirement that migrants provide proof that they are above 18 years of age and have completed at least grade eight in their education. Those who do not meet these requirements instead turn to smugglers to organise their undocumented migratory journeys. Hence, smuggling plays a vital role in deploying Ethiopian labour in Saudi Arabia since the formal, state-led

migration route is too costly, bureaucratic, time consuming, discrimina-
tory and inaccessible to certain migrants due to their gender, age or class.

Smuggling practices presented in this study challenge popular assumptions about smugglers as the main cause of the failure of governments to
control irregular migration.[12] Rather we can argue that clandestine migration and state migration policies are complementary and co-constitutive
processes. As state migration policies select certain types of migrants while
excluding others, smugglers and brokers come in to fill the gap created by
migration policies. What's more, the formal PEAs work with smugglers to
facilitate labour migration from Ethiopia to Saudi Arabia. Smugglers in
Ethiopia, *delaloch* (plural of the singular *delala*), meet migrants who are
looking for brokers in villages and towns throughout the country, guide
migrants in handling phone interviews with potential employers; gain
access to government documents; obtain medical certificates; organise
transportation; arrange employment contracts; and obtain works visas –
which at times are fake tourist visas. These processes are indicative of the
blurred boundaries between formal and informal, legal and illegal, and
state and market, as migrants, smugglers and brokers use various formal
and informal strategies simultaneously.

The knowledge and networks in smuggling

There are various tasks, positions and actors that function together to
facilitate a journey. For example the *lekami* (literally 'picker') is a contact
person who meets potential migrants and collects them in a village or
a town. Another actor is *wana delala* (literally 'main broker') who gives
general guidance and provides directions from a strategic migration
origin, a transit location, or a destination. *Agachoch* (literally 'intercep-
tors') are a group of smugglers, often nomads and armed people in Yemen,
who collect migrants arriving by boat on the Yemeni side of the Red Sea
shores. Each type of smuggler has their own role, though there is sometimes an overlap. For instance, the *wana delala* may also act as a recruiter
or as a *lekami* in a village where they have good social relations and trust
among the local community. The *lekami* may perform the roles of *agachi*
and *wana delala*. The *leqamiwoch* work at the *kebele* (local area) and district
level. Their main job is collecting contact details of potential migrants and
linking them to the *wana delala*.

Hamud, a man in his late thirties, was *wana delala* in Dessie town, the
capital of Wollo district. I met him in March 2018 in Dessie Town Admin-

istration Prison as he was serving a long sentence for human smuggling in the region. He said he worked with many *lekami* in different villages and districts in both South and North Wollo Zone. He spoke of the specific knowledge and resources of smugglers: '*lekami* knows the migrant. I know the routes and I have contacts at all points.'

The role of the main *delala* is providing guidance, transport, food and shelter for potential migrants along transit locations. This is the person who knows about timings, routes, borders and control structures along the routes. Hamud states:

> I was a *wana delala* in Kombolcha town for a long time and I used to send different migrants to the Middle Eastern countries. There were different *lekami* who were working for me. The *lekamis* used to bring or send their clients to Kombolcha. I have [sic] different mechanisms of hiding potential migrants in Kombolcha. For example, there was one grocery in which I used to hide them. If we suspect staying in the grocery might be risky, we usually shift to hotels, different pensions, compounds, and tea shops. After I receive potential migrants from my *lekami*, I, in turn, send them to Afar. In Afar, particularly in Deshoto [a town at the Ethiopia-Djibouti border], I had another person who facilitated everything for me. Taking migrants as far as Deshoto was my role.

Bringing migrants to the Ethiopia-Djibouti border is not a simple task as there are several checkpoints along this migration route. Smugglers carefully work with different actors. They may secure support from border agents at various checkpoints, or they may use diverse transport strategies. Smugglers often transport migrants during the night, and they do not always take their clients by themselves, but instead use a variety of methods, depending on the context. If migrants can be transported in one vehicle, smugglers will transport them by themselves, but when their number becomes too few, smugglers transfer them to another *delala* to take along with his migrants. Migrants claim that smugglers or *delaloch* have their own style of communication, which is full of codes and difficult for others to comprehend when they communicate and broker with one another. During phone conversations, smugglers often use the language of commodities. As Hamud reports: 'When I communicate with my agents over the phone, I tell them I have sent them 10 sacks of sugar, instead of 10 migrants.'

Lorries are used to transport potential migrants from Kombolcha to Desheto. When brokers use lorries they do not load them with people alone, but use other commodities as a cover. One *delala* stated: 'we make the car to have [sic] two partitions by using rope or wood at the bottom and at the top. We often load people at the bottom and other commodities (bottle cases, egg, tomato, and other things) at the top.'

The *agachi* wait for migrants on the Yemeni side. The Yemeni and Ethiopian *agachi* work together. The Ethiopian *agachi* also serve as translators between migrants and Yemeni *agachi* during the deals and interactions in Yemen before migrants proceed to Saudi Arabia. The *agachis* have their own shelters and safe houses in Yemen. They have their own vehicles for transportation, guns and communication devices. Using these resources and connections, they facilitate migrants' clandestine journeys through Yemeni territory and across the Saudi border, despite the ongoing war, violence and tightening border control apparatus along the Saudi-Yemeni border.

The *agachis* collect migrants from the seaside and transport them to their camps or safe houses, often by Land Cruiser Toyota, a four-wheel drive vehicle for off-road driving. The smuggling process beyond Yemen is similar to those within Ethiopia. However, this part of the journey requires more resource and knowledge due to the war in Yemen and tough controls along the Saudi-Yemeni border. According to a returnee who was deported from Saudi Arabia, the *agachi* act like the military soldiers and armed resistance groups in the Yemeni desert:

> They put their vehicles in a row. The car in a front line is always intentionally kept empty. It is used as a gatekeeper and guide ... the rest of convoy which are behind. ... The front car checks and scans the security conditions and passes over information for others. The command is from the front; if they need to retreat or use other short path; all this is determined by the flow of information from [the] front guide car.

This shows one way in which smugglers develop knowledge about the working of borders in a particular location. Smugglers develop these strategies to transport migrants through war-torn and unstable Yemeni territories. Once migrants arrive at the safe house the *agachi* require every migrant to name the *delala* they dealt with. They then ask each migrant to pay money in cash or transfer money via *hawala* agents to pay for the *agachi* and the *meshiwar* (lit. 'smuggler adviser'). The *meshiwar* is a smuggler in

Yemen who guides and transports migrants from Yemen to Saudi Arabia, usually for the fee of SAR (Saudi Arabian Riyal) 6,000 (about €2,000). Transferring money through *hawala* agents is done by migrants who have *anshi*, that is, a relative who resides in Saudi Arabia and is willing to collect them by paying the *meshiwar* in Yemen. For those who have *anshi*, they are simply requested to give the address and contact number of this person. Other issues like negotiations regarding payment are dealt with by the *meshiwars* and the *anshis*.

If a migrant does not have cash to pay, they are first divided into two groups by the *meshiwars*: those who have *anshi* and those who do not. Migrants claim that those who have *anshi* are treated better by *meshiwars*. The *meshiwars* leave migrants who cannot pay by cash or through *anshi* under the burning sun in the desert. If migrants refuse to give an address of someone who can transfer money and pay the smuggling fee, they are beaten. Hamud stated:

> There will be no tolerance for such kind of issues. There are people called *gerafi* [whipping person] who are responsible for beating and torture [sic] migrants. Most people in the beginning used to say, 'I don't have *anshi*'. But when they taste the stick, you find them say that they have many people who can help them.

Under torture, one is forced to fabricate an *anshi* or lie to save themselves. According to the smugglers, migrants are asked whether they have money or *anshi* before they get into the *Donik* (boat) in Djibouti. Boarding the *Donik* is not allowed if they do not have money or *anshi*. Hamud stated:

> Everybody says, I have *anshi* when they are taken to the boat in Djibouti, but refuses to pay after arriving in Yemen. We are not providing services for free. They have to pay us! When they fail to pay, we have no other option than to whip them.

Such are the views of smugglers about their violent actions. They justify beating or torturing migrants as a result of a failure by clients to live up to the agreement.

Sometimes migrants run away from the safe-houses of *meshiwars* and walk to the Saudi border on foot, a journey which is possible thanks to the assistance of local people who offer them food, provide directions and give other forms of assistance. Migrants who had travelled the route previously and have some Arabic-language skills help others with translation and guidance. Migrants take up any employment offered without hesitation once they have crossed the Saudi border. Once they have crossed the border, migrants move towards big cities in Saudi Arabia. Migrants claim that the local people in Saudi border areas are familiar with the arrival of Ethiopian migrants and approach migrants with job offers. Communications and salary deals are done by sign language or writing on the sand when they meet on the streets.

This chapter has so far demonstrated the emergence of smuggling systems between Ethiopia and Saudi Arabia, which can be understood as unpredictable assemblages of diverse actors, operating at different scales and with different objectives that overlap or are in conflict. This system of smuggling is in a state of flux, responding to changes in geopolitics and bordering practices of transit and destination states. Social connections – translocal and transnational – between migrants, smugglers, helpful locals and former migrants in Saudi Arabia have facilitated the development of smuggling knowledge, shared by this community. The connections between these groups are used to generate the information, material and economic resources necessary at a given point in the journey. This forms an alternative infrastructure for migrants who are immobilised due to restrictive migration regulations and border control practices.[13]

Smuggling as a collective enterprise

As indicated earlier, a range of actors engage in smuggling activities during the process of selecting, housing, transporting, harbouring and helping migrants to cross checkpoints and state borders until they reach Saudi Arabia from Wollo. For example, bus, taxi, lorry and *Bajaj* drivers are employed to transport migrants domestically until they arrive at Djibouti. Hotel owners and mini pensions are hired as safe houses for migrants by the *delaloch*.

A number of other actors are engaged in the smuggling process. Collaborating government officials, such as border guards, are paid to open up checkpoints and to overlook border controls; some clan leaders and pastoralists in Afar region also collaborate with brokers in guiding migrants along safe routes and assisting them to escape border checks at the Ethiopia-Djibouti border. The route from Wollo to Djibouti is less active in terms of population movement, for instance, as there is no regular public transportation. Thus migrants, particularly young men and women from rural areas, rely upon rented minibuses or trucks in a group, making them easily identifiable by border guards at the numerous checkpoints along this route. A number of different actors are therefore employed by smugglers in order to bypass internal checkpoints and reach the border areas.

The small town along the Ethiopia-Djibouti border named Galafi is economically deprived, with high unemployment rates, and many young people take on work as brokers and smugglers to help arriving migrants cross the Djibouti border. They help migrants to avoid the checkpoints in the town and use support from local nomadic pastoralists to cross the border with Djibouti. In these border areas, smuggling is embedded in informal cross-border economies such as pastoralism and the contraband trade, which flows across the long and porous border where the populations on both sides are of the same ethnic group – the Afar. Smuggling thrives, based on clan networks that exist between Ethiopian Afar pastoralists and Djibouti Afar pastoralists. The Afar pastoralists have a tradition of crossing the international borders of Ethiopia and Djibouti for social and economic reasons. Thus they are key members of smuggling networks. The Afar pastoralists[14] who reside along Ethiopian-Djibouti border areas have the right to cross borders by law. They possess identification cards that allow them to move back and forth between Ethiopia and Djibouti for trade, family visits, and medical treatments.

Saied Ali worked as *delala* for eight years before he was arrested and sentenced to a long-term imprisonment in the town of Kombolcha, Wollo, where I met him in February 2018. When I asked him about the engagement of Afar pastoralists in brokering and facilitating border crossings, Ali said:

> In Afar we work with some pastoralists and clan leaders. There were *mnged meri* [lit. 'guides'] who are from local Afar pastoralists. They know safe routes via the bush and guide migrants to the other side of the border during on foot journeys or to avoid checkpoints in Galafi or Desheto towns along Ethiopia-Djibouti borders. I have five Afar pastoralist partners in the town of Desheto who helped more than 2,000 clients of mine enter Djibouti.

Sometimes smugglers also help migrants buy local ID cards from Afar district officers. If migrants are intercepted and have their first ID confiscated, they use another one when they travel the next time. Sometimes, with ID cards, migrants can travel by foot unaccompanied, or take a ride on the lorries traveling from Ethiopia to Djibouti. These are the results of the skills and knowledge of smugglers about the (mal)functioning of border regulations and the local lives along the porous borders in East Africa. The smugglers capitalise on the old established travel routes along border areas in East Africa in order to facilitate clandestine migration.

There is local support for migration smuggling practices in Wollo and Afar regions. The communities residing in places of origin and migration routes do not see brokering and smuggling activities as criminal. Rather, smuggling is viewed as a major migration strategy and a livelihood opportunity for young migrants, facilitators and for the family left behind. As illustrated here, different actors engage in and benefit from human smuggling directly and indirectly. Thus smuggling is a socially and culturally embedded practice and becomes a collective enterprise.

The role of religion in smuggling facilitation

In the migration process from Wollo to the Middle East, Islam plays a triple role: the first being that migrant women use a *hajj* visa to enter the country (a visa used for the annual Islamic pilgrimage to the holy city of Mecca in Saudi Arabia). Upon arrival in Saudi Arabia migrants use social and smuggling networks in order to access accommodation and job offers. They usually overstay their visas and find employment as domestic workers. The second role played by Islam is during the overland journey, when Muslims perform rituals known as *du'ua*, which involve group prayer, chewing *kaht* or *chat* and blessings from religious leaders and elders. For many, religious rituals foster courage and hope during risky journeys. Finally, migration from Wollo to Saudi Arabia reaches its peak during the Islamic Ramadan fasting season. This is because the Yemeni-Saudi borders are expected to be more or less open. According to migrants, violence is generally discouraged during Ramadan. Furthermore, many border guards take more frequent breaks and have no energy to patrol. At the same time, employers in Saudi Arabia require more migrant labour as cooks, shepherds, cleaners and for other laborious tasks which the Saudi citizens do not want to take due to the extra need for rest during fasting season.

Smugglers play a pivotal role in arranging *hajj* visas. I met Betelehem Khassa, a young divorced woman, in Kombolcha in March 2018. She had returned from Saudi Arabia after seven years. She migrated to Saudi Arabia using a *hajj* visa in 2010. She was a young Christian woman assuming a

Muslim identity. In response to my question about the arrangements for her *hajj* visa and whether a *delala* was used or not, she responded:

> I went to Saudi Arabia through a *hajj* visa. To travel via *hajj* and *umra* what one needs is travel costs. At that time, the cost was around ETB [Ethiopian Birr] 18,000, nearly €1,000. Medical test [sic] and a man who would act as a muhrim[15] (male representative) were also required. For the health test, I went to Addis Ababa. My *delala* arranged all travel documents, the *muhrim* and also contacts and host family in Saudi Arabia.

Migration brokerage and smuggling arrangements thrive on the production and reproduction of knowledge within smugglers' and migrants' transnational networks. Arranging a *hajj* visa, accommodation and a host family in the destination country requires in depth knowledge about the workings of visa regimes, mobility regulations and the labour market in both Ethiopia and Saudi Arabia. In other words, smuggling relies upon knowledge of states, labour markets, borders and international religious mobility regimes, such as that of the *hajj*.

When it comes to Christian migrants, smugglers guide and train them to 'perform a Muslim identity'. Betelehem was trained in this performance in order to obtain a *hajj* visa. Betelehem recalled:

> I used Muslim name, Hayat. I also changed my wearing style; I wore like a Muslim, [sic] including veils. I went to the Hajji Committee and told them that I wanted to make the *Umra* pilgrimage. I paid my *muhrim*. My *muhrim* handled all my processes by himself. I only gave him the required money. We were four females under our *muhrim*. We covered all his travel cost. I did not know any other person in Saudi Arabia; I had only to trust that man [the *muhrim*]. He knows Jidda very well as he had been there before. He has brothers in Jidda. After we finished the process, we went to Saudi Arabia. I was 16 years old at that time but I raised it to 23 in my passport and national ID because my age was not fit to go there. My *delala* guided me [through] all these process. I paid him.

This reveals the social, economic, political and cultural underpinnings of human smuggling and migration brokerage between Ethiopia and Saudi Arabia. The process involves diverse strategies, plans, techniques, and knowledge regimes. Smuggling networks operate locally and transnationally. Betelehem's story also demonstrates the participation of multiple actors, and how their operations have evolved over time, as well as the kinds of networks they use.

The ethics and politics of smuggling

In 2015 the Ethiopian government issued a new proclamation to control illegal migration named Proclamation No. 909/2015 on Prevention and Suppression of Trafficking in Persons and Smuggling of Migrants Proclamation. Following this, a national committee was established to enforce the legislation. The new proclamation is designed to control human smuggling, to provide humanitarian and developmental assistance for trafficking and smuggling victims, and to facilitate legal migration to the Middle East. Accordingly, several new checkpoints were set up in Ethiopia along migratory exit routes towards the Middle East via Djibouti, South Africa via Kenya and Sudan, as well as the exit route to Europe via the town of Metema at the Ethiopian Sudanese border.

To overcome this policy, smugglers developed new strategies and enlisted several new actors. New overland migration routes were identified by the smugglers, and in order to avoid checkpoints, they changed transport facilities and payment methods: money transfer and payment is now done online instead of in cash. Smugglers also started to make debt agreements with migrants instead of requesting payment on the spot. New partnerships were created, including planting agents in police departments, banks, and telecom companies as well as recruiting local officials to provide necessary documents, SIM cards, and bank accounts registered in false names to brokers. This makes detection far more complicated.

Smugglers work alongside and share the benefits with local residents in border areas. Many people, such as contraband traders, drivers, shop owners, hotel owners, street coffee sellers, unemployed young people, nomadic pastoral communities and even government officials benefit from the smuggling industry, whether directly or indirectly. Borderland communities are attracted to the smuggling business. Smugglers have better resources than state actors to share with the local people. They have more advanced skills and knowledge of changing events domestically and internationally. The state border control policies remain merely rhetorical. This has neither stopped migration nor has it addressed the factors which push people to migrate.

The state and smugglers have different perceptions of their activities. The state's intensification of migration control and regulatory infrastructures are manifest through the criminalisation of brokers and the portrayal of migrants as victims of human trafficking and smuggling practices. The state wishes to portray itself as a champion of migrants' rights and as being morally superior. The smugglers' understanding of protection is different from the state's logic. The smugglers I have met do not believe their activities should be labelled as criminal by the state. Hamud (the *delala*), repeatedly told me that he is opportunity creator and a service provider for migrants otherwise unable to leave Wollo. He says: 'Look at Wollo. Without migration it is nothing. Without *delaloch* there is no such scale of migration. We help them to find opportunities for work abroad.'

Hamud's statement challenges the state's portrayal of smugglers as merciless, heartless people driven solely by profit rather than the needs of the public.[16] Smugglers perceive their activities as morally right and appropriate. This might be a case of smugglers trying to legitimise illicit activities. However, it also shows us the strong social ties that exist between smugglers and their clients, as well as their role in helping migrants navigate the unequal geographies of mobility.[17]

Conclusion

Smuggling thrives, despite the many barriers it faces due to particular ways of generating knowledge about the functions of borders, states and markets that shape contemporary migration. Smuggling practices involve specific strategies, plans, and techniques, as well as local and transnational relations. Each step of transnational migration encompasses multiple layers of relationships, and experiences of the past and imaginations of the future. Smuggling is not an independent criminal activity; rather, it is a socially and culturally embedded collective practice as it functions through the support of local communities and collaborative relationships between migrants, local residents and smugglers. Understanding this requires viewing the role of smugglers as an entry point, and examining the wider organisational logic of migration, as opposed to simply seeing it as the relationship between smugglers and migrants.

The empirical discussions and analysis have demonstrated that smuggling and facilitation of clandestine migratory exits is embedded in and functions within broader translocal and transnational social, cultural and economic relations. This challenges the view reflected in popular discourses that such smuggling is carried out by independent criminal organisations. Smugglers and their intermediaries facilitate Ethiopian migrants' clandestine border crossings via Djibouti, the Red Sea and Yemen, generate support and resources from local communities along the border, bribing border guards and capitalising on their ethnic, religious and economic connections in the Ethiopian-Djibouti and Yemeni-Saudi borderlands. Thus, human smuggling has become a collective economic and social activity. It is deeply integrated into the economic lives of communities in border areas and transit locations and towns.

Smuggling flourishes along migration routes from Ethiopia to Saudi Arabia and border areas partly because actors extend the benefits of smuggling to the economically disadvantaged local community and this in return generates social support and community back-up for smuggling activities. As discussed earlier, in the case of Ethiopian Wollo migration to Saudi Arabia, multiple layers of smugglers, transporters, employers, ordinary residents and *hawala* agents engage in selecting, housing, transporting, protecting, facilitating informal money transfers and helping migrants cross checkpoints and state borders. In such a context smuggling becomes a collective enterprise.

The Ethiopian government tries its best to demonise and prevent smuggling. This is in part to show its importance and legitimacy as a protector of citizens from the 'abuse' of smuggling. However, in reality, smugglers attract more local support than the state in communities living along migration routes. Local residents and migrants alike often do not see smugglers as criminals or morally wicked. Instead, smuggling is seen as a service emerging to meet migration needs in the context of restricted mobility and migration control infrastructures. This is partly why smuggling continues, despite the proliferation of regulations along migration routes and in border areas.[18]

Notes

1. Marina de Regt and Medareshaw Tafesse, 'Deported before experiencing the good sides of migration: Ethiopians returning from Saudi Arabia', *African and Black Diaspora: An International Journal* 9(2), 2016, pp. 228–42.
2. Asnake Kefale and Zerihun Mohammad, *Ethiopian Labour Migration to the Gulf And South Africa* (Addis Ababa: Forum for Social Studies – FSS, 2015).

3. Tekalign Mengiste Ayalew, *Struggle for Mobility: Risk, Hope and Community of Knowledge in Eritrean and Ethiopian Migration Pathways towards Sweden*, PhD dissertation, Stockholm University, 2017; Girmachew Adugna Zewdu, 'Ethiopian female domestic labour migration to the Middle East: Patterns, trends, and drivers', *African and Black Diaspora: An International Journal* 11(1), 2018, pp. 6–19.

4. De Regt and Tafesse, 'Deported before experiencing the good sides of migration', p. 229.

5. The fieldwork is partly supported by the Migrating out of Poverty project, funded by UK aid from the UK government, and the Swedish Research Council (Vetenskapsrådet, grant number 2019-02185).

6. Tekalign, *Struggle for Mobility*, pp.10–25; Fekadu Adugna, Priya Deshingkar and Tekalign Mengiste Ayalew, *Brokers, Migrants and the State: Berri Kefach 'Door Openers' in Ethiopian Clandestine Migration to South Africa* (University of Sussex, School of Global Studies, Migrating out of Poverty research consortium, Working Paper 56, 2019).

7. De Regt and Tafesse, 'Deported before experiencing the good sides of migration', pp. 232–6.

8. Jon Abbink, 'Transformations of Islam and communal relations in Wollo, Ethiopia', in René Otayek and Benjamin F. Soares (eds) *Islam and Muslim Politics in Africa* (New York: Palgrave Macmillan, 2017), pp. 65–83.

9. De Regt and Tafesse, 'Deported before experiencing the good sides of migration', p. 234.

10. Following the enactment of the Overseas Employment Proclamation in 1998 and its amendment in 2015 (proclamation no. 923/2016) more than 400 PEAs have been established in Ethiopia and deployed more than 300,000 Ethiopian domestic labour migrants in Gulf countries. By adapting circular migration management models and policies from Asian countries, the Ethiopian government is playing a triple role in the deployment of migrants: (1) it sets up rules, regulations, and institutions that govern activities of Private Employment Agencies (PEAs); (2) it has signed bilateral labour agreements with receiving countries such as Saudi Arabia and the UAE; (3) it directly engages in the process of recruitment and deployment of workers in receiving countries that have bilateral agreements with Ethiopian state. As such, the government functions both as a migration merchant and regulator. For circular migration management models see Eugene McCann and Kevin Ward (eds) *Mobile Urbanism: Cities and Policymaking in the Global Age* (Minneapolis, MN: University of Minnesota Press, 2011).

11. *Kafala* sponsorship, is an employment framework in the Gulf states that requires sponsorship from a national for migrant workers to be employed and reside in the country. The sponsor, either an individual or a company, has substantial control over the worker. Without their employer's permission, a worker cannot leave their job, change jobs, or exit the country,

and the sponsor is able to threaten deportation if a worker questions the terms of the contract.

12. Gabriella Sanchez and Luigi Achilli, *Critical Insights on Irregular Migration Facilitation: Global Perspectives* (Florence: European University Institute, Robert Schuman Centre for Advanced Studies, 2019).

13. Adugna et al., *Brokers, Migrants and the State*, p. 35.

14. The Afar pastoralists are the largest pastoral communities in East Africa who reside and move between three countries (Ethiopia, Djibouti, Eritrea) often referred to as the 'Afar-triangle', searching for land and pasture for their animals.

15. He is an acting husband or a male Muslim protector in Hajj Umra pilgrimage who can take about four females to Mecca during a single pilgrimage.

16. Sanchez and Achilli, *Critical Insights on Irregular Migration*.

17. Luigi Achilli 'The "Good" Smuggler: The Ethics and Morals of Human Smuggling among Syrians', *The Annals of the American Academy of Political and Social Science* (2018) 676, pp. 77–96.

18. Sanchez and Achilli, *Critical Insights on Irregular Migration*.

2

Aurelian Dreams: Gold Smuggling and Mobilities across Colonial and Contemporary Asia

Nichola Khan

Between 1988 and 1995 Jacek lived in a two-bedroom luxury condominium in Singapore. He had lived in Asia since leaving Poland in the 1960s. Recently released from Delhi's Tihar prison, he revived a profitable gold smuggling syndicate. Many small-scale syndicates operated out of Singapore at that time, handling twenty or so couriers, the largest ones operated by Poles and Iranians. 'Syndicate' refers here to one or more individuals who invested in buying gold in Singapore, established buyers in India or transit countries, and recruited and paid couriers to smuggle it. Gold bars weighing 10 *tola* (116gm) were readily bought tax-free from the bank or Indian money-changers. Import duties on gold into India were high, and smuggled gold could yield 20 per cent profit. A courier received US $2,000 for transporting five kg (44 bars) and returning to Jacek the secreted cash in US dollars (c. US $120,000). Jacek's core couriers rotated bed-spaces in the condominium. In the period 1989 to 1992, they included: Jon, a US Vietnam veteran and his partner Torin, who had an Ivy League degree in Mandarin. They lived on an *ex servicio* teak container boat on Bangkok's Chao Praya river and smuggled gold to finance their heroin habit. Avi, an ex-Israeli air pilot who had fought in the 1967 war, now flew gold runs, using his Australian-based wife and daughter as cover. Darek had been arrested in Delhi with smuggled gold and spent three years in Tihar jail. At the time I met him, he had just been released and was *en route* home to Poland for good. Isabelle, from France, worked with her Vietnamese stepmother to raise funds to release her daughter from Tihar jail, also imprisoned for gold smuggling. Mick, a British citizen in his fifties, had left his family and now did gold runs with his new Thai wife. For now, their marital home consisted of a makeshift tent in Jacek's second bedroom, a room they shared with other couriers. French backpacker Jean-Dominic was planning a future with Nellie, a Chinese-American seeking to escape her humdrum life in Maryland. They smuggled to finance their travels.

Jacek's business partner, a British woman called Sophia, occasionally smuggled gold with her own funds, but mostly met the couriers in Delhi or Bombay, or the transit stops Kathmandu or Colombo, where she sold the smuggled gold to dealers who then transported it by land or ship to India. The profits were higher for direct flights to India that bypassed the associated costs of transiting through third countries and paying middlemen, but these direct flights were also riskier. Security at Delhi airport was low tech, and low key, but undercover police were increasingly vigilant. If several couriers flew together, some might be caught. In India, Jacek would struggle to obtain their release through bribing officers, although customs in Nepal and Sri Lanka were still amenable. Avoiding the Indian High Commission in Singapore, for fear of drawing attention to the multiple, regular trips his couriers were making, Jacek had somehow acquired a real Indian visa stamp somewhere along the smuggling routes; pages crudely pre-treated with paper glue allowed stamps to be frequently erased and re-applied. Money was easily made and spent; few questioned the future.

This chapter comprises research into gold smuggling across Asia with a mobilities perspective, and archival research on gold smuggling between Singapore and urban destinations in India – primarily Bombay, Delhi, Calcutta and Madras (before their name changes after the mid-1990s). It considers the dissolving, re-forming, and adaptable route as a variable of rapid transformation in the ways the gold smuggling trade in the last two decades of the twentieth century reshaped Asian cities and their interconnections, and the ways its profits changed urban and social landscapes. It further develops the nexus of commodities and cities, mobility and routes, and some temporal and historical transformations in order to track and analyse the motile logic of illicit trades in gold between Asian cities. Beginning with the postcolonial island city-state of Singapore, it follows the legal export of gold through its transformation into an illegal commodity entering India.

The chapter draws on extensive archival research at the National Archives of Singapore, where using the keyword 'gold smuggling' to search all English-language newspapers from 1900 to 2014 (after which the trade declined) produced 1,840 results. Reflecting the trade's fully international character, it additionally draws on the stories of a Polish and an Iranian syndicate chief respectively, a British handler, and Western smugglers. I met these actors when I lived in Singapore between 1989 and 1992. I maintained contact with them intermittently and made extensive notes in my personal diaries on their stories, as well as during several meetings between 1995 and 2009, with the aim of fictionalising them someday. These stories were elicited with consent, are fully anonymised, have been updated for this chapter, and verified with their authors where possible. Identifying features have been removed or changed. They illustrate the easy slippage between il/legality characterising the city's social landscape at that time, and the human economies of trust, cohesion and secrecy that enabled high-risk networks to flourish while endangering individual and collective freedoms in playing for high financial rewards.

This chapter aligns broadly with anthropological studies of single everyday commodities, and their social, economic and global networks and histories of circulation. These include Sidney Mintz's study[1] of the place of sugar in the Euro-American history of colonialism and slavery through to its shaping of capitalism, class, and modern eating habits; Emma Tarlo's study[2] of global and local networks through which human hair circulates; and Frederick Errington, Tatsuro Fukijura and Deborah Gewertz's study of the global rise of the instant noodle as an industrial food.[3]

Following an object like the gold bar also enables a questioning of the trade's social and economic organisation; ways the trade shaped the international, highly mobile social fabric of the city; and Singapore as a regional pull-factor for smuggling syndicates, and its relation to cities along other il/licit trade routes across Asia. It reveals the ways profits from gold smuggling were channelled into legalised businesses (hotels, property), alongside how networks became entrenched in parallel illegal activities involving smuggling of drugs, antiquities, rare animals, gemstones, currency – and later the smuggling of people to Europe. It also implicates gold's use as a hidden currency to buy weapons for insurgency movements (e.g. in Khalistan and Kashmir).

Several existing studies have examined territorialised attempts to mine and profit legally from gold locally or between states, or else focused on power and wealth dynamics between global mercantile communities, global corporate businesses, liberalisation and modern finance.[4] Complementary to this study's approach, Nisha Mathew[5] explores how mercantile communities, Hindu, Jewish, Muslim and Christian communities in Dubai, and global businesses in gold became integral to trading networks in gold reaching from Malabar on India's south-west coast to South-East Asia, wherein the legal and illegal merged, often inseparably, in the late twentieth and early twenty-first century. Also drawing colonial and post-colonial connections, she shows how illegal flows from Dubai to Bombay were constituted by international monetary politics in the Persian Gulf that shaped gold smuggling as a trans-regional economy operating in the interstices of the retreating British empire, Partition, and Bombay's post-colonial history.[6]

While there have been various historical attempts to mine, trade and profit from gold on a legal basis in colonial Singapore and the region,[7] a focus on gold smuggling offers productive insights into the mobility, fluidity, and swift adaptability of people and trade across markets in Asia. That is, when seen from places such as Singapore, and from a smuggler's perspective, a picture of mutability and mobility involving multiple circuitous maritime, terrestrial and aerial routes in the il/licit movement of gold across states, markets and places emerges more clearly. Gold (Au, Latin *aurum*), is a transition metal in the Periodic Table of the elements; it transmutes in form and value. As a commodity, its value lies in its materiality: in its chimeric capacity to rapidly change from the rough spoils of mining to fine-crafted jewellery, coinage, bride-wealth, bullion, shares, bribes and investments, to connect with the illegal traffic of money, weapons payments, investments in property, prison terms, and people. Likewise, the overland, aerial or maritime character of routes through cities that enable less tracking of movements of gold can divert analytic attention away from state-ism, territoriality and fixed materiality towards a more fluid and joined-up perspective involving social and human connections.

The conditions for gold smuggling to India emerge within a relatively neglected aspect of economic growth in Singapore's distinct history. Singapore offers an interesting vantage-point to investigate gold smuggling as it entangled with urban diversity, shifting boundaries, and social relationships evolved through waves of migration, trade, and gold's distribution across Asian cities. Although gold smuggling to India involving the Middle East and South Asia spans the entire period after the Second World War, this chapter focuses on a 'boom' period during the 1980s and early 1990s, when Polish and Iranian syndicates dominated gold smuggling in Singapore. The period coincides with Poland's transformation post-1989 from a socialist to a market economy, and Iranian migrations across the world after the 1979 revolution.

The confluence of state complicity in illegal trades, British colonial infrastructures, and international monetary politics enabled smuggling markets, routes, networks, and a highly mobile cartography of licit and illicit money flows to traverse different time zones, historical moments, and Asian cities. Singapore's infrastructural significance lies in its colonial legacy as a free port, established in 1819 by the British East India Company (EIC). Likewise, gold has been instrumental to reviving connections from Britain's imperial past, and creating new connections between mining companies, banks, bullion dealers, refiners, cartels and states.[8] Singapore thereby assumes historical importance in thinking about state complicity, the advantages to the state of the existence of illicit trades, and the state's role in brokering relations between licit and illicit money. Emphasising the significance of an early financial system that profited from inter-regional maritime and terrestrial trade routes, with clear links to present-day trades, the chapter also urges paying attention to cyclicality, and to ways old trade routes and 'silk roads' are repurposed and reimagined in the movements of gold across Asia. It views the social and human embroidery of the region, city, route, trade, and licit and illicit urban fabric as inextricably connected.

Singapore: duty-free-smuggling, reciprocity and connection

In 1819 Stamford Raffles founded Singapore as an imperial outpost of the EIC which would be 'open to ships and vessels of every nation, free of duty', in order to destroy the Dutch monopoly in the East Indies.[9] By the 1850s, Singapore was the principal trading centre in the South-East Asian Nusantara – encompassing a maritime network of approximate 25,000 islands traversing contemporary Singapore, Indonesia, Malaysia, southern Thailand, the Philippines, and Cambodia – and strategically connecting west and east Asia, and Europe and China. Colonial accounts detail British struggles to tame a crocodile-infested backwater and immoral quagmire of gambling, squalor, and opium addicts (migrants were first brought from China addicted to opium which the British imported from India). Under British rule, opium was legal, taxed and highly profitable: between 1825 and 1910 the income accrued accounted for 30 to 55 per cent of total revenue.[10]

Singapore became a Crown colony in 1867. Its population expanded with migrants from the Malay Archipelago, China, Hadhramaut on the Arabian Peninsula, and South Asia. While many were traders, many more worked in

Malayan mines and plantations. Malayan rubber and tin drove Singapore's growth as an international export and financial centre. In its early years, Indian convicts were sent to Singapore to build roads and government offices.[11] By the 1830s, Chinese were the largest ethnic group and Chinese merchants (*towkays*) dominated commerce for most of the nineteenth century. In the 1920s and 1930s, goldsmiths established businesses along South Bridge Road – with some Chinese family businesses, such as Poh Heng, still popular for their traditional *si dian jin* ('four touches of gold') wedding sets.[12] Indian entrepreneurs, latterly Sikhs, engaged areas of finance: insurance, banking, and money-lending. The money-changers involved in twentieth-century gold smuggling were also Indians, and the gold dealers in India were mostly Sikhs, demonstrating the historical entanglement of licit moneylending and conditions developed in the nineteenth and twentieth centuries through Indian migration flows.

Smuggling anywhere emerges symbiotically and relationally with regard to market restrictions, tax conditions and economic geography. For example, in the early twentieth century an increase in opium smuggling at the Malay-Singapore border was reported after an increase in opium taxes in Singapore. Subsequent reports detailed cases in Singapore of arms smuggling, hog smuggling, tin smuggling, and large-scale smuggling networks in rubber and spices from Indonesia involving government officers. Gold smuggling spanned Asia and was also smuggled in large quantities into Europe throughout the twentieth century. The post-Second World War scenario involving Singapore reveals a continuous history of gold smuggling that profited from high import taxes in destination countries including India, Malaysia, Thailand, and Indonesia.

Archival research on patterns of gold smuggling in the post-war decades uncovers a regional picture involving different scales and actors, including government officials, government ministers, British, Singapore and Chinese national airlines staff and pilots, diplomats, parliamentarians, governors, ambassadors, UN officials, foreign nationals, small-time smugglers, and links reported in the Singapore press between gold smuggling, arms and heroin smuggling, and separatist and so-called terrorist groups. Heads of small syndicates (say, with ten to twenty couriers, such as those mentioned earlier) and larger-scale smugglers were imprisoned across Asia, in Taiwan, Indonesia, Malaysia, Thailand, Japan and the Philippines. Gold smuggling into India increased exponentially after 1963, following changes to the 1948 Gold Act. Arrests increased significantly in the four principal destination cities of Bombay, Delhi, Madras and Calcutta – as well as the transit countries of Nepal, Pakistan, Sri Lanka and Bangladesh. The key origin countries for gold smuggling were the duty-free ports and former British colonies of Singapore and Hong Kong, and also Dubai. While throughout the 1980s gold was smuggled across East and South-East Asia, the largest market in the world by far was India.

To briefly historicise the trade, the year 1948 heralded India's golden age of smuggling.[13] In 1948 the Indian government placed a ban on gold imports to limit domestic consumption of gold, conserve foreign exchange reserves for more essential commodities, and boost India's economy. Demand for gold continued, however, and an illicit market profited from the gap in domestic gold production and consumption. Pakistan was an important early transit country; camels transported gold across the border with India. While in the mid-twentieth century fencing was erected along the Western coastal Pondicherry and Karaikal borders to curb smuggling to India from Persian Gulf ports in *dhows*, the measures were largely ineffective as gold continued to be found along Indian seashores.

Subsequently, in 1962 the India Gold Control Act banned all forward trading in gold. This preceded a ban in 1963 on gold jewellery production, and a gold bond scheme with tax incentives in 1965. The measures were ineffective, leading to the 1968 Gold Control Act and an era of licensing. The act prohibited citizens from owning personal gold in the form of bars and coins, goldsmiths from owning more than 100g, and licensed dealers more than two kg. Prohibitions on trading and mobility banned dealers from trading with each other, and permits were required to transport gold between cities. The legislation quashed the official gold market, and set the conditions for an unprecedented cash-based black market in bullion and illegal mobilities. These, in turn, attracted Polish and Iranian migrant entrepreneurs, such as I write about, on the move after massive political and economic upheavals in their countries, as well as Western backpackers and Vietnam veterans such as Jon.

Throughout the 1970s and 1980s, gold smuggling entered a golden age with syndicates sending ten to twenty carriers per flight, and crew members of Singapore International Airlines (SIA) heavily involved. During this period we can read reports about gold smuggling to Jakarta and South Korea from Singapore, large caches seized in Nepal, a 'business boom for gold smuggling in Asia',[14] and the 'threat posed by smuggling' to India's economy.[15] Reports detailed seizures of gold worth several millions of US dollars and high-profile arrests across a network of routes from Dhaka to Colombo, Islamabad, Bangkok, and Indian ports and airports. By the late 1980s, sentences were harsher as national economies suffered. Bangladesh introduced the death penalty, and many SIA crew members were imprisoned. To deter smuggling syndicates, SIA issued a list of thirteen 'forbidden cities' crew members could not request to fly to because they had featured in arrests of SIA crew, or attracted smuggling syndicates. These were: Jakarta, Seoul, Kathmandu, Colombo, Bombay, Madras, New Delhi, Calcutta, Karachi, Dacca, Istanbul, Tokyo and Osaka.

In 1978 the Indian government proposed selling gold reserves to check smuggling, inflationary pressure, and meet a large budget deficit. Control measures failed to quell domestic demand, and consumption increased from 50 tonnes in 1980 to 175 tonnes in 1985, including recycled and smuggled gold, which bullion experts believed was under-estimated by around half. Bullion market watchers estimated government losses of more than US $2.5 billion annually in money smugglers repatriated outside the country; in 1988 customs authorities seized 6.1 tonnes, but an estimated 80 tonnes entered India that year. The situation continued until 1990 when severe foreign exchange problems led to the repeal of the Gold Control Act. Through taxes and restrictions, the government sought to divert profits from smugglers.

India simultaneously embarked upon economic liberalisation benefiting the gold market on payment of an import duty of Rs 250 per 10g. From practically no gold being officially imported in 1991, India imported more than 110 tonnes of gold in 1992. Smuggling increased accordingly. In 1991 the amount of gold smuggled annually was valued at US $3.5 billion. This figure was extraordinary given India was negotiating standby credit of US $2.1 billion that year from the International Monetary Fund: a full 60 per cent of the value of gold smuggled into the country. An Asian state where gold was readily available to be exported tax-free, Singapore was at the frontline.

Enter foreign smugglers

Lee Kwan Yew, Singapore's prime minister between 1959 and 1990, was hugely successful in the economic development of the country. He did not apply tariffs to gold imports or exports. By the 1980s Singapore was a major financial centre and established stopover for Western tourists and backpackers; migrant workers from Asia and Europe; foreign syndicates (Australian, English, Polish, Iranian smugglers) who traded in fake passports, gold smuggling, and human smuggling. In 1989 I was living in a family apartment in Singapore and teaching English. I met Sophia, an English woman who worked for a Polish gold smuggling syndicate and we became friends. She was based in Singapore but dispatched by handlers to live in Colombo from time to time. Smuggling, as with all social or economic activity in Singapore, was racialised and gendered, reflecting colonial discourses of white female innocence and brown male criminality. As a white middle-class British woman living in postcolonial Singapore's highly racialised and racist society[16] – who socialised with British expatriate workers and attended embassy parties, Sophia appeared an unlikely smuggler. Directly arising from Singapore's racialised legacy of empire, white Western women were preferred as couriers, and Polish smugglers were putatively less suspicious than Iranians or brown-skinned migrants from poorer countries across South Asia.

Many Poles living in Singapore in the late 1980s on repeated 90-day tourist visas had embraced Poland's era of post-socialist economic liberalisation. One consequence of liberalisation after 1989 was a host of Polish traders and crime syndicates across Asia seeking investment funds. Poland had a long history of economic and cultural cooperation with India from the 1950s to 1990s that reflected a search for alternatives to the Western modernity model, and the national 'socialist modernisation' discourse.[17] This was accompanied by a cultural and spiritual fascination with the 'East'. Such links enabled the development of an early informal 'suitcase trade' in household goods. In the 1960s and 1970s Polish mountaineers in Nepal and India smuggled drugs overland to fund expeditions. In the 1980s, assisted by regular flights of LOT Polish Airlines, enormous quantities of wholesale goods were exported to India, and Indian textiles travelled back.[18] Other entrepreneurs concentrated on gold smuggling – in Jacek's case, developing existing Polish networks in drugs and currency smuggling in Asia. Jacek's business partner Sophia, who received and sold on the gold when it arrived in India or transit places, first encountered smuggling in 1988 in Thailand, through a Canadian woman Karin. Karin worked for Polish and Yugoslavian syndicates to recruit couriers from budget hostels, and introduced Sophia to Jacek. Karin typically received US $200 for referring Western European passport holders, less for non-white or single male 'tourists' more likely to appear suspicious to Indian customs officials and be checked. In Singapore, Sophia met Jacek seeking to start afresh following a prison term in Delhi, and they joined forces as business partners.

Initially, couriers carried tax-free electronics from Singapore to India, where import duties were high: Sony M7 video cameras, MC10 VCRs, and cameras were all valuable for India's booming wedding party market. Syndicate heads profited ingeniously from the Singapore-Delhi route with a transit to a domestic carrier in Bombay. As Sophia described, on arrival couriers tried to avoid getting a TBRE ('to be re-exported') stamp in their passport which preventing them selling the electronics. Later, when Jacek and Sophia began adding gold bars to M7 battery compartments, a TBRE stamp was desirable so goods could not be seized. In transit in Bombay, the courier would hand over the electronics to a contact, take a domestic connection, collect more electronics on the Bombay luggage belt with the *same* serial numbers, transfer the additional goods there, and receive payment. On the return flight to Singapore they collected the TBRE'd electronics and transferred them in transit in Delhi. Jacek and others in higher ranks re-marked the serial numbers in Singapore multiple times so batches appeared the same. Gradually they added gold bars to VCRs or video cameras, and gold took over.

Polish couriers flew mostly on Western European passports with the air of 'wealth' they imputed to their holders, depending on which passports the smugglers could acquire. Pre-Schengen, falsification was simple. As direct flights became riskier and losses more costly, couriers flew to transit countries – Sri Lanka and Nepal – from where dealers transported the gold overland or by ship. These routes yielded lower profits. The Sri Lankan civil war meant bombs, bomb-scares, and the presence of army personnel all over Colombo. Sophia lived there for some months, but few tourists and too many middle-men involved in transportation to India lowered profits. She drew attention as a single white 'business woman' living alone during the war, and returned to Singapore.

Couriers rarely absconded; if, like Alex, an apparently well-off Belgian backpacker in his twenties, they did, they were usually found in Western backpacker centres in Bangkok, Nepal, or Hong Kong, and beaten until they returned the money. Polish smugglers exchanged currency and bought gold from Singapore money-changers. Larger-scale smugglers sent containers carrying tons of gold from Nepal to India; and by ship to Bombay and Colombo. Later, when the risks pertaining to gold-smuggling outweighed profits, and smugglers turned to drugs, absconders or dishonest dealers were killed.

The Poles' dealers in Delhi were Sikhs, small business owners. According to Jacek and money changers in Singapore, gold was the currency used to buy weapons destined for Kashmir, for Pakistani militant groups in Kashmir, and the Sikh nationalist movement for an independent Khalistan. After anti-Sikh riots in Delhi in 1984, the movement gathered strength. In 1986, Sikh separatists declared Khalistan a sovereign state. A major insurgency against the Indian government was suppressed in the early 1990s. Khalistan nationalists bought and manufactured fake dollars on a massive scale to raise money for the cause, flood the market, and further destabilise the national economy. The market in fake dollars also attracted Pakistani drugs and arms syndicates operating across Asia (including in Singapore and Hong Kong).

By 1990 gold smuggling was more risky. Increasingly, couriers were captured, consignments lost. Marek, who also ran a syndicate in Singapore, occasionally carried gold himself. Wearing a jacket capable of holding over 10 kg, he took the KLM flight to Amsterdam that transited in Delhi. When the cleaners boarded the flight in Delhi, they collected the jacket. The procedure seemed foolproof until he was removed from a flight by the police, whom he surmised were informed in advance of his flight, beaten in the airport, and sentenced to three years in prison. The Poles considered Delhi 'closed' thereafter; Bombay airport soon followed after metal detectors were installed. In Colombo, Sophia's dealer, a gold jewellery shop owner, was apprehended and arrested on capital flight related charges, his properties seized, and bank accounts frozen. He would reappear years later in Dubai as the owner of a small suite of hotels.

After India repealed the Gold Control Act in 1990, profits dropped to 10 per cent; each flight constituted a significant risk because of the numbers of successful flights needed to recover a loss. By 1992 smuggling had almost ceased. Groups disbanded. During this period Singapore bosses who also smuggled gold themselves such as Jacek, and his subsequent courier, Isabelle's stepsister were jailed; posters around the backpacker area Pahar Ganj in Delhi, and in Bangkok, invited tourists to visit Western prisoners in Tihar jail. Large Bangladeshi and Chinese syndicates were broken up and many members sent to jail. The Reserve Bank of India set up a gold bank for household depositors to earn a small interest rate, and allowed Non Resident Indians (NRIs) to import small amounts, with duty paid in foreign exchange – hoping thereby to accrue taxes from privately held gold gained from rampant smuggling and to dent the country's financial problems. Yet smuggling remained highly lucrative because of the price differential, $21 per gram in Singapore and over $30 in India.

In Singapore's Little India district interviews with money-changers revealed a shuttle trade, wherein Indian couriers and Singaporeans legally carried gold bars in exchange for free tickets. With 55 flights from Singapore to India a week, newspaper sources based on informal activities and approximations estimated that 1,650 couriers carried 8,250 kg of gold into India per week.[19]

In 1992 India halved gold import duty, calculating that smugglers' margins were already dented and their risks too high. After further big arrests, the trade largely stopped. At this point other groups of smugglers in the region, not usually Poles but Pakistanis, Chinese and Nepalis working out of Hong Kong, turned to smuggling other commodities through Asia. These included weapons, drugs, rare animals, banned animal products (ivory, rhino horn, snakeskins), plant species and animals (parrots, small monkeys, tortoises, reptiles), with much transiting through Frankfurt. Furthermore, migrants and refugees travelling from Asia to Europe would use the same routes, indeed paying former gold smugglers who had accrued 'mobility capital' in the form of skills in illegal cross-border smuggling.[20] A few former Iranian gold smugglers in Singapore, such as one I was acquainted with called Reza, turned to human smuggling.

Some Nepalese syndicates operated from Hong Kong then turned to trafficking Nepalese women and girls to Japan for sex work. Hong Kong took over from Singapore. Western tourists there signed up for the 'milk run' (exporting gold from Hong Kong, and returning with other goods to sell). Hong Kong was also a hub for fake dollars, manufactured by Japanese mafia groups. These travelled into Russia, where foreign currency was scarce, and exchange rates high. With the Russian money some bought rare illegal animal parts to sell in Beijing, such as black bear feet, an expensive food delicacy. One Englishman, Peter, partnered with a Pakistani dealer, Hasan, who bought rare golden eagle chicks from thieves or dealers in Urumqi who had contacts with hunters in the Altai mountains in western Mongolia, and transported them to Hong Kong where his English partner sedated them before flying them (in plastic tubes) on to the Arabian Gulf. These examples demonstrate how gold smugglers were not simply homogeneous national groups moving from one commodity to another, and connected to more serious 'crimes' as represented in popular journalistic media. Rather they represented a fully international heterogeneity of actors, different aspirations, different levels of involvement and trade across diverse places and time periods.

In Singapore, it transpired that Marek's arrest in Delhi had been due to information passed on to Indian authorities by a rival Iranian gold smuggler there, Farhad. One of Farhad's techniques was to fashion gold bars into coat hangers, with couriers passing as well-dressed 'businessmen'. After crossing paths several times around Singapore, Farhad and I struck up conversation. We occasionally met up. Gradually he divulged his story, although I would not know his real name for 20 years. During the 1979 Iranian revolution, he fled, like many, to Pakistan where he lived a year in Karachi, and met dealers in fake passports. Using one, he moved to Delhi where, moving through Iranian networks, he eventually arrived in Singapore. Here he sold stolen passports to gold smuggling syndicates, and falsified passports to smuggle Iranians to Europe. Although he described himself as a 'Robin Hood' character who helped his countrymen, he carried a knife around Singapore in case of attack by rival Iranians, and his help was indubitably partial. On one occasion, I struggled to assimilate the information that he had informed Indian customs about a plane with 18 Polish gold smugglers aboard. This particular flight was diverted to Delhi, all 18 couriers arrested, and the syndicate destroyed. One courier I heard about through her subdued flatmate was raped by several Indian customs officials in exchange for her freedom. While I did not encounter similar incidences perpetrated against male couriers, certainly the risks to women, if apprehended, included sexual violence in airports, in police custody, and prisons – as well as forfeiture of the smuggled gold.[21] Farhad subsequently continued smuggling gold and people to Europe until he and several migrant 'customers' were apprehended and imprisoned in Syria *en route* overland from Iran to Europe. He was able to bribe his way out, with immense difficulty, but could not help the others and stopped thereafter. Having lost his money in Syria, he settled in Europe where he now runs an Italian restaurant.

Through Western travellers in Singapore I met other Iranian syndicates and smugglers. Arash and Hussain's condominium, for example, was well-furnished and, aside from two bags containing Western passports in their living room, appeared like any middle-class Singapore apartment. However, illustrating the propensity of smugglers to fall victim to other long-established il/licit trades, Arash began spending more time in the Chinese opium houses around Bugis Street and, unable to manage his smuggling operations, drifted into more desperate means of survival, providing security to sex workers and massage parlours, stealing, and robberies.

Gold smuggling eased until in 2009 the Indian government doubled gold import tax. After 2009, Singapore, Dubai, Bangladesh and Sri Lanka remained popular origin and transit points, but in the drive to evade authorities, Thailand, Vietnam and Myanmar became prominent, highlighting the adaptability of the route to changing conditions. Fears circulated in the Indian press that, due to interlinkages of smuggling networks and illegal trades, some smugglers might now use profits to finance arms-on-credit for terrorist and secessionist groups, in a confluence of sensationalised threats to national interests.[22] This putative linkage may indeed have applied to some, but certainly not all and, as with all journalistic data, it requires interpreting with caution. The year 2013 witnessed a surge, as India raised gold import duty to 10 per cent in another attempt to decrease demand and the current-account deficit. Smuggled gold increased 365 per cent in the first quarter of 2013, with most coming from Bangkok and Dubai; smugglers' profit margins reached US $4,200 per kg; courier use revived.[23] By the end of 2013 gold prices were down, but taxes up. In 2014, India eased regulations to curb smuggling.

In the period from the late 1990s, some of those smugglers I knew returned to Poland empty-handed after long prison terms in India. Several Iranians in Singapore turned to smuggling people to Europe. While human smugglers would become notoriously unscrupulous, certainly Jacek *did* pay bribes to release his captured gold smugglers on several occasions (when, for example, one of them, Jean-Dominic, was arrested in Bombay and another, Torin, too obviously high on drugs, was arrested in Colombo) – whether out of moral imperative, a desire to protect his business, friendship, or likely a mixture of all of these. In other instances couriers turned to drug smuggling across the Nusantara; some women, former gold smugglers, sold sex in escort agencies in Singapore and Hong Kong alongside migrant women from China, Nepal and India. Exemplifying everyday interconnections of 'rival' syndicates in a small city-state like Singapore, some marriages ensued between Polish and Iranian smugglers. Jacek served several additional prison terms for gold and drug smuggling. Jon remained in Thailand and still battles his addiction; Torin operates a successful tourism agency. Sophia adapted her entrepreneurial flair to directing a successful, legitimate business.

Concluding thoughts

The conditions for the merging of legal and illegal movements of gold out of Singapore were set, not exclusively, by a convergence of the Indian 1968 Gold Control Act and its repeal in 1990, economic liberalisation and migration from Poland, liberalisation in India, the regrouping of individuals fleeing the Iranian revolution into smuggling networks, and a concentration after the 1960s of Western backpackers and travellers across Asia. The legacy of the British empire in Asia is at the centre of this historical interplay of global political-economic conditions, cosmopolitan social networks, social navigation, and altered life-courses that compelled a particular type of racialised illegal mobility and subject. The dimensions of risk and endangerment that smugglers assumed bear in interesting ways on Kleinman's arguments that the ways individuals respond to uncertainty and danger, to challenges posed by societies and to existential moral experiences, are definitive of what it means to be human.[24] They imply a dimension of extraordinary but also ordinary ethics enfolded into social life and human existence, and into ways people relate to each other – for example, how we respond to our ability to afford to travel, maintain dignity, or act in a way that is 'good'.[25] The moral economy of bosses and couriers fostered interdependencies that, here, led smugglers and handlers to live together, develop intimacies, transient loyalties, and to accept shared risks to liberty and life that also did not preclude betrayals, abandonment, lengthy prison terms, violence, sexual assault, lasting physical and psychological effects, and sometimes death. These forms of protection and care belie the common image of smuggling as only exploitative. Others, Farhad for example, were more ruthless in the levels of violence they calculated they were willing to inflict and accept. For all described here, excepting Jacek who intermittently revived his business, gold smuggling was time-limited. Given smuggling's furtive and illegal nature, this short chapter represents a small snapshot. The data is necessarily second-hand, and derived from a priori long-standing relationships of established trust that made confidences about the trade possible. However, what is clear is the entanglement of gold smuggling with illegal movements of drugs, arms, and people as commodities to exploit and profit from; the willingness of individuals to knowingly endanger themselves and others; and the conspiracy of political, economic, and historical conditions to allow such conditions to flourish.

Acknowledgements: My thanks to the University of Brighton for providing me a research sabbatical for six months during 2017–18, and to the Asia Research Institute at the National University of Singapore for hosting me as a Visiting Scholar during this period which I used in part to conduct the research for this study.

Notes

1. Sidney Mintz, *Sweetness and Power: The Place of Sugar in Modern History* (New York: Penguin, 1986).
2. Emma Tarlo, *Entanglement: The Secret Lives of Hair* (London: Oneworld, 2016).
3. Frederick Errington, Tatsuro Fujikura and Deborah Gewertz, *The Noodle Narratives: The Global Rise of an Industrial Food into the Twenty-first Century* (Berkeley: University of California Press, 2013).
4. Samuel Knafo, *The Making of Modern Finance: Liberal Governance and the Gold Standard* (Abingdon: Routledge, 2013); Nisha Mathew, 'God, gold and invisible routes to a cosmopolitan society in Malabar', ARI News, September 2017; Catherine Schenk, 'The global gold market and the international monetary system', in Sandra Bott (ed.) *The Global Gold Market and the International Monetary System from the Late 19th Century to the Present* (New York: Palgrave Macmillan, 2013), pp. 17–38.
5. Mathew, 'God, gold and invisible routes to a cosmopolitan society in Malabar', p. 8.
6. Nisha Mathew, 'At the crossroads of empire and nation-state: Partition, gold smuggling, and port cities in the western Indian Ocean', *Modern Asian Studies* 54(3), 2020, p. 204.
7. Charles Buckley, *An Anecdotal History of Old Times in Singapore* (Singapore: Fraser and Neave, 1902); J.A. Richardson, *The Geology and Mineral Resources of the Neighbourhood of Raub Pahang* (Kuala Lumpur: Geological Survey Department Federated Malay States, 1939).
8. Schenk, 'The global gold market and the international monetary system'.
9. Buckley, *An Anecdotal History of Old Times in Singapore*; Joh Crawford, 'Crawford's mission to Siam and Hue', *Quarterly Review*, 110, 1826, p. 110.
10. Carl Trocki, *Opium and Empire: Chinese Society in Colonial Singapore, 1800–1910* (Ithaca, NY: Cornell University Press, 1990), pp. 96–7.
11. John Frederick Adolphus McNair, *Prisoners Their Own Warders* (London: A. Constable and Co., 1899).
12. Daniel Tham, Curator, National Museum of Singapore. Personal communication, 5 December 2017.
13. See Mathew, 'At the crossroads of empire and nation-state'.
14. *Straits Times*, 'Business boom for gold smuggling in Asia', 9 September 1984.
15. *Business Times*, 'Smuggling threatens India's economy', 16 July 1984.
16. Mary Judd, 'Is harmony possible in a multiracial society? The case of Singapore', in Rik Pinxten and Ellen Preckler (eds) *Racism in Metropolitan Areas* (New York: Berghahn, 2005), pp. 107–11.
17. Janek Simon and Max Cegielski, 'Polish-Indian shop', Art Musuem, 2017. https://artmuseum.pl/en/wystawy/sklep-polsko-indyjski (accessed 17 October 2018).

18. Ibid.
19. *Straits Times*, 'Indian couriers in gold trade', 14 October 1993.
20. Jason de Leon, *Land of Open Graves: Living and Dying on the Migrant Trail* (Oakland: University of California Press, 2015).
21. While the gender division of couriers was fairly equal, most syndicate heads were men.
22. Andy Mukherjee, 'Indians' love for gold puts govt in a spot', *Straits Times*, 24 April 2012.
23. Krittivas Mukherjee, 'India's gold smugglers back in business', *Straits Times*, 15 August 2013.
24. Arthur Kleinman, *What Really Matters: Living a Moral Life Amidst Uncertainty and Danger* (Oxford: Oxford University Press, 2006).
25. Michael Lambek, *The Ethical Condition: Essays on Action, Person and Value* (Chicago: University of Chicago Press, 2015).

3

The Border Merchant

Aliyeh Ataei

Even under the full moon, the red revolving floodlights along the border between Iran and Afghanistan are easily visible. My guide is asleep in the next room. I wake him up, so we can get a head start toward the border village of Gazik. We are going to meet Mohammad Osman. 'I'll be up and running at 5:00 a.m.,' he'd said. 'Be there before me.'

Mohammad Osman Yusefzai has been arrested three times by Iranian border police for trafficking undocumented immigrants, and every time they've had to let him go for lack of evidence. His area of operation is the South Khorasan province of Iran, which borders Farah in Afghanistan. 'I have no idea where this guy is from,' an Iranian Border Police colonel told me later. 'He's got both Iranian and Afghan papers. The illegals we catch never testify against him. Even when we lock them up, they still won't testify. We know for a fact this man is moving people, but without witnesses stepping forward our hands are tied.'

I grew up near the border, on the Iranian side. In these in-between regions we have an entire vocabulary for the geography of our lives. Some places we simply call *the border*, some we call *border-plus*, some are called *this-side-of-the-border* and some *that-side-of-the-border*. It is a vocabulary that can be exhausting, and dangerous. Gazik is *border-plus*. It is on the very cusp.

Our aim is to meet Mohammad Osman early, before he dashes across to retrieve his human cargo. There's no sign of him in the designated parking lot, just a lone gray Peugeot. He shows up right before dawn, looking fearless and sure of himself. He is tall and has the tan of the desert. I've been told he's about 35, but he looks ten years older. Loose pants taper at his ankles and he wears a noticeably long white shirt – typical attire for Iranians and Afghans of the border areas. It's his leather jacket, though, that stands out in the intense, dusty summers around here.

As an excuse to meet him, I told Mohammad Osman I wanted to sneak into Afghanistan to avoid being fingerprinted by the Taliban. He doesn't believe me. 'Everybody wants to leave that cursed land to come here, and you want to go *there*?' I stare at him, unsure of what to say. 'What is it you really want? … I know a bit about your clan, you know. The Yusefzai over in Farah.' He's unimpressed, and looks at me in silence.

'Look, I just want to learn about the business of border traffic.'

The 'business' of the border is a thousand different things. Fuel, rice, sugar, beans, opium, humans. I'd always wanted to know the people who worked the *line*. For the first time in our brief conversation Mohammad Osman returns my gaze, and then he starts rattling off specific information about my family. Information is his job, and he has me down cold. He says, 'Listen, I'm not about to create a headache for myself by revealing the secrets of my trade to you.' I promise not to get in his way.

He replies, 'I still don't understand what it is you do.'

Life in Iran might not be easy for a lot of people, but compared to life in Afghanistan it's a cakewalk. For one thing, there are no suicide bombings every other day. In fact, there are two reasons why an Afghan risks the border crossing at all: to get work in Iran that Iranians won't do, or to find transit into Turkey to get to Europe. Either way, the border has to be crossed.

A pair of young men appear in the dim light of the parking lot. Assistants. Immediately they get to work, and start taking off the car's licence plates. Mohammad Osman curses under his breath the whole time. When he curses, his Afghan accent completely takes over. I ask my guide, *what's with the fake Iranian accent he puts on the rest of the time?*

'What's the difference what accent he fakes?' my guide shoots back. 'Do any of us living around here really know which side of the border we belong to?'

He has a point. On the other hand, border people have an almost obsessive relationship with identity – their own and everybody else's. We tend to immediately want to know where someone is from. We ask them questions about their geography; we want to pin them down in space and time. Mohammad Osman takes a spiral notebook out of the pocket of his leather jacket and waves it at me. 'Don't ask questions,' he says. 'Just go with it. The names you see in here, they are the names of my travellers.'

Yaqoob Salehrafi, Kunduz, January 28; Misaq Mohammadi, Anar-Dara, April 8th; Masumeh Yadegari, Faryab, January 5 …

I have no idea what the dates signify. Are these the dates they crossed the border? Or the day they signed up to cross? I try to show off the little bit I do know about the border business, and tell him how easily I can pick out the cars and buses that have been outfitted to cross over illegally. His laughter is like the neighing of a horse. 'I take care of my people, understand? I don't make them suffer sending them here and there. God takes care of Mohammad Osman and his work.' His two young assistants take all the seats out of the car. The stench that rises from the carpeting envelops us, difficult to take.

'What is that smell?'

'Don't ask,' he says automatically. 'Just take it in. That's fear you're smelling. A person can't hold much inside when they're that scared.'

The Border Patrol reports that approximately 3,000 Afghans try to cross into Iran from Afghanistan and Pakistan every day. Half of them are caught right away and turned back. The other half make a beeline for the big cities, hoping to blend in and disappear. As I'm wondering how Mohammad Osman and his cargo will fare today, he says, 'If for any reason the police stop you and ask questions, you tell them I used to work in your father's house. Got it?'

I nod.

The assistants walk off with the car seats while Mohammad Osman loads several gas cans in the trunk.

I muster a casual tone and say, 'We'll follow you in our own car.'

He doesn't bother to reply. 'Take this woman away from here now,' he says to my guide.

'But I want to learn how you get across the border!'

'Wait for us tomorrow at the Shamsabad Junction. We'll be back with our load between 4:00 and 6:00 a.m. That's as much as I'm going to show you.'

They set out.

For Mohammad Osman, who has spent his entire adult life hauling humans back and forth, there's never a question of why things are done, only the question of how. On the other side of the border there are no jobs, and a war, and there are men and women trying, somehow, to get to this side. But crossing the line comes with a cost. They need passports and visas and letters of invitation – things an Afghan who is not an expert at anything, and whose existence is of no consequence to anyone, will never get. The *why* is self-evident. Mohammad Osman says his job is to 'make people's lives better'. What I don't understand is the mechanism.

The next morning we hit the road at 3:00 a.m. There are a half-dozen ghost villages in the vicinity of the border. The one we drive to, the village of Shamsabad, was a lively place until a couple of decades ago, even boasting a marketplace. Then special Border IDs were issued to area residents, the authorities clamped down on who belonged to which side, and the market was closed. Choices had to be made; folk had to decide if they were Afghans or Iranians. Abandoned mud huts and rusting shipping containers are fading testimony to that time, a reminder of the realities of border life that loom over people here.

At the Shamsabad Junction we turn the engine off and wait. Afghan music wafts low over the radio, and unease sits in the car like another passenger. What if Mohammad Osman has gotten caught this time? It's still dark, but I get out. The wind and dust are overwhelming. At last we hear a car approaching. It's him, driving with no headlights. He signals us to follow. Inside the dead village we stop in front of one of the old shipping containers. Mohammad Osman jumps out of his car and unlatches the trunk; six people straggle out.

I stand there watching in disbelief. In the backseat are an impossible number of people, all tied down together with rope. On the top is a visibly pregnant woman, staring up at the car's ceiling. Beneath her is man who is more than likely her husband. No one speaks until the rope is pulled off. Each traveller gets out, then turns back to give Mohammad Osman a hand. There are people in the front seat, too. All in all, I count a total of eighteen. The pregnant woman can barely move, moaning quietly to herself. I can already tell that she and her husband are Pashto speakers, from a region close to Pakistan. The rest of the passengers speak Persian. In all of them there's fear, anxiety, fatigue, and frustration. Afghans have an expression for this particular combination: it's called *zende-margi*, living-death.

Mohammad Osman is holding the hand of an older man and speaking to him in a thick Afghan accent, far more respectfully than I'd heard him speak before. I have no idea who this man is, and I'm not supposed to ask any questions or talk to anyone. Of the eighteen, seven are obviously *Hazara* Shia, with very distinct Central Asian features. They will probably be easy pickings for the Iranian authorities. The rest might have a fighting chance if they don't open their mouths to let their accents give them away. How this is possible, I am not sure.

Mohammad Osman steers everyone toward the shipping container. None of the eighteen carries a single piece of luggage, or even a small bag.

My guide takes out a few packets of biscuits and soda from the back of our own car and lays them out for the travellers.

Mohammad Osman turns to me, 'A bad dust storm is on the way. Your eyes will suffer.' My discombobulation must be showing. He takes out a pouch of kohl from his pocket and offers it to me. 'Blacken your eyes. Kohl is magic for the eyes. Gives you the power of sight in the desert.'

A gentle side of him. Far too gentle for my idea of how a smuggler is supposed to act.

To the eighteen travellers, I am invisible. They don't see me. They've come out of hell and they're grateful just to be alive. I imagine them on the road, the hours they've spent tied down like that, and the way they look now, unsteady, murmuring to themselves. What do they hope to gain in Iran?

The wind picks up and Mohammad Osman's voice is barely audible. 'Ayoub and Yaqoob will be here soon. Before midday they'll get these people to Zabul. Our job is to get them that far; after that they're on their own.'

'And if they're caught? What border crossing do the police use to ship them back to Afghanistan?'

'The 78 Mile Road from Birjand.'

The 78 Mile Road from Birjand. It sounds like a song.

I still haven't seen any money change hands. Now that he's no longer insisting I keep my mouth shut, I say, 'You must be a rich man.'

'No. This is not money that lasts. Depending on who I'm transporting, I take anywhere between 100 and 500 dollars before the trip.'

He says 'dollars' like an American would – or like an Afghan would, after having had Americans invade his country and stay for going on two decades. Once again I'm unsure about this man. I want to believe him when he talks about making people's lives better, easier. I want him to confess to me that he doesn't take money from those who are too poor, or whose lives are in too much danger. But he talks quite readily about money – about the dollars on the other side of the border, and what he has to do to get them to Iran. He's a real smuggler, after all. This border might be a terrible thing for most people, but for Mohammad Osman it's been profitable.

I ask him, 'Who do you think builds borders?'

He shrugs. 'The barbed wire was probably built in Birjand.'

The question is too philosophical for him, or else he doesn't want to answer. For Mohammad Osman, the person who makes the barbed wire also makes the border. Both he and the wire-maker earn a living from the border.

The Afghans gather inside the shipping container and Mohammad Osman closes the hefty metal door behind them. The next step is for his assistants to arrive and collect the travellers for the next stage of their journey.

I watch Mohammad Osman get in his car, most of his work done. He turns to me and calls, 'You never told me what you do for a living.'

'And you never told me where you're really from,' I say. 'But if anyone ever asks you, tell them you're from the Khorasan province.'

He might or might not get it. Khorasan is a huge swath of the earth that has eternal significance for us Afghans. It's that territory of the real and of the imagined that connects Afghans to Iranians and to Central Asia – the cradle of Persian civilisation. Now we have the barbed wire, which cleaves Khorasan in two. It doesn't take much introspection on my part to realise what I've told Mohammad Osman is my own issue, not his. He waves a hand indifferently and drives away.

Eight months later, in April 2018, I receive word that Mohammad Osman has been caught and is being kept at the Ferdows prison. It's a substantial drive to get to the town of Ferdows, and I'm uncertain if it's worth it to go. They might not let me see him; I'm not close kin, nor do I carry a journalist identification card. I go anyway.

The officer in charge says, 'Of course we know this guy. He insists he's Afghan and carries an Afghan passport. But that could be a fake. Or maybe his Iranian passport is fake. Or maybe they're both fake. Who knows! I can't tell you what exactly will happen to him. If, as always, he turns out to be Afghan, we'll just throw him back to the other side. But if he should ever turn out to be Iranian, well, then his offence is pretty serious.'

We drink tea and chat, about the misfortunes of the Afghan people, the ongoing negotiations with the ruthless Taliban – who, even while negotiating, keep murdering fellow Afghans – the statistics on the dead and maimed, the numbers. We speak like newscasters, about everything and anything except the one thing that really matters: why the border is there at all.

The officer is from Shiraz, a laidback city in the south, far from any of Iran's numerous borders. On his desk sit an Afghan-made bracelet and a package of Indian green tea.

He volunteers, 'Gifts from these Afghans who are our "guests" for a while. When we finally send them back home, they always leave something behind and invite me to visit them if I'm ever in Afghanistan.' In that moment, this officer and Mohammad Osman and I seem to me to be one and the same person.

Three hours later they haul Mohammad Osman in. He's visibly happy to see me, and starts chattering in the thick Pashto that no Iranian speaks. He's trying to establish his Afghan bona fides for the authorities, but even while speaking Pashto he reminds me of the fiction we agreed upon eight months before, that he used to work for my father.

'Where have you been?' I ask.

Again he bursts into Pashto. 'I was supposed to bring my uncle's daughter from Kunduz and decided to take on a few other people who wanted to get to Iran. What harm's in that? But the woman, my cousin, what can I tell you! I heard she's already married an Iranian while I'm rotting here in jail.'

I have no idea if he's making this up. He's playing a whole other role today. A soldier, who's been standing at attention next to the door, brings him a glass of water, and Mohammad Osman offers a flurry of thank-yous in Pashto. It looks like they're inclined, as always, to accept him as an Afghan. The officer says, 'We'll send him back to Afghanistan soon.'

This time Mohammad Osman murmurs in the more familiar accent of the border, 'So much the better. Who wants Iran anyhow!'

The soldier, standing at attention again, sighs, as if agreeing with him. There's something utterly absurd, even sentimental, about our situation in this room, and this mix of sympathy and unforgiving law. After more than a year trying to figure out the human smuggling trade in this region, I finally understand that what I've really been trying to put my finger on is identity. Who is Mohammad Osman? A smuggler, neither Afghan nor Iranian. A person of the border. Mohammad Osman, like many border people, can shapeshift; he can be Robin Hood or Noah. He can make people's lives better, as he claims, or he can funnel them into this prison.

The officer excuses himself and leaves the room for a minute. With the soldier still with us, I ask Mohammad Osman if he needs anything. He continues to play the innocent – the lovestruck, clueless, Pashto-speaking Afghan. A clever narrative, but he still has to put in his six months behind bars and pay a fine before they throw him out.

I recall that last image of us in the desert, him asking me what I do for a living.

'We're both merchants, you know.'

He eyes me, and I want to believe he is as smart a smuggler as I wish he were.

'I'm a writer. I sell words to people. And you sell them the border.'

I take out of my wallet the little pouch of kohl he had given, and leave it for him on the table. The dreamy private pays no mind.

4

Smugglers and the State Effect at the Mexico-Guatemala Border

Rebecca B. Galemba

Introduction: looking for the law

Alonso[1] hardly considered himself a smuggler. A primary school teacher
in his mid-forties, he has lived in Chiapas, Mexico, but less than a mile
from the Guatemalan border, for his entire life. He, like most border residents, had family straddling the border. In the spring of 2007, however,
he decided to try to supplement his income by smuggling gasoline from
Mexico to Guatemala. Alonso's salary as a teacher earned him $700 per
month, but he could earn $1,600 per month smuggling gasoline.[2]

Smuggling pervades the daily life of those who reside along an unmonitored road crossing the Mexico-Guatemala border, which is one of the
busiest routes for contraband in the region. Local residents, whether they
participate in smuggling or not, rarely use the term 'contraband'. What
they call 'business' is conducted by truckers, businessmen and merchants
– not smugglers. Even residents who engage in smuggling often do so
to supplement other income-generating activities. They are unlikely to
identify as smugglers – or even primarily as businessmen. While there
is no one identifiable smuggler, few areas of the border economy are left
untouched by smuggling. Men who own multiple 10-ton trucks and who
smuggle coffee, sugar, and hire other drivers often identify as transporters.
Female vendors purchase clothing to resell to their neighbours on either
side of the border depending on prices and currency differentials. Guatemalan store-owners take advantage of currency differentials and cheaper
prices in Mexico to stock their inventories. Youth load cargo into trucks to
be smuggled across the border for a fee and widows charge businessmen to
use their fields to transfer and disguise cargo between trucks.

Smuggling is critical to community subsistence in this rural region.
Most smuggled goods are mundane: corn, coffee, clothing, fruits and veg-

etables, sodas and canned goods, but may include anything that fits inside a truck. Business occurs in broad daylight without official interference, provides jobs to local residents as merchants, truckers and cargo loaders, and generates economic ripple effects throughout the border communities. Residents admit that most of the profits remain with the businessmen, but without the smuggling economy, the communities would fail to thrive. In contrast, inhabitants occasionally used the terms 'contraband' or 'illicit commerce' to more quietly describe the trafficking of drugs, weapons and migrants.

Border inhabitants historically relied on corn farming, growing small amounts of beans and coffee, migrating for seasonal labour to southern Chiapas to work on coffee plantations, and some cattle ranching (for those with sufficient capital). Residents have also long depended on the price and regulatory differences generated by the border and their own cross-border networks to supplement their incomes by smuggling small quantities of goods. Yet Mexico's economic and agricultural reforms in the 1990s, which liberalised the corn sector in preparation for the North American Free Trade Agreement, made it increasingly difficult for Mexican corn farmers to sell their harvests. In this context, Mexican border residents increased their reliance on smuggling goods, especially corn, across the border. They took advantage of larger social upheavals in Chiapas in the 1990s that challenged the corruption of state officials and the exclusion of peasants to expel authorities who once monitored this route and nearby inspection posts.[3] Inhabitants on both sides of the border united to demand their right to smuggling as a form of livelihood, constituting a kind of citizenship right based on their border residence.[4]

After expelling authorities in the mid-1990s,[5] two Mexican (Santa Rosa and El Nance) and two Guatemalan communities (Nueva Vida and El Girasol)[6] along this road erected what they call *cadenas*, or chains (see Figure 4.1). The *cadenas* are toll-booths where the communities levy taxes on passing smugglers. Some smugglers are locals and others come from other regions and states, but they pass through with enough regularity to become accustomed to the tolls. The communities each drape a chain across the road to regulate entry and exit. In doing so, they offer an alternative interpretation of border control and the right to exact tolls. All household heads take turns guarding the *cadena* and funds are used for road maintenance, school and community building upgrades, electrical services, fairs, and other community projects. Many residents who guard the *cadena* also inevitably participate directly or indirectly in the smuggling economy. Yet local smugglers who have built larger businesses tend to pay other residents to work their turns.

Through these *cadena* tolls, the wider border communities benefit from smuggling, whether it be from local or long-distance smugglers. Residents do not view border smuggling as illicit nor the *cadena* tolls as predation. Locals consider these fees to be legitimate and necessary and likewise they go largely undisputed by truckers and merchants.[7] In contrast, due to a history of state officials entering their communities to collect bribes misconstrued as taxes, community members perceive official interference in smuggling to be extortion. Smuggling is largely dominated by border residents, regional merchants and their kin and social networks, even as these networks connect to larger formal businesses and transnational legal and illegal commercial chains.

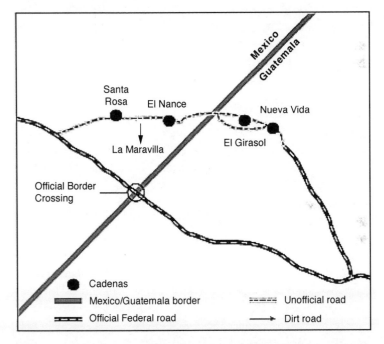

Figure 4.1   Map of border communities with rough position of *cadenas*. The official border crossing passes through the towns of Las Champas and Ciudad Cuauhtémoc, Chiapas, Mexico and La Mesilla, Huehuetenango, Guatemala.

Source: Drawn by the author based on the map in Rebecca B. Galemba, *Contraband Corridor: Making a Living at the Mexico-Guatemala Border* (Stanford, CA: Stanford University Press, 2018), with permission from Stanford University Press.

State regulations at the nearby formal border post at Ciudad Cuauhtémoc, Mexico and La Mesilla, Guatemala (see Figure 4.1) restrict most cross-border commerce that is not prearranged with a customs agent. The Mexican government authorises Ciudad Hidalgo, four hours to the south, the official crossing point for commerce with Guatemala whereas it designates Ciudad Cuauhtémoc as a crossing for tourism purposes. These restrictions make it nearly impossible for small businesses and peasants to participate in legal cross-border trade. Exclusion from formal trade opportunities and the Mexican state's abandonment of the corn sector left border residents with few options. As one resident related, 'This is a border famous for contraband, but there is nothing else.' Another added, 'It should not be contraband. Business provides work here ... business and the *cadena* benefit the entire community.' In this context, residents and border smugglers view the smuggling of basic goods as an ethical livelihood strategy and legitimate business. Their residence near the border, and their reliance on it, govern a sense of local ethics regarding who should control the border and how border commerce should be organised. However, such local ethics are not necessarily in opposition to, or external to state logics, even if smugglers defy state regulations by subverting border controls.[8]

As Alonso organised local truckers to participate in the gasoline smuggling business, he encountered a major stumbling block. Even though authorities rarely entered in their vehicles to inspect the route, he knew that all smuggling required relationships with, and the payment of regular bribes to, multiple state officials. However, he didn't know where to start. Was it with the customs agent? The highway police? How many people should he pay, how much, and how frequently? Which authority provided access to the others? Alonso lamented one day in frustration, 'We still need to look for the law.' By articulating his challenges, Alonso demonstrated how smugglers depend on the state to operate.[9] He also signalled how border residents and smugglers see, as well as effectively conjure, the state (or the law) as a unitary actor that exercises an all-encompassing, ghost-like power over the world of smuggling.[10]

This chapter demonstrates how smuggling does not necessarily undermine the state or espouse an alternative 'ethics of illegality'.[11] Instead, border residents' and smugglers' practices and discourses are integral to the maintenance and reproduction of the state as a 'structural effect', cloaking the power dynamics that uphold the division between the state and smugglers.[12] Smuggling practices produce state-effects from the margins that are critical to the maintenance of state power.[13] The smuggler as a 'figure of resistance' does not exist outside of, or necessarily in opposition to the state. Rather, the smuggler is constituted 'within the organizational terrain we call the state'.[14] The chapter examines how smuggling and alternative border control reproduce the state as structural effect through legibility, isolation, identification and spatialisation effects.[15] Smuggling, and the local border control practices and discourses it invigorates, reveal much about how the state continues to be recreated as a unitary, powerful abstraction. Seeing like a smuggler challenges normative scholarly, policy and social assumptions that morally and conceptually divide states from illegal practices like smuggling.[16]

The cadenas: local taxation as state effect[17]

In the 1990s, four communities residing along this unmonitored road crossing the Mexico-Guatemala border began levying tolls on smugglers to traverse the road. Rather than erecting chains at the geopolitical dividing line between the countries, the communities each placed their own chains at the borders of their own territory so that a trucker will encounter, and pay each, sequentially (see Figure 4.1). This enabled each community to benefit from the commerce using this route. Inhabitants realised that state agents who intermittently patrolled this border crossing frequently personally pocketed what they claimed were taxes. State officials are usually not native to the region and rotate frequently, and are thus delegitimised as 'de afuera', or from 'outside'. The communities therefore usurped this function and sought to delegitimise the state's role to perform it, at least at this particular crossing. In doing so, the border communities question the state's sovereign right to control what passes through its territory and appropriate taxes. The communities on both sides of the border communicate to ensure officials do not intervene and to maintain consistent toll prices to facilitate commerce.

The border, residents argue, is experienced at the cadenas, materially bordered with chains at each border community's territory, rather than at the international geopolitical division. These local informal practices appear to displace border authority from either national state. In doing so, they undermine central principles of state planning, in particular the state's function to make territory and populations legible, simplified and ordered to facilitate governance, and to monitor and shape citizen behaviour, and enable taxation.[18]

James Scott[19] contends that state attempts to execute such ordering often fail because they neglect, as they attempt to engineer over, complex social realities that are characterised by contingency and 'informal practices and improvisations'. Such tensions are often most visible in borderlands where individuals possess cross-cutting social, ethnic and economic allegiances that render the state's attempt to map, render legible, and order through the imposition of borders all the more unnatural.[20] In Scott's analytical framing, efforts to impose formal order are inevitably 'parasitic on informal practices'.[21] However, this assumes that border residents operate in ways that frustrate the central planning and sovereignty of the state to promote an alternative ethics. Instead, digging deeper into the *cadena* system demonstrates the ways that smugglers and border residents reproduce state effects of isolation, identification and spatialisation.

The border communities justify the right to regulate entry, exit and the flow of goods through their claims to territory. As residents argue, 'We live here and built [and maintain] the road ... so we have the right to work here.'[22] They do not contest state-like associations between territorial boundaries, power and taxation, but attempt to appropriate it for themselves. When I inquired whether other communities could erect *cadenas*, residents used state-like logics to argue that such taxes could only be levied at borders. Residents took for granted that *cadenas* could only be erected 'here because it is a border.... Other communities not on the border cannot have them.' Border communities question the authority of state actors to control their territory,[23] but in doing so, they produce state effects that fall well within prevailing understandings of the relation between authority, territory and taxation.[24]

The *cadena* system also exerts an 'identification effect', whereby 'individuals come to recognise themselves as the same ... a homogenising process', whereby individuals understand themselves as belonging to 'imagined communities'.[25] The *cadenas* generate an identification effect by uniting the communities that depend on them regardless of nationality; as one resident articulated: 'We are coyotes from the same wolf ... we are the same.'[26] Simultaneously, *cadena* practices and the connections facilitated by smuggling also produce identification effects with each respective nation-state. A Mexican corn smuggler noted that, 'Guatemala is another country, but we are also neighbours.' By delineating each separate community with a chain, and evidenced by times when the communities have used the chains to obstruct each other's commercial access, the *cadenas* also create localised identification effects. Internal community rules and obligations regarding each *cadena* create legibility and isolation effects, rendering individuals knowable, governable and accountable. At monthly assembly meetings, community leaders announce how much money each pair collected during their shifts, enabling surveillance into community profits and over particular individuals.

The border communities grasp that decisions enacted on one side of the border inherently impact the other. In response to a dispute between competing groups of Mexican gasoline smugglers in the spring of 2007, each Mexican border community raised its *cadena* to obstruct the other's commerce and *cadena* revenues. This was possible because the road from El Nance serves as the entry point to the border with Guatemala while Santa Rosa, on the same road but further from the border, provides the access point to the Mexican highway (see Figure 4.1). Within a few days, community leaders from a Guatemalan border community, which shares the same road, drove to the Mexican communities to complain and offer to mediate. One of the Guatemalans lamented, 'By being at the border, [this closure] affects us as well ... [and] what comes in.' Blocking the *cadenas* on the Mexican side meant that Guatemala border residents had no smuggling work opportunities (or trucking or cargo loading) and no income coming into their *cadenas*. Demonstrating how the *cadenas* also reproduce national identification effects, the Mexican communities at first claimed that the dispute did not concern those in Guatemala. They soon realised, however, as one Mexican resident put it, 'We need to unite the communities on both sides since commerce affects all of our interests [and] ... in order for the chain to function.'[27] The Mexican border communities have also coordinated to close their *cadenas* strategically when state authorities have attempted to intervene. In one instance, the communities each raised their *cadenas* and gathered in the middle of the road to prevent authorities from exiting to the Mexican highway. In doing so, they forced Mexican authorities to cross into Guatemala and loop back through the official crossing point to re-enter their own country.[28]

The *cadenas* may generate a wider identification with a transborder community that depends on smuggling and *cadena* revenues, but justifications for having *cadenas* also inherently draw on, and reiterate, nation-state logics that extend the racialising effects of bordering practices. In the 1930s, Mexico pursued strong nationalist campaigns in the borderlands to forcibly assimilate indigenous peoples who shared ethic identities with Guatemalan indigenous groups as part of a nation-state making process.[29] This left a legacy whereby many Mexicans in the borderlands conflate Guatemalan nationality and indigenous identity, using these ethno-nationalist assumptions to preclude indigenous peoples from belonging in Mexican border spaces. However, the ethnic composition of the borderlands was reshaped by the exodus of thousands of indigenous Guatemalan refugees fleeing at the height of the Guatemalan conflict in the early 1980s.[30] After the war, most refugees returned to Guatemala, but others settled in Mexico or relocated closer to the border. Within this particular route, one community, La Maravilla, was settled in 2000 by former refugees who naturalised as Mexicans, and on the Guatemalan side, Nueva Vida was established by former Guatemalan refugees who had lived in Mexico during the conflict. Instead of returning to their homeland in the Guatemalan highlands, residents of Nueva Vida purchased this land abutting the borderline. These communities experience a tenuous inclusion at the border. For example, the Mexican border communities prohibit La Maravilla from erecting their own *cadena*. They justify this exclusion by invoking ethno-nationalist associations between territorial borders, identity, and rights to the border. The other Mexican communities assert that La Maravilla does not technically lie along the actual border road (it is located up a small path emanating from the main road) and that it was settled after the other communities had already constructed the road.

In this relatively non-indigenous region of Chiapas, some Mexicans claim that former refugees who naturalised in Mexico are still Guatemalan and belong in Guatemala. This rationale perpetuates the 'national order of things',[31] whereby identity and a world of territorial nation-states neatly align and exclude. Local perceptions about belonging at the border reproduce what Shahram Khosravi[32] refers to as a racialised 'border gaze', such that racialised populations are excluded from belonging and considered suspect and out of place. One Mexican resident erased indigenous peoples from the borderlands, stating that, 'There are no indigenous people here [referring to the Mexican side of the border].' He believed that indigenous peoples present in the borderlands could not be Mexican, but instead were 'really from Guatemala'.[33] The linguistic use of the term '*here*' effectively positions indigenous peoples as outside of the national space. *Cadena* practices do not represent an alternative logic of border control that revolves around smuggling outside of the state; but rather mimic statist logics while also laying bare the 'untenable hyphen' between nation and state.[34]

Spatialisation effects: a patchwork of control

Michel-Rolph Trouillot[35] argues that 'regardless of the relative effectiveness of governments at border patrol, the national state still produces – and quite effectively – a spatialisation effect' whereby individual citizens accept themselves as a '*we* [that] live in a place usually defined in part by a political border'. Alleged gaps in state sovereignty, like this unmonitored border route, are integral to upholding the spatialisation of the state as one of territorial integrity.[36] The border road resembles a patchwork of state and local bordering practices and control, intermittently composed of pavement laid by the municipality with dirt portions constructed by the communities. When the respective municipalities on both sides of the border offered to pave the entire road, local smugglers helped convince their communities to refuse. They feared that this would provide the government with a mandate to intervene in their business. The road's patchwork reflects the ways that smuggling economies and local border control do not exist outside of the state, but instead, help constitute the state's authority and territorial integrity through their very transgressions.

When I asked border residents who depend on the smuggling economy, 'Who controls the border?', their responses revealed a patchwork of control that reproduced the state's spatial hierarchy. One resident, Edgar, reasoned that, 'The government controls [the border],' referring to the international division marked by white monuments. 'But,' he continued, 'they don't have control over the actual border ... the [community] has autonomy ... the communities control the path and commerce going through.... The border is free for all to pass through.' He reflected how border residents spatialise their own forms of border control in relation to the state's. Inhabitants and smugglers respect the authority of the state to control the geopolitical division while they assert that they control the access to the border because they own the property along the road. Another resident clarified, 'The land [along the road] belongs to the landowners whereas the state and municipal government keep the line and monuments [that demarcate the geopolitical border] clean.' According to Carlos, a Mexican border resident and corn smuggler, 'The government controls the border, but we organise [among ourselves to control the border] too.... The [geopolitical border] line belongs to the government.... The path belongs to the communities so [there is] control by the government and by the people too.' Through these explanations, residents and smugglers produce a state effect of seeing the border as a 'line in the sand'[37] even as they frustrate the ability of the state to control flows of goods across its borders. The description of the line controlled by the government over there, and the path controlled by the communities here, spatially reflects this patchwork of control. At the same time, this very distinction is a product of, and internal to, the very organisational terrain of the territorial state.[38]

When I interviewed him in 2006, Fernando, a farmer, was also serving a term as a community authority in one of the Mexican border communities. He too smuggled corn and gasoline to supplement his income. Smuggling and subsistence blurred; he was in the corn [smuggling] business, he stated, both 'to sell and to eat'. Fernando expressed a sentiment echoed by many border residents that 'Corn is not contraband ... it is a basic grain.'[39] He appreciated how living at the border provided opportunities to earn a living selling goods across the border. He asserted that the border communities collaborated to prevent authorities from interrupting their businesses: 'We are united here ... if I had a problem with my business [with authorities] everyone would come to help me ... the authorities are now afraid of the people.' Fernando explained how the communities make rules and that merchants respect the communities more than the government; as he noted, 'the businessmen mock the laws'. In the same sentence, however, Fernando admitted that, 'we govern some things, but not all.... In some parts the government governs, in some parts us.' He stressed the community's independence to engage in smuggling, but qualified that, 'Autonomy can be good, but it can be bad to just declare to do whatever you want [to do]. We also need to respect the government.' Governance is exercised, according to Fernando, 'a little bit [by] the government ... a little bit [by] us'. At times strongly defending their right to control the border and benefit from smuggling, residents and smugglers also recognise that they do not solely control the border outside of the role of the state. Like Fernando, few border residents contest the sovereign right of the state to control official border inspections points at the international line or the state's 'exclusive rights to create and implement laws.'[40]

Local framings of border control around the smuggling economy contribute to the spatialisation of the state through verticality (the state is 'above' society) and encompassment (the state contains its regions and localities).[41] Border residents realised that they had more power to negotiate with municipal officials than with state and federal units. One resident explained:

> The communities here control the flow.... [But] with other officials not from the municipality [federal, state], we learn how to talk with them to ... negotiate with [these] units that have more influence than the municipality.

As another Mexican border resident continued:

> If someone makes a denouncement ... saying someone is taking bribes for example, and the merchants are paying the federales locales, Mexico will send someone to investigate here. But when they come, the federales locales know when they are going to come and advise the merchants ... [and] nothing moves [across the border].

Even in their efforts to subvert state authority and facilitate contraband, residents and smugglers rely on, and help bring forth the state's spatial ordering and aggregation of jurisdictions under a central vertical and encompassing authority, naturalising a hierarchy from the local to the regional, state, and federal levels.

Border officials use similar spatialised language to justify turning a blind eye to contraband on unmonitored paths. Some officials and residents called such unmonitored routes *extravios*, or deviations, implying that they exist outside of state regulation and are deviations from regular commercial routes. This term positions unmonitored routes outside of the state's jurisdiction, but simultaneously leaves them open to potential intervention to reclaim territorial integrity. As one resident noted, 'There is no law for gaps [unmonitored routes].' These perceptions reinforce official convictions that this is a relatively forgotten border with little commerce. A Mexican fiscal inspector confirmed how seeing like a state reinforces the idea and myth of the all-powerful state as structural effect:

> The image is that Mexico is controlling borders, but in practice, no. What the government wants to do most is demonstrate an image that it is controlling things, but of course, in practice, if you actually see, you know that it isn't true.... The government likes images of control, but to actually make control implies costs.[42]

Seeing like a state reproduces the image of the sovereign container nation-state controlling its borders as territorial gaps are embedded in, and used to reinforce, this very fiction.[43] This depiction, however, obscures how most commerce in the region passes through unregulated channels and intertwines with legitimate commodity flows and businesses.[44] Guatemalan coffee is smuggled to Mexican warehouses to be packaged with other Mexican coffee (as if it were all Mexican) and legally exported to Europe. Smugglers' proceeds are reinvested into legitimate stores and businesses that pay local taxes even as they necessarily deprive the state of other revenue from circumventing official border inspections and duties. Seeing from the vantage of point of smuggling corridors reveals that clandestine routes are not marginal or irrelevant to the economy, but integral to it.[45]

Local efforts to displace and usurp the border and its functions from the state exist within the system of state relations; not outside of it. This point became evident when residents evaluated rumours that the government would close their border access by installing more surveillance within the route. The terminology of 'closure' references a state-centric materialisation of the border as a discrete object or line. In response to the rumours, one resident reified the law as unitary abstraction when conceding that he heard the government was going to make their law, depicting a ghost-like swooping in of the law applied onto their territory. Such discursive abstractions perpetuate the 'depoliticising effects of abstractions of "the state" … [that enable it to appear] as an autonomous … all-powerful and mysterious' actor.[46]

Even as some residents' perceptions about closing the border reinforced the fiction of the state as an integral, unitary and abstract entity, others pointed to the variegated geography and uncertainty of the division. One elderly Mexican resident reminded me:

> We would adapt because [the border] has changed before. Before the [monuments] at the line weren't there, but we got used to it. People find another place to pass things … it would be a bit more difficult, but we would adapt.

Seeing like a smuggler reveals the multiple ways of experiencing the border beyond the state's line of division, but in ways that do not exist outside of, or necessarily undermine the state. Instead they are integral to how the state is continually constituted and reconstituted from its margins.

Identification effects: living at the border

> Many have now forgotten agriculture and learn how to engage in business as their inheritance [or heritage]…Because they are from the border, this same border offers us this [opportunity to engage in smuggling]. (A border resident)

Understanding how border residents and smugglers see and talk about living at the border revealed how discursive bordering practices produce identification, as well as spatialisation effects. Below, I detail how border residents responded to the question: What are advantages and disadvantages of living at the border? Do you identify with Mexico, Guatemala, or both?

Many families span the border; residents constantly reminded me that Chiapas was once part of Guatemala and that most Mexican families in the region traced their roots to Guatemala. Although border residents often articulated strong nationalist sentiments, their daily lives also revealed the ways that the border generated a transborder identity, which also grounded the right to engage in smuggling. What tied residents together, as well as separated them, was intimately related to the state effects of the border. Discourses about the border produced identification effects as residents personified and objectified the border. As one resident responded, 'Only the line divides [us].… We are more or less the same,' invoking a two-dimensional line separation while also recognising the ways borders can inculcate a broader transborder identity. Most residents and local smugglers portrayed living at the border as a particular advantage, or as an inheritance, that offered them the opportunity to engage in smuggling and its related occupations.[47]

Border inhabitants frequently personified the concept of the border as a provider for the community, in similar fashion to how they discussed the discrete *cadenas* and their tolls. As one resident stated, 'I like the border. It is good because of business … more work.… It provides work for people here and the *cadena* [as well].' Residents questioned dominant policy rhetoric that called for the need to control borders to stem possible threats, often associated with the breach of territorial integrity, state sovereignty, and the ethno-racial national space. Some residents feared that although the border was tranquil, risks remained because it is a pathway for everything. Residents also associated outsiders with possible threats, but displaced the division between us and them from the geopolitical border to the Guatemalan interior. For example, Mexican residents possess close social relations with Guatemalans in the border region, whom they often called *paisanos* (countrymen). They therefore extend the border to include Guatemalans living in the borderlands as insiders in a larger conceptual-isation of border citizenship. On the other hand, dangers were associated with individuals from the other side, with the other side as a possible threat re-spatialised from the geopolitical division between Mexico and Guatemala to the Guatemalan interior and other Central American coun-tries. However, the complexities of ethno-nationalism limit the inclusion of indigenous peoples on both sides of the border, most of whom settled in the region during and after the Guatemalan conflict. Non-indigenous Mexican and Guatemalan border residents are more likely to marry one another than their indigenous conational neighbours.[48]

State effects of identification are not only extended to include wider geographic spaces; the border is also embodied by residents in literal con-formation with statist geographies. For example, some Mexican residents in Santa Rosa asserted that Mexicans in the neighbouring community of El Nance were *más frontera*, or more border-like (implying they shared more ties with, and were more like, Guatemalans), because El Nance's territory geographically touched the border. In contrast, Santa Rosa's inhabitants felt distinctly more Mexican although one community is located just a short walk down the same road from the other (see Map).[49] Yet Mexicanness also pervaded the Guatemalan side of the border, where the customs, music, food and linguistic terms share more in common with Mexico than Guatemala. 'Because we are borderlanders, we do [and] have a lot in common,' mentioned one Guatemalan border resident. However, former Guatemalan refugees claimed that the regional dominance of Mex-icanness made it difficult for them to reclaim their indigenous customs and language. As for former Guatemalan refugees, their Mexican neigh-bours often reasserted the border to remind them that they could never be Mexican enough; for example, some Mexicans still called them refugees.

The identification effect generated by living along the border grounds local ethics governing the smuggling economy. Border residents form rotating associations for smuggling businesses based on a local ethic that 'Everyone who lives here [along the border] has the right to work [in the smuggling industry and its associated occupations like trucking and cargo loading].' They also rely on this ethic to identify and exclude outsiders, which referred to individuals from communities not residing along this

border road, from participating in the smuggling economy. Border inhabitants invoke a similar spatialising logic to justify their own control and
delegitimise the right of outside officials to interfere in their business
on their property. In contrast, state officials also employ similar binaries
between the state and smugglers to further pathologise petty smugglers
and border residents as criminals or mafia who attempt to make their own
law.

Legibility effects: middlemen smugglers

To effectively circulate and escape sanction, contraband goods must be
disguised or transformed. Relationships between middlemen smugglers
and state agents reveal how contraband is rearranged and classified into
legitimate national goods, which generates legibility effects, or the ability
to render society and activities legible to facilitate practices of governance.[50] In this fashion, smuggling is not illegible to the state, nor does
it always frustrate state tax collection efforts. Instead, state agents help
render contraband legible to foster prevailing forms of governance and
accumulation in the region. For example, municipal officials in La Democ-
racia, Guatemala, have arranged to tax Mexican smuggled corn entering
Guatemala, providing it with a semblance of legality, legibility and state
oversight even though the practice remains against national laws. Because
this municipality suffers from perpetual corn shortages, it tolerates corn
smuggling through this particular route in exchange for a small fee per
truck. However, whenever authorities rotate posts or are replaced, this
agreement is threatened, often leading to raids, arrests and new negotiations that re-demonstrate the power of the state to selectively enforce the
law, look the other way or attempt to regulate smuggling.

Mexican border resident Tito also relies on relationships with different
state authorities to enable coffee smuggling. Each year his family frets over
whether Mexican officials will allow him to work. He must often negotiate
with different Mexican authorities each year, lamenting that 'There are
always more [state officials] to pay [to look the other way or to help facilitate contraband].'[51] These negotiations enable smuggling, but also permit
authorities to maintain a degree of surveillance over smugglers and their
activities. Tito also works with a contact in the nearby Mexican municipality who provides him with *constancias*, or forms, so that he can certify that
the Guatemalan coffee he smuggles to Mexico originated in Mexican communities. The verb *constar* means to establish, state or render official and,

as such, represents the space in which the state and illegal practices come together as state authorities help make contraband legible.

Upon further introspection, it is unclear whether Tito is a smuggler, a businessman or a middleman. He runs a business to smuggle coffee between Guatemala and Mexico and the direction of the commerce depends on prices, types of coffee beans, and the demands of formal sector companies and warehouses. Tito and his drivers, meanwhile, bear the risks and stigma of illegality, whereas his clients supplement their inventories and profit by mixing in the smuggled coffee with little risk to themselves – and facilitated by municipal authorities who add bribes to otherwise low salaries. The terminology of contraband implies a moralistic assessment applied to the product or person, when in fact it is the outcome of seeing like a state. As one resident put it, 'The problem is to cross a border … that is what makes it contraband they say. But then [once] in Guatemala, it is no longer contraband.'

Tito is essentially a middleman, a term which frequently invokes a pejorative assessment of individuals who profit from exploiting producers and consumers. Instead, border residents use their social and geographic positions of being in the middle, between Mexico and Guatemala, to ethically justify their roles in business – they know people and facilitate access to markets on both sides. Spatialising the border as such a middle space also carries a moral stigma of inevitable transgression that derives from a state-driven logic. It reflects assumptions of a coherent, territorial integral state on each side where people and things belong.[52] Accordingly, the state has the sole right to determine who can cross the line in an orderly fashion. Hence deviations always pose a latent risk. These discursive moves abstract the role of the state in producing such dislocations, middles and edges. The state does not stand apart from, or in fundamental opposition to allegedly deviant or illegal practices; instead these practices inhere within, and are made possible by, the concept of the state. Critically examining how the state is produced as structural effect demonstrates how the state and formal actors benefit from such blurred arrangements of power. One resident related what becomes hidden with the focus on the intermediary and border zone: 'If I am going to conduct business, I would rather put someone in the middle … put other people … so I don't get in trouble.… Usually the ones who are caught are the intermediaries … not the big [players].' Seeing like a smuggler challenges moralistic assumptions that associate middlemen and borders with deviance, assumptions which are shaped by statist discourse that positions borders as moral and physical risks to territorial integrity, sovereignty and national identity.[53]

Similar parallels can be drawn regarding who is considered a smuggler and what constitutes legitimate business in a region where corruption and informality also pervade the formal sector. As Alonso reminded me, many teachers also pay bribes or cultivate personal relationships to acquire permanent posts. Mexican customs agents admitted that most commercial fraud was committed by legitimate companies that profit from mispricing their wares and falsifying invoices.[54] Even as smuggling interferes with the state's sovereign authority to control its borders, smuggling inevitably depends on, and 'reaffirm[s] the very borders which they seek to subvert'.[55]

Conclusion: Smugglers and the state

Beginning with Alonso's case, this article demonstrates how smugglers and the state depend on one another, even though officials rarely visibly intervene in this border route. Knowing who, where and how much to bribe is a constant source of unpredictability for border residents when state officials frequently rotate. The inherent threat of state intervention, as well as periodic dramatic displays of state authority, including a military raid on gasoline trucks in 2008,[56] serve to remind people, and summon the magic-like aura of the state.[57] The illusion, ambiguity and mystifying power inspire fear, anxiety and obscure relations of domination.[58] Intense performances of power demonstrate how smuggling practices are situated within the organisation of the state and how they serve to discipline actions, obscure state complicity, and inculcate fear that is difficult to locate.

The juxtaposition between smugglers and the state reinforces the structured abstraction and power of the state while neglecting the ways that smuggling and state power constitute one another in the borderlands. Smugglers depend on state authorities in order to operate and to certify their goods, officials depend on smugglers to augment meagre salaries, and smuggling provides livelihoods and maintains stability in a marginalised region. The threat of smuggling and unmonitored crossings keeps border security in business as the law, sovereignty, and the gaps in both, make smuggling possible and lucrative.[59] It is in the transgressions and disruptions that sovereignty inheres.[60] In the borderlands, the right to smuggle is also an assertion of the right to citizenship, belonging and resources that are frequently denied to marginalised populations at the fringes of the nation-state and economy.

The figure of the smuggler does not exist apart from, in opposition to, or underneath the state, as is often implied by language like 'the dark side' of globalisation,[61] 'the other side' of globalisation,[62] or 'the black market'. These terms reproduce the fictional dichotomy between states and illegal practices, and depoliticise the power dynamics upholding it.[63] It is the very state system of organisation and categorisation; its workings of power, discipline and surveillance; and the relationship between power, discourse and knowledge that make the criminal or smuggler possible, knowable and thinkable as a discrete, unitary Other. The state requires, as Begoña Aretxaga[64] contends, 'constant exclusions'.

Unpacking how the state/smuggler binary is reproduced further points to how it serves to divide humanity into those who deserve rights, and who are legitimate business actors and legal border crossers, while conjuring the mirror image of the criminal or deviant who becomes relegated to the realm of the unnatural to be subjected to criminalisation and stigma. The figure of the criminal smuggler, and the fantasies and fears it animates, makes the idea and structure of the state possible and desired, which in turn produces as structural effect – the criminal smuggler.

Notes

1.   All names are pseudonyms to protect identities.
2.   Case elaborated in Rebecca B. Galemba, *Contraband Corridor: Making a Living at the Mexico-Guatemala Border* (Stanford, CA: Stanford University Press, 2018), pp. 188–208.
3.   Highway improvements, the extension of electrical and phone service, and rise in car and truck ownership (often purchased from the United States or with migrant remittances) also facilitated the growth of smuggling.
4.   See Galemba, *Contraband Corridor*.
5.   Ibid.
6.   Names of communities are pseudonyms to protect residents and the specific location.
7.   In the past, corn producers in the region complained about the tolls, but eventually acquiesced because they relied on the road to sell their corn to Guatemala and lacked an alternative means to do so. The border communities also maintain respect for the tolls by not charging individuals transporting goods for their own consumption; only goods intended for business exchange. According to residents, smugglers do not mind the

tolls, and some even give additional voluntary contributions, because
they appreciate that the communities maintain and repair the road and
largely keep state authorities at bay (see Galemba, *Contraband Corridor*).

8. See Hastings Donnan and Thomas M. Wilson (eds) *Borders: Frontiers of
    Identity, Nation, and State* (Oxford: Berg, 1999).
9. Peter Andreas, 'Smuggling wars: Law enforcement and law evasion in a
    changing world', in Tom Farer (ed.) *Transnational Crime in the Americas*
    (London: Routledge, 1999), pp. 85–98.
10. See Timothy Mitchell, 'The limits of the state: Beyond statist approaches
    and their critics', *American Political Science Review* 85(1), 1991, pp. 77–96.
11. See Janet Roitman, 'The ethics of illegality in the Chad Basin', in Jean
    Comaroff and John L. Comaroff, (eds) *Law and Disorder in the Postcolony*
    (Chicago: University of Chicago Press, 2006), pp. 247–72.
12. Mitchell, 'The limits of the state', p. 95.
13. Veena Das and Deborah Poole (eds) *Anthropology in the Margins of the
    State* (Santa Fe: School of American Research Press, 2004).
14. Mitchell, 'The limits of the state', p. 93, drawing from Michel Foucault,
    Discipline and Punish: The Birth of the Prison, trans. Alan Sheridan, 2nd
    edn (New York: Vintage Books, Random House, 1995).
15. Michel Rolph Trouillot, 'The anthropology of the state in the age of glo-
    balization: Close encounters of the deceptive kind', *Current Anthropology*
    42(1), 2001, pp. 125–38.
16. Josiah McC. Heyman and Alan Smart, 'States and illegal practices:
    An overview', in Josiah McC. Heyman (ed.) *States and Illegal Practices*
    (Oxford: Berg, 1999), pp. 1–24.
17. Some excerpts in this section appear in Rebecca B. Galemba, 'Remap-
    ping the border: Taxation, territory, and (trans)national identity at the
    Mexico-Guatemala border', *Environment and Planning D: Society and Space*
    30(5), 2012, pp. 822–41.
18. James C. Scott, *Seeing Like a State: How Certain Schemes to Improve the
    Human Condition have Failed* (New Haven, CT: Yale University Press,
    1998), p. 2.
19. Ibid., p. 6.
20. Donnan and Wilson, *Borders*, p. 13.
21. Scott, *Seeing Like a State*, p. 310.
22. Cited in Galemba, 'Remapping the border', p. 825.
23. See Itty Abraham and Willem van Schendel, 'Introduction: The making
    of illicitness', in Itty Abraham and Willem van Schendel (eds) *Illicit Flows
    and Criminal Things: States, Borders, and the Other Side of Globalization*
    (Indianapolis: University of Indiana Press, 2005), p. 14.
24. Roitman, 'The ethics of illegality in the Chad Basin'.
25. Trouillot, 'The anthropology of the state in the age of globalization',
    pp. 126, 132.
26. See Rebecca B. Galemba, 'Report: Coyotes from the same wolf', *NACLA
    Report on the Americas* 51(1), 2019, pp. 49–54.

27. Cited in Galemba, *Contraband Corridor*, p. 196.
28. See ibid., pp. 116–17.
29. R. Aída Hernández Castillo, *Histories and Stories from Chiapas: Border Identities in Southern Mexico* (Austin: University of Texas Press, 2001).
30. Ibid.
31. Liisa H. Malkki, 'Refugees and exile: From "Refugee Studies" to the national order of things', *Annual Review of Anthropology* 24(1), 1995, pp. 495–523.
32. Shahram Khosravi, *'Illegal' Traveller: An Auto-ethnography of Borders* (London: Palgrave Macmillan, 2010), pp. 76–7.
33. Cited in Galemba, *Contraband Corridor*, p. 36.
34. Begoña Aretxaga, 'Maddening states', *Annual Review of Anthropology* 32(1), 2003, p. 396.
35. Trouillot, 'The anthropology of the state in the age of globalization', p. 133, emphasis mine.
36. Das and Poole, *Anthropology in the Margins of the State*, p. 4.
37. Chris Rumford, 'Towards a multiperspectival study of borders', *Geopolitics* 17(4), 2012, p. 887.
38. Mitchell, 'The limits of the state', p. 93.
39. See Rebecca B. Galemba, '"Corn is food, not contraband": The right to "free trade" at the Mexico–Guatemala border', *American Ethnologist* 39(4), 2012, pp. 716–34.
40. Alison Mountz, 'Human smuggling, the transnational imaginary, and everyday geographies of the nation-state', *Antipode* 35(3), 2003, p. 637.
41. James Ferguson and Akhil Gupta, 'Spatializing states: Toward an ethnography of neoliberal governmentality', *American Ethnologist* 29(4), 2002, p. 981.
42. Cited in Galemba, *Contraband Corridor*, p. 157.
43. Susan Bibler Coutin, 'Being en route', *American Anthropologist* 107(2), 2005, pp. 195–206.
44. Carolyn Nordstrom, *Global Outlaws: Crime, Money, and Power in the Contemporary World* (Berkeley, CA: University of California Press, 2007).
45. Ibid.
46. Mountz, 'Human smuggling, the transnational imaginary, and everyday geographies of the nation-state', pp. 637–8.
47. See Galemba, *Contraband Corridor*, pp. 160–87.
48. Ibid., pp. 49–73.
49. Donna Flynn, 'We are the border: Identity, exchange, and state along the Bénin-Nigeria border', *American Ethnologist* 24(2), 1997, pp. 311–30.
50. Scott, *Seeing Like a State*; Trouillot, 'The anthropology of the state in the age of globalization'.
51. Cited in Galemba, *Contraband Corridor*, p. 171.
52. Malkki, 'Refugees and exile', p. 516.
53. For example, see Abraham and van Schendel, 'Introduction: The making of illicitness'.

54. Also see Nordstrom, *Global Outlaws*, pp. 199, 206.
55. Donnan and Wilson, 'Introduction: The making of illicitness', p. 105.
56. See Galemba, *Contraband Corridor*, p. 204.
57. Michael Taussig, *The Magic of the State* (New York: Routledge, 1997).
58. Aretxaga, 'Maddening states', pp. 400–1.
59. Andreas, 'Smuggling wars', p. 96.
60. Ferguson and Gupta, 'Spatializing states'.
61. Moisés Naím, *Illicit: How Smugglers, Traffickers and Copycats are Hijacking the Global Economy* (New York: Random House, 2005).
62. Abraham and van Schendel, 'Introduction: The making of illicitness'; see their book title for example: *Illicit Flows and Criminal Things: States, Borders, and the Other Side of Globalization.*
63. Mitchell, 'The limits of the state', p. 90.
64. Aretxaga, 'Maddening states', p. 407.

5

Kolbari: *Workers not Smugglers*

Amin Parsa

'We are not smugglers, we are only searching for an income to provide for ourselves and our families', says Attaullah, a 38-year-old *kolbar*.[1] *Kolbari* refers to a form of transportation of goods across borders between Iran, Iraq and Turkey. This form of smuggling occurs within the Kurdish territories, which are divided by the sovereign spaces of these countries. The naming of the practice is descriptive of its punishing nature. *Kolbari* literally means to carry goods on one's back and shoulders. *Kolbars* – those who engage in *kolbari* – regularly carry heavy loads of goods on their backs, or on a mule for those who are lucky, across the mountainous border separating the Kurdish homeland from the states whose borders it lies across. The Kurdish cities in Iran are the typical destination of such journeys. This chapter focuses on *kolbari* on the Iranian side of the border as an informal cross-border trade.

Decades of economic and political marginalisation have made chronic unemployment a permanent feature of life for the Kurdish population living in Iran. The Kurdish provinces of Iran suffer from the highest unemployment rate in the country.[2] In this environment, *kolbari* has become an alternative form of employment for many Kurds – spanning all age ranges (including teenagers and the elderly), genders and levels of education.[3]

On average, a *kolbar* carries between 50 and 100 kg of goods per trip. The smuggled goods are usually common goods, such as cigarettes, car tyres and home appliances like washing machines and refrigerators, but also include products that are prohibited in Iran such as alcoholic beverages, satellite dishes and receivers. A round trip for *kolbars* is approximately 15–20 km. What makes this form of smuggling particularly difficult is the physical toll that it takes on the body of *kolbars*, as well as the life-threatening dangers that lie along their route. Treacherous mountains with heavy snow and freezing temperatures, slippery roads and deep valleys are among the natural hazards facing *kolbari*. Added to this are the armed

Iranian border guards – stationed atop mountains with a panoramic view of the *kolbars'* passage – who regularly shoot to kill and injure *kolbars*.

In 2019 alone, Iranian border guards shot and killed 54 *kolbars*. A further 26 individuals died from the hazards of border crossing, including hypothermia, avalanches or stepping on land mines – reminders of the Iraq–Iran war. During the same year, 183 individuals were injured through what appears to be a mixture of the above-mentioned causes. *Kolbars* typically are not owners of the goods they carry. Local business owners or traders from major cities like Tehran, Isfahan and Shiraz place large orders online to be delivered to the border point on the Iraqi side, from which point *kolbars* load the goods on their back and begin their journey *en masse* across mountains. After delivering the goods on the Iranian side, *kolbars* are paid and the smuggled goods are transported by car to local bazaars in cities such as Marivan, Sar-Dasht and Baneh.

The estimated value of the trade (including smuggling) between the Kurdish territories and Iran is US $8 billion annually.[4] The average wage a *kolbar* receives for one trip is between US $15 and US $25 from which 30 to 40 per cent is spent during the journey on food and often on bribing the border guards.[5] *Kolbars'* wage depends on the weight and value of the products entrusted to their shoulders. Ironically, according to Iranian laws, the punishment for smuggling is also determined according to the weight and value of the improperly imported goods.

Unsettling the legal reality

Branding *kolbari* as smuggling may imply it is a secret activity. In reality, however, nothing about *kolbari* is secret. The actors involved, the routes, the goods, the buyers, the sellers, and the markets in which the goods are traded are all known to local and national authorities. *Kolbari* and its punishing conditions are also reflected in numerous cultural productions in the form of poems, films, investigative reports and photo exhibitions.[6] Furthermore, the eastern Kurdish territories – *Rojhilat* – have been and continue to be a site of historical struggle and contestation between the independence-seeking Kurds and the Iranian government. As a result, these areas have always been under close surveillance by the sovereign states of the region. In this region, activities such as *kolbari* are an openly kept secret between various local, national and international actors who organise both the trade and the rules and regulations of this informal practice. Perhaps one of the most convincing myths of a state is that its

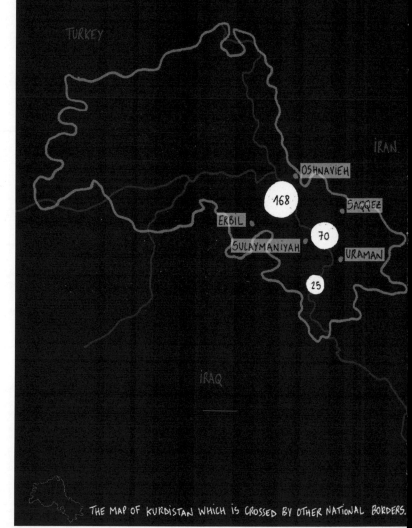

IN 2019 A TOTAL NUMBER OF
263 KOLBARS HAVE BEEN KILLED AND
INJURED BY BORDER GUARDS OR
DUE TO BORDER DANGERS.

(THE NUMBER REFERS ONLY TO THE DOCUMENTED
CASES ON THE IRANIAN SIDE OF THE BORDER)

TURKEY

IRAN

OSHNAVIEH

168

SAQQEZ

ERBIL

70

SULAYMANIYAH

URAMAN

25

IRAQ

THE MAP OF KURDISTAN WHICH IS CROSSED BY OTHER NATIONAL BORDERS.

PEOPLE KILLED IN 2019 *
54 SHOT BY BORDER GUARDS
 3 FELL OFF A MOUNTAIN
17 FROZEN TO DEATH
 6 OTHER CAUSES
80 TOTAL

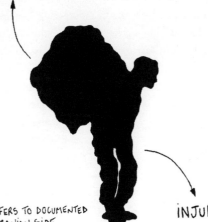

THE NUMBER REFERS TO DOCUMENTED
CASES ON THE IRANIAN SIDE
OF THE BORDER.

INJURED PEOPLE
153 SHOT BY BORDER GUARDS
 13 FELL OFF A MOUNTAIN
 10 BY MINES
  7 OTHER CAUSES
183 TOTAL

THE NUMBER OF KILLED AND INJURED KOLBARS IN EACH SEASON :

WINTER 68   SPRING 58   SUMMER 66   AUTUMN 71

Source: Map and illustration by Lucie Bacon, based on 'Koolbar News Annual Report 2019',
https://www.nawext.com/fa/post/view/۲-نیوز-کولبر-یکساله-گزارش%D9%A0۱۹
(accessed 25 May 2021).

laws are the sole source of order in society, its apparatus the most effective guarantor of obligations among people. Accordingly, the absence of law would result in lawlessness, disorder and irremediable sufferings.

For *kolbars*, however, the main source of disorder and suffering in their lives is not the illegality of their labour, but the systematic and institutionalised ethnic discrimination they face, and their exclusion from meaningful political participation and economic prosperity. In establishing the legal foundation of the crime of smuggling, Iranian laws ignore the political, social and economic context that promotes and sustains *kolbari* as a source of livelihood for the inhabitants of the borderlands. The causes of *kolbari* are deemed irrelevant factors in the overall assessment of its legality.

Concealing the descriptive and socio-political context of legal norms is a common feature and function of any state's juridical form. Law solidifies a monopoly of relevance by ignoring the wider contexts which might explain the emergence of practices such as informal cross-border trade. In the case of *kolbari*, the context that is erased includes historical factors emphasising how ancestral land has been divided by borders. The economic context is also missing, which reveals the necessity for informal cross-border trade as a dependable source of income. Social norms are also excluded by the legal framework: these can function to establish alternative modes of order that emerge from the unofficial economic interactions of various actors, and serve to sustain livelihoods more effectively than official laws.

In stripping away the wider context, smuggling laws ignore the social complexity of *kolbari* and the plurality of its actors. This reductive understanding of smuggling is reflected in the ways in which law enforcement authorities concentrate their violence on *kolbars* who labour across the borderland. A report published by the Kurdish online journal *Nawext* in 2020 describes one of the markets organised around *kolbari* in the city of Baneh:

This city is one of the central locations of the activity of *kolbars*. People come from all around Iran to buy goods that *kolbars* bring to their modern bazaar. Goods are spread out on the window sills and on the sidewalks. The city is rich with the presence of businessmen who organize border trades. We can see them driving foreign impressive new 4×4s.[7]

Business traders buy and sell the smuggled goods transported by *kolbars* openly, because officials deem transportation across borders to be the core criminal element of this activity. A widespread alternative source of income therefore can be presented as a punishable action of a limited few. As Patricia J. Williams notes, the language of law is designed to mask the intersubjectivity of legal process and state violence. Legal language, she writes: 'flattens and confines in absolutes the complexity of meaning inherent in any given problem'.[8] Accordingly, the power to select the legitimate and relevant descriptions of reality allows the state to mask its own culpability for the violence which results from activities that have been made illegal. In other words, labour can be presented as smuggling once it is disconnected, through the force of the law's authoritative narrative, from a complex intersubjective legal process that forgives certain actors as traders and punishes others as smugglers.

When it comes to *kolbari*, by presenting a reductive version of reality and focusing on the smugglers as the prime subject of regulation, the Iranian officials also allow themselves to describe and frame *kolbari* at will. The Iranian officials, at times, frame *kolbari* as an economic disturbance, while at other times they define the practice as a national security threat, for the purpose of importing weapons or members of the Kurdish militia into the country.[9] At the same time, the Iranian government sees *kolbari* as a viable method of easing the effects of international sanctions through the import of goods of which there are shortages in the market. By oscillating between different framings of *kolbari*, the state can deny it as a form of alternative employment which is used by many, and conceal its own role in creating the conditions for this form of trade – while simultaneously justifying the ongoing killings of *kolbars* by its border guards. This means that the state's legal operations are not interventions external to the practice, but an integral part of the violence that is involved in it.

Unsettling the legal production of irresponsibility

In his book *Law and Irresponsibility*, Scott Veitch elaborates on ways in which modern state law can be seen as means of not only legitimising different scales of human suffering but also guaranteeing and securing the lack of responsibility of state officials for causing such suffering.[10] Veitch uses the legal philosophy of Robert Alexy and highlights two main features of the modern judicial form, namely coercion and the claim to correctness.[11] It is through these two features, Veitch argues, that 'legal normativity brings with it a socially effective institutionalised force and a claim that this force (state monopolised violence) is right or just'.[12] In other words, the legal system uses its socially effective coercive force to promote its own operation as legitimate, just and correct – regardless of its material effect. With this in mind, suffering and irresponsibility are outcomes of favouring certain regimes of knowledge over others. Legal responsibility comes from acknowledging a certain normative order as just and enforcing its descriptions of the social reality as accurate and authoritative.[13]

Unsettling the built-in lack of responsibility of the state officials for their ongoing border killings requires a shift in subject position. Such a shift requires a subversion of the authority claimed by law to describe the social reality of *kolbari* as a criminal activity. This requires pointing to the empirical reality of *kolbari*, which reveals alternative descriptions of this practice, which contradict the legal/illegal dichotomy. Such an alternative understanding could show it to be a complicated form of labour involving various power relations that bind individuals to one another and create a mutual sense of obligation and responsibility.[14]

Unlike the reductive portrayal presented in the smuggling laws, activities like *kolbari* are highly organised practices involving numerous actors. The most visible actors are *kolbars*, drivers, brokers, retail sellers, buyers, animals (mules and horses) and border guards. Similar to other informal markets, in *kolbari* there are also less visible actors such as the Iranian government, the autonomous Kurdistan Region in Iraq, Kurdish Peshmerga militia and, not least, the US Department of the Treasury. From this perspective, *kolbars* do not appear as a central figure in an economic conspiracy against the state. They are instead transport services contracted by business owners operating in markets across the country. This unofficial trade relation imposes its own norms among the actors, and it does so through starkly asymmetrical power relations. For instance, similar to the rules of formal trade and transportation, any loss or damages to the product are deducted from *kolbar*'s pocket and not from the other parties. A *kolbar*'s wage is dependent on whether they deliver the goods on time to the owners on the other side of the border. Neither *force majeure*, the extraordinary risks involved nor the physical toll of this work exempt *kolbars* from liability. In lieu of the protections which exist in formal trade practices – such as insurance – *kolbars* are constantly negotiating the terms of their agreements and obligations, rather bleakly with their lives.

Kamal Soleimani and Ahmad Mohammdpour describe one such example, shared with them by a *kolbar*:

> I never forget the day when a friend of mine, who was also married, fell on the ground with his load on his back … I approached him to help … He was crying, shivering from the cold and exhaustion … The weather was frigid and biting, and his load was heavy. With a shaking voice, he said that he no longer wanted to live. He handed over his knife to me: 'Please end my life with this knife ….' I took his loads down and hid it somewhere to deliver it to the owner by the next day. Had I not stopped him, he would have killed himself right where we were.[15]

To negotiate the terms of border passage and trade is a constant process that also involves state officials. It is common for border guards to let *kolbars* pass in exchange for a share of the smuggled products, such as cigarettes. This is a common practice to which Karwan – a 25-year-old *kolbar* – refers as 'stealing' during an interview with *Foreign Policy*.[16] *Kolbars* use different tactics to negotiate and manage their passage. Jiyan tells *Nawext*: 'Sometimes, I would take my children with me so the agents would have mercy on them and would allow us to pass. We were around 10 to 15 women. They also took their children with them.'[17] Stealing, bribery or the occasional display of pity from a border guard may momentarily reformulate norms of border passage, but *kolbars* see the arbitrariness of border laws above all through the actions of the state itself.

As a result of decades of US-imposed sanctions, the Iranian government regularly faces severe difficulties in importing products through its official ports. Keeping informal markets like the ones organised around *kolbari* outside the realm of legality means that the government can partly count on these clandestine trade practices as a means of circumventing international sanctions and ensure the availability of certain products in its markets. A significant international relations conflict between the Iranian legislature and the US Department of Treasury therefore also forms part of the complex social reality through which *kolbars* navigate their day-to-day life and labour.

In 2017, in an attempt to organise *kolbari*, the Iranian government passed a formal administrative regulation titled: 'Organising Trade in Informal and Temporary Border Markets'. Through this, *kolbars* who had been living for three years anywhere within a 20 km radius of the border could receive permission to transport goods through certain designated corridors. Furthermore, to promote trade through these corridors, the regulation offered tariff discounts on certain goods listed in its annex.[18] This list included ordinary products such as cooking oil, rice and sugar. In addition, to compensate the shortages caused by the international sanctions, the tariff discount included products such as spare parts for heavy agricultural machinery and spare parts for boat and truck engines, along with more mundane items like hair dryers, coffee makers, printers, and diapers.[19]

No part of this regulation recognises *kolbari* as part of a formal trade process or affords it with basic trade and labour protections. In fact, the regulation refers to its aim as 'directing informal trade towards the formal border bazars' rather than legalising the practice. As a result, the illegal smuggling carried out by *kolbars* could become certified once, and only if, the employer and the list of items were to change from local business owners to the state itself. Meanwhile, under the same law, the trade is kept as an informal temporary practice.

For *kolbars* who carry the goods listed by the government, across the same border area but illegally, using different routes and for a different client, changes like this are further evidence that state normativity is one of many, and its laws surrounding border crossing are arbitrary and lack any intrinsic value.

The arbitrariness of state laws and the plurality of actors and norms involved in *kolbari* is further evident in the complex geopolitics of the region. The temporary relaxation of rules regarding the informal trade by the Iranian government coincided with the imposition of a second tranche of US sanctions against Iran in November 2018. In its attempt to block the informal economic flow and further seal the porous borders of the region the US government involved an unlikely actor.[20] According to the publication *Foreign Policy*, by December 2018 Peshmerga forces – the military of the autonomous Kurdistan Region of Iraq – were coordinating with the USA. The Peshmerga displayed a radically changed attitude towards *kolbars*, often redirecting them to longer and more dangerous routes or at times preventing *kolbars* from passing with their goods altogether.[21]

Looking from the other side of the border, as Shahram Khosravi writes, 'unfolds a continuum of oppression and expulsion across place and time'.[22] It summons up histories of erosion, eradication and exploitation, reinserting them into an otherwise thinned out, state-oriented perspective on border crossing. For the *kolbars*, the illegality of their work is directly connected to the global geopolitics of the region. The informality of their trade is necessitated by a national policy, which on the one hand relies on untraceable and clandestine trade markets, and on the other maintains them as means of economically excluding and subordinating minorities.

From informality to parallel formality

Informal markets are not just spheres of clandestine economic activity, they are also spaces of economic self-determinacy, of alternative norms regarding border crossing, of different orders of trade, and of a plurality of sources of obligations. Furthermore, in their exceptionality, informal markets simultaneously engender systems of power as well as making possible otherwise unimaginable social allegiances which undo opposing orders and forces.[23]

A brief look at *kolbari* reveals it to be a normatively cluttered practice, despite being outlawed entirely as smuggling. Plurality in the context of *kolbari* at times emerges as the result of various degrees of governance of the border trade – manifested in the shifting legal framings of this practice. Plurality is also manifested through the radical change of attitudes among officials on both sides of the border. In turn, *kolbars* also constantly reshape their own normative codes, allowing them to negotiate the terms of their border crossings and trade with border guards, business owners and the state. Out of these interactions emerges a social practice of border trading that holds significant empirical value for understanding smuggling not as a lawless and disordered activity, but as a highly organised and ordered small-scale trade. This practice is one which is connected to the history of a divided ancestral territory, economic disenfranchisement of an oppressed minority, and the global politics of the region.

We must also observe the reality of the high stakes at play in this practice, which are paid through the physical deterioration of *kolbars* and their constant exposure to death at the border. In Iran, the legal punishment for smuggling products other than alcoholic beverages, weapons and drugs, is a fine and imprisonment. Nonetheless death, both directly – at the hands of the Iranian border guards – and indirectly – as the result of the punishing conditions of this labour – is a constant feature of *kolbars'* daily life. It is important to end this chapter by questioning the function that death performs for the management of smuggling, while the law prescribes fines and prison sentences.

The internationally sanctioned and economically isolated government of Iran finds itself in part dependent on the services of informal trade corridors. Killings at the border, as Karwan says, is the government's way of asserting its control and reminding the *kolbars* that they can work as long the state allows it.[24] In other words, to compensate for its reluctant permission to transgress borders, the state finds it necessary to assert its authority and jurisdictional presence elsewhere – if not on the territory then on the bodies that inhabit the land and travel through the territory.

Notes

1. For the interview in Farsi see: *Borna News*, 1 October 2019, https://www. borna.news/fa/tiny/news-904659 (accessed January 2021).

2. See Hamshahri Online, 5 April 2020, https://hamshahrionline.ir/x6fw7 (accessed November 2020). The official unemployment rate in Iran is regularly contested, yet according to these estimates the provinces of Kurdistan, with 20 per cent, and Kermanshah, with near 18 per cent unemployment, are among top three.

3. See Kamal Soleimani and Ahmad Mohammadpour, 'Life and labor on the internal colonial edge: Political economy of kolberi in Rojhelat', *British Journal of Sociology* 71(4), 2020, pp. 741–60.

4. Sergio Colombo and Andrea Prada Bianchi, 'For Kurdish smugglers, Iran sanctions are starting to bite', *Foreign Policy*, 24 February 2019, https:// foreignpolicy.com/2019/02/24/for-kurdish-smugglers-iran-sanctions-are-starting-to-bite/ (accessed November 2020).

5. IRNA, Islamic Republic of Iran News Agency, 8 August 2020, https:// plus.irna.ir/news/83897923/ (accessed November 2020).

6. For instance, and most notably, see: Bahman Ghobadi's critically acclaimed film: *A Time for Drunkenness of Horses* (2000). As an example, see also Morteza Bahami's photo exhibition: *Rigai Zhan 'Rah-e-Dard'* (2019). There are numerous journalistic accounts of *kolbari* in, among others, Kurdî, Farsi and English. In this chapter I refer to a number of such reports. Similar reports can be found in both mainstream governmental media in Iran and in the opposition media outside Iran.

7. Hataw and Loez, 'Between Iran and Iraq: Kolbars do not bend', *Nawext*, 17 January 2020, https://www.nawext.com/post/view/between-iran-and-iraq-kolbars-do-not-bend (accessed November 2020).

8. Patricia J. Williams, *The Alchemy of Race and Rights: Diary of a Law Professor* (Cambridge, MA: Harvard University Press, 1992), pp. 6–7.

9. For instance: Hamshahri online, 9 September 2020, http://hamshahri online.ir/x6G5c (accessed November 2020).

10. Scott Veitch, *Law and Irresponsibility: On the Legitimation of Human Suffering* (Abingdon: Routledge-Cavendish, 2007).

11. Ibid., pp. 25–6.

12. Ibid., p. 26.

13. See ibid., p. 22.

14. For legal pluralism see Emmanuel Melissaris and Mariano Croce, 'A pluralism of legal pluralisms', *Oxford Handbooks Online*, 2017, doi: 10.1093/oxfordhb/9780199935352.013.22.
15. Soleimani and Mohammadpour, 'Life and labor on the internal colonial edge', p. 751.
16. Colombo and Prada Bianchi, 'For Kurdish smugglers, Iran sanctions are starting to bite'.
17. Hataw and Loez, 'Between Iran and Iraq'.
18. Islamic Republic of Iran Government, Ministers Cabinet Administrative Regulation, 'Organising Trade in Informal and Temporary Border Markets', 2017, http://qavanin.ir/Law/PrintText/227175 (accessed November 2020).
19. Islamic Republic of Iran Government, Ministers Cabinet Administrative Directive, 'Amendment to Article 1 of Directive concerning 41 items essential for border inhabitants', 2018, available on epe.ir/News/19894 (accessed November 2020).
20. Ibid.
21. Ibid.
22. Shahram Khosravi, 'What do we see if we look at the border from the other side?', *Social Anthropology* 27(3), 2019, p. 421.
23. Peter Mörtenböck, Helge Mooshammer, Teddy Cruz and Fonna Forman (eds) *Informal Market Worlds Reader: The Architecture of Economic Pressure* (The Netherlands: NAI010 Publishers, 2015), p. 17.
24. Quoted in Colombo and Prada Bianchi, 'For Kurdish smugglers, Iran sanctions are starting to bite', p. 6.

6

From the Smuggling of Goods to the Smuggling of Drugs in La Guajira, Colombia

Javier Guerrero-C

In their 2018 film *Pajaros de Verano* ('Birds of Passage', 2018) the direc-tors, Ciro Guerra and Cristina Gallego, present a story set roughly during the period known as the *La Bonanza Marimbera* ('the Marijuana Boom') a period characterised by the surge in marijuana cultivation, production, and smuggling, which spanned the period from the mid-1970s to the mid-1980s in La Guajira Peninsula and the neighbouring Sierra Nevada de Santa Marta. The film avoids the many clichés of Hollywood-style drug trafficking movies, such as mob bosses, cartels, and the like. Instead, the film shows a more horizontal development of the marijuana smuggling business. The story takes place in the desert landscape of La Guajira in the north-east region of Colombia and spans the slopes of La Sierra Nevada de Santa Marta in the north of the country. After it was harvested, marijuana was moved either to the makeshift landing strips where small aeroplanes could come and go, or to the many natural ports along the coast where smuggler boats would start their journeys. In its aesthetic treatment of the landscape, the movie exposes the more prosaic side of drug traffick-ing. In various scenes, the camera gazes into the distance and reveals the utter emptiness of the desert, as if to highlight an idleness in which nothing happens, quite different from the accelerated pace of a Hollywood blockbuster.

The film's most telling scene is the attack on a luxurious house in the middle of the desert. The house also functions as a marijuana warehouse and weapons depot. Despite its location in the middle of the desert, the house connects the many activities involved in marijuana cultivation and smuggling. It is not there for long, however. We are led to assume that, after the attack, the house is abandoned and soon lost in the desert sand. Such is the fate of the infrastructures created or utilised by drug smugglers.

This chapter explores the transitory arrangements of prosaic artefacts, cutting-edge technologies, and local knowledge needed to transport drugs. I argue that such infrastructures intersect with local views on the licit and the illicit. As Diana Bocarejo[1] demonstrates, during the Bonanza, peasants dealt with legality and illegality in the context of their own experiences rather than in the context of the state. In this chapter, I do not attempt to present a detailed history of smuggling in La Guajira, for which there are many excellent sources, Lina Britto,[2] most recently. Instead, I argue here that focusing on socio-technical arrangements to transport illicit things helps produce a narrative in which the focus is not the state or state-developed concepts such as organised crime or transnational organised crime.[3] The long history of contraband in La Guajira demonstrates how the combination of different technologies and cultural resources co-evolves with the value system. As a result, smuggling and the infrastructure that supports it is considered a legitimate activity.

Scholars have used the long history of contraband in La Guajira to explain the recent involvement of *guajiros*, as the people born in the Department of La Guajira are colloquially called, in the traffic of marijuana and cocaine. According to this literature, there is a traditional acceptance of contraband or contraband culture in La Guajira, which allowed the shift from the smuggling of household appliances, cigarettes, alcohol, and coffee to smuggling marijuana and cocaine. While I do not attempt to discuss such arguments, I consider that most interpretations have focused on the cultural practices of contraband, the consequences of legal commerce, and the rule of law. Less attention has been paid to the material culture and everyday practices of smuggling. Scholars continue to focus on organisational arrangements and make hierarchical assumptions. They have adopted the frames of 'organised crime', breaking the law, and the cost of such practices to the state's fiscal integrity as central themes. These interpretations argue that a lack of control, the absence of state agents, and the so-called 'culture of contraband' are the leading causes of smuggling.

What is clear from the many historical accounts of smuggling in La Guajira is a sense of continuity.[4] Historians of seventeenth- and nineteenth-century smuggling mention the ships that transported contraband from the Caribbean islands, and contraband accounts in the early twentieth-century mention routes, while histories of the *Bonanza Marimbera* allude to the presence of aeroplanes and boats. These accounts neglect to examine these aeroplanes, cars, ships, and other practices of moving illegal cargo in favour of focusing on the boundaries between legality and illegality. A focus on the modes of transport and infrastructure which enable smuggling and drug trafficking, and the local practices surrounding these, opens up an alternative interpretation of smuggling in La Guajira, however. This chapter focuses on this alternative approach.

The long history of smuggling in La Guajira

The Department of La Guajira, established in 1964, retained the same borders as the previous administrative unit ('*intendencia*'), the province of Riohacha (also the name of its capital), had during colonial rule. La Guajira was both a point of entry and departure for different products brought into the country without a proper customs registry. A brief history of contraband in La Guajira would show that indigenous people traded pearls directly with Dutch and English pirates in exchange for cattle, alcohol, and other goods during the seventeenth century. Such trade was risky due to the punitive measures imposed during Spanish rule; it is worth noting that the indigenous population continued to be subject to slavery long after slavery was prohibited in 1851. Relationships between the local population of La Guajira and traders from the French, Dutch, and English Antilles strengthened during the eighteenth and nineteenth centuries. Contraband products were introduced to the country via the main port in the region, the port of Riohacha, and the many natural ports around La Guajira.

By the mid-eighteenth century, La Guajira was considered by the central government to be the region through which most contraband en route to the cities inland of Nueva Granada passed. Tobacco and cattle were brought to the La Guajira coast by English smugglers, transported via various modes to the town of Mompox on the Magdalena River, or to other ports along the coast, such as Cartagena or Santa Marta, to be shipped upriver. Smuggling of Brazilwood, a natural dye, connected the illicit traffic of goods with the Caribbean basin and the centres of the Industrial Revolution due to the demand for such dyes, which were used for textiles. Throughout the nineteenth and early twentieth centuries, La Guajira continued to be considered a gateway for contraband.[5] During the early nineteenth century, alcohol smuggling from the Caribbean islands was a lucrative business due to the high taxes on liquors and the prohibition of sugar cane alcohol commerce in Nueva Granada. The English smuggled Jamaican rum, and the Dutch brought gin from Curaçao to La Guajira. Locals also smuggled salt during the late nineteenth century, an activity that reveals some of the early practices of smuggling and conceal-ment methods. In 1878, customs officials in Barranquilla reported the interdiction of a shipment of salt from Curaçao and Aruba, in which the salt was covered and mixed with locally produced salt.[6] The smuggling of salt also reveals the uneasy relationship between local people and the government. While the central government in Santa Fé de Bogotá pushed for the use of mine salt produced in Zipaquira, the locals preferred to consume imported salt.

While alcohol, salt, textiles, and cattle were being smuggled in, the Guajira smugglers further strengthened their ties with Curaçao and Dutch smugglers. Communication with the Caribbean islands was more frequent than with the Colombia's capital. There was an extended practice of bar-tering. Smugglers used ships carrying goods from the Antilles to transport local products back there, without the intervention of monetary exchange. Until the middle of the nineteenth century, smuggling in La Guajira con-sisted of exchanging goods and raw materials. Dutch boats played a central role in smuggling goods during the nineteenth century. Smugglers used the lack of knowledge about maritime jurisdiction on the part of Colom-bian authorities to evade governmental interdiction. Offshore jurisdiction and sea borders have traditionally been grey areas. During the early to mid-twentieth century, the smuggling of alcohol and cigarettes attracted the attention of local and national customs officials. As a result, smugglers built a network of rendezvous points and hiding places throughout La Guajira, building upon earlier smuggling routes. Another critical moment in the history of contraband in La Guajira was the start of coffee smuggling that, according to Britto,[7] paved the way for marijuana smuggling. Trade in contraband of coffee became a profitable business during the 1950s and 1960s, one that, despite being illegal, became a legitimate commercial activity in which both local elites and marginalised groups participated. Contraband coffee helped create connections between a dispersed set of actors and the utilisation of several strategies later used to transport marijuana and cocaine. With coffee, smugglers subverted the infrastruc-ture and logistical chains of legal coffee export for their gain. In addition, they were able to build transient infrastructures to bring coffee from the Andean mountains to the Caribbean coast.

The first significant period of trading criminalised drugs was the *Bonanza Marimbera*. The marijuana trade with the United States from the early 1970s until the early 1980s operated mainly from the Colombian Atlantic coast. Although there is evidence of marijuana plantations from the early 1940s on the Sierra Nevada de Santa Marta slopes, there were no commercial fields until the end of the 1960s, and most were small scale. With no tradition of farming marijuana prior to this, the primary explanation for the surge of marijuana seems to be the so called 'balloon effect'.[8] The aerial fumigations mandated by the American government using the herbicide Paraquat over the marijuana crops in Mexico and Jamaica in 1974 moved the trade to Colombia, similar to the way air in a balloon moves to an area of less resistance. From that year onwards, production and transport of marijuana increased, specifically from the slopes of the Sierra Nevada de Santa Marta.[9] During the 1970s, Colombian smugglers established contacts with American smugglers and buyers to distribute the marijuana. By 1974, local authorities estimated that 80 per cent of La Guajira peasants cultivated marijuana. By 1978, 'Colombia had between 25,000 and 30,000 hectares of marijuana crops. Of the approximately 10,000 tons introduced to the United States, between 60 and 65 per cent came from Colombian smugglers',[10] most of it smuggled through La Guajira. The decline of this industry came with the fall in the benefits of marijuana production due to several causes (consumer taste changes, expansion of a seedless version, and the state's interdiction efforts), which motivated the search for new business opportunities, found in importing coca paste from Bolivia and Peru.[11]

In discussions of smuggling in La Guajira, there is a focus on well-known places for trade and the relationship that *guajiros* have with their many borders. In the middle of La Guajira, there is a small town with around 166,000 inhabitants named Maicao. The town's origins are similar to those of most towns in La Guajira: it was an older indigenous settlement given a new name and an official foundation date, which is usually a consequence of the central government's attempts to control and pacify a territory. Maicao has been known as a place where selling contraband products and smuggling have been the leading commercial activities of its inhabitants for decades. But contraband in La Guajira has moved across different areas and in many directions. The history of smuggling with the Caribbean islands goes back to the colonial era. Smugglers – then and more recently – became folk heroes with nicknames such as 'the Marlboro man' as the cigarette and drug smuggler, Samuel Santander Lopesierra Gutiérrez was known.

Illicit and illegal activities in La Guajira have played a central role in the lives of its inhabitants. They have actively prevented the deployment of state control and demanded their rights to contraband. Contraband has been a source of income since the sixteenth century, benefiting both the elites and ordinary people, including indigenous peoples and Arab immigrants, mostly established in Maicao as traders. Britto[12] points out how, during the 1960s, politicians benefited from their alliances with coffee smugglers. They invested in the business, and both the economic benefits and the relationships built around smuggling allowed them to solidify their base. In a region with few industries, peasants and day labourers found a route to upward social mobility. Meanwhile, Arab traders encountered a market for their products, as seen in the growth of commerce in Maicao. By the 1970s, 80 per cent of shops in the town were owned by Arab descendants. Since the decline of the marijuana trade, La Guajira has been active in the smuggling of cocaine. The tradition of smuggling in the area has created unique socio-material relationships. Since the early days of marijuana smuggling from the La Guajira region in Colombia, smugglers have used maritime transport methods. The use of traditional smuggling routes continued during the marijuana boom. The same routes that were intensively utilised during the cartels' era in the early 1990s survived the demise of cartels by the early 2000s and passed into the age of *cartelitos* and *networks*.

Moving contraband in La Guajira

Smuggling in La Guajira reveals the overlap between illicit and licit, summarised in the phrase, 'The Guajira is a region where legality and legitimacy do not coincide.'[13] Here, academic and state interpretations alike agree that this is genuinely a 'contraband culture', where breaking the law is possible because contraband permeates all aspects of everyday life and is celebrated in popular music. Nevertheless, for some, contraband goods and drug trafficking have different moral connotations. As one former cigarettes contrabandist makes clear, 'Let's be precise: when we say smuggling (*contrabandear*) we talk about illicit economies, but when we talk about trafficking (*traficar*), we are talking about something different.' The former contrabandist describes the difference between the movement of things in and out of the country. While contraband products are brought to the country to evade customs and other taxes in order to sell at a lower price than chain stores, trading marijuana and cocaine benefits from inflated costs due to their illegality.

Boats, aeroplanes, and trucks used for smuggling are often dismissed as serving only as tokens when captured by state agents. Until recently, there have been few studies exploring the vehicles used in smuggling. Craig Martin[14] emphasises the need to include the seemingly mundane modes of transport used to move contraband. As well as the vehicles themselves, disguises such as double hulls and hidden compartments also warrant attention.

Scholars working on the 'new paradigm of mobility' has argued for the inclusion of studying artefacts and technologies that facilitate or impede mobility within the social sciences. While scholars in mobility studies have focused on legal mobility, others have shown how various forms of mobility, both legal and illegal, have become intertwined[15] and how, despite the enormous efforts to control and monitor illicit modes of movement, they continue their flow. Moreover, different configurations of socio-technical systems combine both legal and illegal flows. As William Walters argues in his analysis of the role of vehicles in immigration, it is important to study these elements of criminalised activity as it allows for a less vertical perspective.[16] Bringing to the fore the vehicles involved in moving contraband deepens our understanding of the flow of illegal activity. It shows that mobility is produced through the continuous interaction of forms of transport, regulatory frameworks, and socio-technical systems.

Cocaine and marijuana are moved from producer to consumer countries. They are moved from production centres to shipment points, often involving further movements to complete the journey from 'south to north'.[17] Once the peasants, who earn a negligible amount, harvest the marijuana, it must be packaged in a way that both avoids detection from state agents and gives it protection from water, sand, heat, and insects. One of the transportation strategies used by marijuana smugglers in the 1980s consisted of 'air drops', where carefully assembled packages of several kilos of marijuana were thrown from small aeroplanes to the sea, to be recovered by speedboats and transported to the United States. The properties of cocaine allow for the use of more varied methods. The extraction of the alkaloid and conversion into cocaine salts was mostly done in rudimentary laboratories in the jungle. The cocaine could be mixed with other products to be separated and distributed at a later stage. The cocaine departing from

La Guajira came mostly from the interior of the country, hidden inside double hulls in cars and trucks, and moved to ships or aeroplanes.

In the process of moving illicit drugs, smugglers are able to acquire knowledge of logistical networks.[18] Drug smugglers can also appropriate this knowledge through their structural and social embeddedness,[19] as they take advantage of existing social ties. Authors from the cultural sociology tradition, Bourdieu and de Certeau, emphasise the need to focus on skills, tacit knowledge, and embodied ways of doing things, as they consist of unspectacular forms of resistance. James Scott highlights the importance of local knowledge, which he describes using the term *metis*.[20] Scott presents several examples of how locally situated knowledge is often superior to formalised methods in solving problems.

The journalist Juan Gossain provides an accurate description of the traffic of marijuana in La Guajira in their novel *La Mala Hierba* (The Bad Weed). The events narrated in the book take place between the 1970s and the early 1980s, the *Bonanza Marimbera*, which later gave way to cocaine trafficking. The novel describes the social transformations of the region and delves into the minutiae of the transport of marijuana. A key element of the detail explored is the way in which local knowledge is expressed. These local forms of knowledge include the appropriation of technologies to create temporary logistics; the knowledge of local routes, hiding places, and trading customs; and the management of the paradoxical results of enforcement on contraband and drug trafficking, such as how the focus on some methods or areas opened up new areas for smuggling.

Enforcement actions are ineffective because removing some players merely creates the conditions for exploiting new opportunities. Even back in the nineteenth century, the competition between smugglers and state agents featured greater resources on the smugglers' side. Laurent narrates the story of a Dutch schooner that set sail from Curaçao.[21] The *Zeester* was well known by local authorities as a smuggler boat, but it was impossible to interdict. This was because customs officials only had a *falua*, a small vessel, which was not powerful enough to reach the place where the *Zeester* would dock. As shown previously, the methods used to smuggle drugs cannot simply be classified as new or old.[22] They can be used, dismissed and, typically, recycled once state agents have set their eyes on other smuggling methods.

A common explanation for the fluid boundaries between legality and illegality in La Guajira given by state agents and academics is weak governance. It is true that there are under-governed areas of La Guajira, where smuggling is carried on without interference and facilitated by a relative lack of control. Nevertheless, significant amounts of smuggling in La Guajira produces visible traces, despite being temporary. Such traces exemplify the entanglements of legality and illegality.

Current drug trafficking in La Guajira has built upon knowledge acquired during decades of smuggling. A critical component of this is the traditional knowledge of the sea and legal smuggling and fishing routes in the north of the Colombian Caribbean. Discussing the transition from marijuana smuggling to cocaine trafficking, a retired drug smuggler explained: 'There were a lot of people who moved from smuggling illegal goods, the old guys, they had to, they had everything, and they had the routes, the ships.'

Smuggling and drug trafficking infrastructures

Martin proposes that drug smuggling practices fall into two categories regarding the relationship with socio-material artefacts, the first comprising of shadow networks and supply chains and the second being the harnessing of legitimate transportation networks and supply chains.[23] Infrastructures for drug smuggling are often built temporarily. Rather than being made to last, drug smuggling technologies are forgotten or destroyed once their goals have been fulfilled. Boats bought to transport one shipment can be left to rot afterwards, while some submarines are designed and built to make one trip. Airfields are quickly abandoned as a strategy to avoid detection or capture by law enforcement, or to hide from competitors, SUVs are repurposed, makeshift docks are discarded, and transitory logistic chains are established.

Inscribed in these transient infrastructures and technologies for smuggling is the emergent nature of smuggling technologies. Through dynamic interactions, they produce new properties and patterns in the existing system.[24] These emerging patterns are the result of a process of mutual co-evolution and adaptation. Each actor co-evolves while developing capacities to reposition the system's macro properties and generate new properties.[25] In La Guajira, multiple temporalities, artefacts, and practices coalesce. Rather than a 'cartel' taking control, smuggling possibilities are realised due to the combination of geography with local socio-material culture and traditional values regarding the legitimacy of the smuggling business.

The socio-material character of smuggling in La Guajira resulted from the combination of different material and cultural resources, such as the combination of various forms of transport and concealment methods.[26] A good example is the capture of a truck carrying a small, dis-assembled aircraft from one part of La Guajira to another in early 2018.[27] Rather than being indicative of constant innovation, this was an example of the continuous recombination of different resources. This provides a challenge to the over-emphasis on developing new modes of transport, with greater flexibility and speed. In this case, the knowledge of terrestrial routes, rendezvous points, and makeshift airstrips enables constant development of existing methods.

Descriptions of networks have concentrated on analysing the forms of communication available to trafficking organisations for adapting both to the market and the strategies developed by security agencies.[28] The interpretations of trafficking organisations as networks, made both by academics and state agents, assume a desire among traffickers to explore new routes and new transportation methods.[29] Traffickers with knowledge of the terrain, rather than looking for other localities, recalibrate existing routes. The complexity of the routes and organisational forms should be understood as a result of constantly shifting interrelationships between different locations and materialities, and the fluctuating conditions of legality and illegality of certain practices.[30]

Consumer goods, coffee, marijuana, and cocaine have been transported thanks to a continuous readjustment of old and the new practices. Rudimentary *pangas* equipped with advanced communication and positioning systems, single-engine aeroplanes, old trawlers, brand new speed boats, handmade submarines, old cargo trucks, new SUVs, and pick-up trucks are all used for transportation of illicit cargo. Local knowledge regarding tides, seasons, highways, and local geography, and the understanding of smuggling as an everyday activity, is fundamental to its success. Locals easily spot the vehicles and routes used by smugglers to transport contraband or drugs. An excellent example of the shifting nature of infrastructures used for drug trafficking is the transport of goods, marijuana, and cocaine by land, sea, and air, demonstrating the overlapping use of these different means of transportation.

SUVs and pick-up trucks play an essential role in contraband logistics and smuggling in La Guajira. When it comes to transport by land, smugglers often transported their cargo in plain sight. SUVs and pick-up trucks used by smugglers mostly had double hulls and bigger fuel compartments, as well as other modifications to adapt to the desert area's particular geography. They also signalled values of masculinity, risk-taking, adventure, and aggressiveness:

> The Ford and the Ranger, those pick-ups with an open cargo area, they became the referent of the *marimberos* [marijuana smugglers], so those pick-ups were very common. You can still see these pick-ups, some of them are tuned up and kept as a memory, as a relic. Then whoever had at that time a pick-up of those ... that was a symbol of power, economic power.... I do not know what to call it, the term is not military ... status yes, but this truck was associated with weapons, whoever had one of these also used to bring along a small personal army of 5 or 10 armed boys.[31]

Knowledge of local geography was an integral part of smuggling in La Guajira. While smugglers did make use of the poor local infrastructure and public transport systems, it was mostly the knowledge of the traditional *trochas*, unpaved roads, which were opened by locals and required an understanding of the correct vehicles to use and skills for driving on them, that facilitated the smuggling.

Contraband products, marijuana, and cocaine have been transported using all kinds of boats, big and small, fishing trawlers, go-fast boats, and dry cargo ships. The *Margoth* was a 50 tonne cargo ship captured in Cartagena with 470 packages of marijuana shipped from La Guajira. The newspaper that reported this capture does not specify the weight of the cargo or its value, only that it was one of three ships captured in the same week carrying a total of 1.1 tonnes of marijuana.[32] Smugglers using speedboats have also developed a considerable knowledge of evasive mechanisms, using speed as stealth, and continuously introducing improvements, usually more engines. Most of the speedboats that have been seized have been modified off-the-shelf boats. During the 2000s, there were several reports in Colombian newspapers of the use of submarines as a transportation method. Intelligence reports based on eyewitness accounts suggested the presence of a submarine loaded with drugs in the La Guajira region that had sailed to supply the European market.[33]

The transportation of contraband, marijuana, and cocaine using aeroplanes is suggestive of the building of makeshift airstrips (and sometimes aeroplanes). The DC-3 plane was a popular plane for drug smugglers, and packed full with marijuana, commonly used for flights from La Guajira to Florida via Jamaica.[34] During the *Bonanza Marimbera*, American smugglers began arriving in Cessna, Fairchild, and Piper Cub aeroplanes. The flat and sandy geography characteristic of the north of La Guajira facilitates the construction of airstrips for light aeroplanes. According to Fabio Castillo, in a report of the former Administrative Department of Security (DAS) dated September 1975, there were 131 illegal tracks around the marijuana crops of the Sierra Nevada de Santa Marta, and the average load of a package of marijuana in an aeroplane was approximately 1,000 kilos.

The smuggling of marijuana during the 1960s and 1970s, and later cocaine, from the desert areas of La Guajira is a clear example of the emergence of the interrelationships and co-development of technologies used for drug trafficking and social order. This understanding is consistent with a contingent discourse on the use of infrastructure.[35] Infrastructures can be transient and, in La Guajira, they served the goal of transporting a vast range of goods. As a retired smuggler, who used to drive a truck bringing contraband goods to the town of Maicao, and later marijuana from the slopes of the Sierra Nevada de Santa Marta to the north of La Guajira, remembers: 'I had a truck, it was a good one, old, very good, but very old, we used to bring TVs and sound systems and transport marijuana, it was all the same thing.'[36]

Drug smugglers combine different forms of knowledge to create new transportation methods. They do this by combining available conventional technologies with local adaptations, as well as using traditional local knowledge, such as dead reckoning sailing, information from fishermen and goods' smugglers about unpoliced areas, and maritime routes. I have presented an overview of the long history of smuggling in La Guajira, focusing on understanding the transitory arrangements of vehicles and cutting-edge technologies, combined with local knowledge, as critical to understanding how 'illegal things' are moved in La Guajira. The smuggling of consumer products, cigarettes, alcohol, and coffee, which evolved into the trade of marijuana, and later cocaine, from and to La Guajira, is seen by academics and state agents alike as indicative of well-organised action and the existence of a 'contraband culture'. A focus on the vehicles and practices of smuggling reveals the critical role of socio-materiality and the infrastructure used in the movement of illegal things. This focus shifts the discourse from organised crime and 'talking like a state' in order to examine the everyday practices as smugglers move around.[37]

The study of drug smuggling has often taken an organisational perspective, whereby the way smugglers organise is regarded as the key to understanding smuggling and its consequences for society. I have argued for the need to include the study of infrastructures to overcome the traditional dualisms between legal/illegal, licit/illicit, local/global. Taking smuggling and drug trafficking in La Guajira as an example, I stress the importance of studying infrastructures. Infrastructures are crucial points in the geography of drug trafficking and essential for its global reach. I propose that grappling with the temporality of infrastructures is vital if one wants to understand how illicit drugs are moved and arrive at a more nuanced explanation of the movement of goods considered illicit. Some drug smuggling infrastructures possess apparent permanence, while others are short-lived socio-technical assemblages that leave few marks on the landscape. Such infrastructures result from combining several practices and kinds of knowledge, combinations between old and new technologies, local knowledge, and smuggling traditions. We need to document such infrastructures and, when possible, to describe their palimpsestic qualities. Attending to these infrastructures allows a more hybrid and less vertical view of criminal organisations. The chapter advances a research agenda that pays greater attention to the socio-technical change in the grey areas of illegality and informality.

Notes

1. Diana Bocarejo, 'Thinking with (il)legality: The ethics of living with bonanzas', *Current Anthropology* 59(18), 2018, pp. 48–59.
2. Linda Britto, *Marijuana Boom: The Rise and Fall of Colombia's First Drug Paradise* (Oakland, CA: University of California Press, 2020).
3. Michael Woodiwiss, *Double Crossed: The Failure of Organized Crime Control* (Chicago: University of Chicago Press, 2017).
4. See Vladimir Daza Villar, *La Guajira, el tortuoso camino a la legalidad* (Bogotá, Colombia: Dirección Nacional de Estupefacientes – Oficina contra la Droga y el Delito de Naciones Unidas, 2003), pp. 16–37; Santiago González-Plazas, *Pasado y presente del contrabando en La Guajira: Aproximaciones al fenómeno de ilegalidad en la región* (Bogotá, Colombia: Editorial Universidad del Rosario, 2008); Muriel Laurent, *Contrabando en Colombia en el siglo XIX: Prácticas y discursos de resistencia y reproducción* (Bogotá, Colombia: Universidad de los Andes Facultad de Ciencias Sociales – CES, 2008); Yoleida Mercado, Seili Quintero, and Yenis Sierra, *Riohacha en tiempos de marimba*, Honours thesis, Universidad de la Guajira, Riohacha, 2000.

5. S. Vásquez Cardoso, *La Guajira, 1980–1935*, Honours thesis, Universidad de los Andes, Bogotá DC, Colombia, 1983.
6. Laurent, *Contrabando en Colombia en el siglo XIX*, p. 273.
7. Britto, *Marijuana Boom*, pp. 59–72.
8. Francisco E. Thoumi, 'The Colombian competitive advantage in illegal drugs: The role of policies and institutional changes', *Journal of Drug Issues* 35(1), 2005, pp. 7–26.
9. Andrés López Restrepo and Álvaro Camacho Guizado, 'From smugglers to warlords: Twentieth-century Colombian drug traffickers', *Canadian Journal of Latin American and Caribbean Studies* 28(55–6), 2003, pp. 249–75.
10. Asociación Nacional de Instituciones Financieras, *Marihuana, legalización o represión* (Bogotá, Colombia: ANIF, 1979).
11. Restrepo and Guizado, 'From smugglers to warlords', p. 255; Francisco E. Thoumi, 'Illegal drugs in Colombia: From illegal economic boom to social crisis', in Menno Vellinga (ed.) *The Political Economy of the Drug Industry: Latin America and the International System* (Gainesville, FL: University Press of Florida, 2004), pp. 70–84.
12. Britto, *Marijuana Boom*, pp. 59–72.
13. Francisco E. Thoumi, 'Legitimidad, lavado de activos y divisas: Drogas ilegales y corrupción en Colombia', *Ensayo y Error* 1(1), 1996, pp. 22–45.
14. Craig Martin, 'The socio-material cultures of global crime: Artefacts and infrastructures in the context of drug smuggling', in Tim Hall and Vicenzo Scalia (eds) *A Research Agenda for Global Crime* (Northampton, MA: Edward Elgar Publishing, 2019), pp. 147–59.
15. Craig Martin, 'Smuggling mobilities: Parasitic relations, and the aporetic openness of the shipping container', in John Urry, Thomas Birtchnell and Satya Savitzky (eds) *Cargomobilities: Moving Materials in a Global Age* (New York: Routledge, 2015), pp. 65–86.
16. Peter Adey, 'Surveillance at the airport: Surveilling mobility/mobilising surveillance', *Environment and Planning A: Economy and Space* 36(8), 2004, pp. 1365–80; Sanneke Kloppenburg, 'Mapping the contours of mobilities regimes: Air travel and drug smuggling between the Caribbean and the Netherlands', *Mobilities* 8(1), 2013, pp. 52–69; Mimi Sheller, 'Air mobilities on the US–Caribbean border: Open skies and closed gates', *Communication Review* 13(4), 2010, pp. 269–88; William Walters, 'Migration, vehicles, and politics: Three theses on viapolitics', *European Journal of Social Theory* 18 (4), 2015, pp. 469–88.
17. Paul Gootenberg, 'Cocaine's long march north, 1900–2010', *Latin American Politics and Society* 54(1), 2012, pp. 159–80.
18. Craig Martin, 'Desperate mobilities: Logistics, security and the extralogistical knowledge of appropriation', *Geopolitics* 17(2), 2012, pp. 355–76.
19. Henk van de Bunt, Dina Siegel and Damián Zaitch, 'The social embeddedness of organized crime', in Paoli Letizia (ed.) *The Oxford Handbook of Organized Crime* (Oxford: Oxford University Press, 2014) pp. 321–39.

20. James C. Scott, *Seeing Like a State: How Certain Schemes to Improve the Human Condition Have Failed* (New Haven, CT: Yale University Press, 1998).

21. Muriel Laurent, 'Contrabandistas y aduaneros en la costa Caribe en el periodo federal', in José Polo Acuña and Sergio Paolo Solano D. (eds) *Historia social del Caribe colombiano: Territorios, indígenas, trabajadores, cultura, memoria e historia* (Cartagena: La Carreta Editores/Universidad de Cartagena, 2011), pp. 162–202.

22. Javier Guerrero C., *Narcosubmarines: Outlaw Innovation and Maritime Interdiction in the War on Drugs* (Palgrave Macmillan, 2019).

23. Martin, 'The socio-material cultures of global crime', p. 154.

24. John Law and John Urry, 'Enacting the social', *Economy and Society* 33(3), 2004, p. 401.

25. Nigel Gilbert, 'Emergence in social simulation', in Nigel Gilbert and Rosaria Conte (eds) *Artificial Societies: The Computer Simulation of Social Life* (London: Routledge, 2006), p. 150.

26. For such combinations and bricolages see Scott H. Decker, and Margaret Townsend Chapman, *Drug Smugglers on Drug Smuggling: Lessons from the Inside* (Philadelphia, PA: Temple University Press, 2008); Guerrero C., *Narcosubmarines*.

27. Francisco de la Hoz, 'Incautan avioneta que era transportada en un camión por la alta Guajira', *El Heraldo*, 6 January 2018, https://www.elheraldo.co/la-guajira/incautan-avioneta-que-era-transportada-en-un-camion-por-la-alta-guajira-444120 (accessed 23 May 2021).

28. Michael Kenney, *From Pablo to Osama: Trafficking and Terrorist Networks, Government Bureaucracies, and Competitive Adaptation* (University Park, PA: Penn State University Press, 2007), pp. 25–47.

29. Thoumi, 'Illegal drugs in Colombia', pp. 70–84.

30. Ray Hudson, 'Conceptualizing economies and their geographies: Spaces, flows and circuits', *Progress in Human Geography* 28(4), 2004, pp. 447–71; Ray Hudson, 'Economic geographies of the (il)legal and the (il)licit', in Tim Hall and Vincenzo Scalia (eds) *A Research Agenda for Global Crime* (Northampton, MA: Edward Elgar Publishing, 2019), p. 12.

31. Interview by author with a retired marijuana smuggler, August 2019.

32. R. Ortega, 'Al mar once mil kilos de marihuana', *Diario del Norte*, 20 October 1977, p. 5.

33. *Semana* (2003) 'El fugitivo', 14 September 2003, http://www.semana.com/nacion/articulo/el-fugitivo/60642-3 (accessed 10 May 2021).

34. Eduardo Sáenz Rovner, 'Entre Carlos Lehder y los vaqueros de la cocaína: La consolidación de las redes de narcotraficantes colombianos en Miami en los años 70', *Cuadernos de Economía* 30(54), 2011, pp. 105–26; Eduardo Sáenz Rovner, 'Colombians and the drug-trafficking networks in New York in the 1970s', *Innovar* 24(53), 2014, pp. 223–34.

35. Stephen C. Slota, and Geoffrey C. Bowker 'How infrastructures matter', in Ulrike Felt, Fouché Rayvon, Clark A. Miller, and Laurel Smith-Doe

(eds) *The Handbook of Science and Technology Studies* (Cambridge, MA: MIT Press, 2016), pp. 529–54.

36. Author interview with a retired marijuana smuggler, August 2019.
37. Paul Gootenberg, 'Talking like a state: Drugs, borders, and the language of control', in Willem van Schendel and Abraham Itty (eds) *Illicit Flows and Criminal Things: States, Borders, and the Other Side of Globalization* (Bloomington, IN: Indiana University Press. 2005), pp. 101–27.

7

Contesting Common Sense: Smuggling across the India-Bangladesh Border

Debdatta Chowdhury

Cartographic borders of states are spaces where the state's project of asserting its sovereign presence is at its strongest and most visible. The borderland is the platform for the state to 'perform' its nationality, including the embodiment, symbolic or material, of its national character and identity, as well as its vision and the principles around which it frames itself. In the process of doing so, states not only ascribe meanings to what its borders are meant to be interpreted as, but also lay down what rightful citizenship demands entail. It is at the borders of the states that binaries like legal/illegal, licit/illicit, inclusion/exclusion, formal/unofficial, victim/perpetrator are unveiled, most often in ways that the state wants them to be understood by its subjects. But borders are also the spaces where such definitions are questioned, upturned, and redefined. Cross-border transactions, mostly for economic reasons, but driven and solidified by other socio-political concerns, are examples of the kinds of practices which challenge the state at the borders. Cross-border smugglers, by their very existence and resilience (in the sense that they continue to resurface despite the state's best efforts), challenge the ways in which states lay down definitions of acceptable (read official) and unacceptable (unofficial) economic transactions. Smugglers trade between this acceptability and unacceptability, making the unofficial as much a part of, and even of great value to, the official. States' knowledge of such cross-border transactions, along with their inability to undo them, hints at how, despite being mocked by such practices, states are not entirely inclined to erase them because of the value they add to the states' coffers.

As smuggling evolved into the version we understand it to be today, the characterisation of those involved in such acts has also evolved, largely into a negative connotation of being a threat to the state, a challenge to sovereignty, morally corrupt and characteristically dubious. At the same time, and from a different perspective, smugglers have also come to symbolise freedom and a sense of power.[1] And it is this very ambiguity that is built into the act of smuggling and has characterised such acts all along. As Harvey points out, the 'there is no smuggling' response most often indicates the obviousness of the practice as part of daily life rather than its actual 'absence'.[2] This also explains, to some extent, why local smugglers are rarely demonised by the people – their 'trade never considered criminal by anybody except governments'.[3] Local, everyday smuggling practices, in fact, provide more interesting explanations than the laissez-faire doctrine that led smuggling beyond the local into the realm of global geopolitics, even though the local is, very often, linked to, or a part of a global network. In fact, it is these local 'armpit smugglers'[4] who constitute the more intriguing narratives of 'everyday' smuggling practices across borders, and who will be the focus of this chapter. These practices reveal the depth and strength of kin and community networks at play – networks and transactions which have existed for centuries. South Asian borders, and the India-Bangladesh border in this case, is a perfect example of ruptured links that have turned into illicit networks.

Closer understandings of such practices indicate the limits of 'seeing like a state' – the limits of taking the existence of the state *a priori* and then labelling certain practices as legal or illegal, and the limits of imagining 'that mobility is border crossing, as though borders came first and mobility second'.[5] This is also why it makes sense to differentiate between legal/illegal and licit/illicit – perspectives which help us to understand the precise difference in the perceptions of the states whose laws are being flouted and those of the people involved in smuggling practices, who merely see themselves as pursuing not just traditional but perfectly logical livelihood choices.

The West Bengal-Bangladesh border[6]

The international border between India and Bangladesh forms a very interesting case study of what was said in the previous section. The Partition of India in 1947 resulted in newly created borders between India and Pakistan (West Pakistan cut out from Punjab province, and East Pakistan cut out from Bengal province). The newly formed borders disrupted age-old transactions and linkages. But instead of bringing cross-border transactions to an end, the border rendered such transactions illegal – once-official trade was now turned into illegal transactions. Rather than the nature of the practices themselves, it was how the practices were labelled that became decisive in how they came to be understood in official and public discourses. The border itself gave rise to certain practices which emerged as smuggling from their very inception – hinting at the prospects and possibilities that the new border opened up for the people who negotiated it every day. It shows how understanding smuggling practices in these areas gives a sense of how past affects evolve and change form, to become what we understand as our present. It also shows how the illicit, and its success, is built right into the licit game of affairs of the states.

The West Bengal-Bangladesh border has been unique in more than one way right from its inception, in the haphazard way in which it was conceived and drawn, followed by its physical execution along its length of more than 2,000 km – running through courtyards, cutting across agricultural fields, disrupting communication links and community networks at large. Even compared to the immediate confusion and violence resulting from the formation of the border, its long-term consequences for the lives and livelihoods of the people who settled along and across it seem to have been more impactful. While considering themselves as 'border people', the border dwellers have, in fact, made the border the 'centre' of their existence and, often, the main source of their livelihoods – legally and/or illegally.

The West Bengal-Bangladesh border, as an interdependent borderland, was characterised by symbiotic links between societies on both sides. Cross-border smugglers are as much a part of this community as any other border dwellers. A study of their practices helps us understand how pre-existing social groups diffuse into the new economic structures, while still conserving the mentality, ideology and aims of their traditional linkages.[7]

Things that move, people who make it happen

The widespread nature of smuggling practices along this border, and the range of contraband items involved, indicates that cross-border smuggling practices are integral to the daily life across this border. From drugs to domestic and household necessities (crops, spices, utensils, cattle and fish), from rare/exotic animal species to fuels, from electronic goods to luxury/lifestyle items, from fake currency notes to newspapers – every conceivable item is being smuggled across the Bengal border.[8] As land borders have been fenced by India (beginning in the 1980s), the riverine borders have become more active as smuggling routes, with innovative ways being devised by smugglers to carry goods, animals, and humans across the water.

Drugs, especially Phensidyl, alongside heroin and marijuana, are the most commonly smuggled items at this border. Given how easy it is to produce this drug, and that it is unavailable in Bangladesh, it is one of the more lucrative items smuggled all along the length of this border. Local factories along the length of this border, disguised as other kinds of manufacturing unit, deal in these drugs. Seizures of large and small consignments of the drug from both big traders and petty carriers are a common feature in almost all areas across this border, as are scenes of drug smuggling in broad daylight by young and aged alike.[9]

Heroin smuggling links the Golden Crescent (central, southern and western Asia/Afghanistan, Iran, and Pakistan) to India and Bangladesh. Heroin and other such light-weight drugs are smuggled through various methods, within tool boxes of bullock carts, the folds of women's sarees, underground canals (built to drain excess rain water) and boats, trucks carrying trade items and, even hidden inside corpses' beds taken for cremation or burial. Mini trucks, small utility and public vehicles, and even ambulances are used for ferrying smuggled items along and across the border. The everydayness of the means adopted for smuggling indicates how such practices have become integral to the quotidian lives of the residents.

Cannabis, as a hugely profitable smuggling item, is based almost entirely out of the North Bengal, Assam and Tripura regions – all being border states. Smugglers usually make use of the night-service buses running between north and south Bengal to transport illegally produced cannabis to cities or centres of distribution – almost all of which are, again, border areas.

Yaba, a lightweight pink tablet drug, has been the most recent addition to the drug smuggling scene across the Bengal border, especially with the crackdown, or at least renewed focus on, cattle smuggling (discussed later). Yaba smuggling, in fact, has been seen to follow the cattle smuggling route, indicating the pre-existing smuggling network in place. The presence of Kolkata (capital of the Indian state of West Bengal) not too far from the border contributes to Yaba smuggling by creating a ready market for the drug.[10]

The border guards can rarely lay their hands on the contractors of these trades. It is the carriers, known as *dhoors* in local parlance, consisting mostly of local villagers, who are mainly nabbed by the border guards. The *dhoors* are assigned the 'job' by the manager of the smuggling network, locally known as the 'lineman', who is responsible for maintaining the liaison between the carriers and the border guards. The linemen are often locally known faces, but are rarely reported to the border guards or the police by the local people, either for fear of being harassed or because many of these people are themselves involved in such illegal transactions and need the services of the lineman for things to go smoothly. More often than not, border guards themselves profit from these transactions, and they too need the lineman's services. The linemen in border areas are often more powerful, and have more authority than either the border guards or the local administrative leaders – given their role in running the economy of the border areas. The linemen are well aware of their power and are, hence, seen operating openly all across the border.

Illicit border crossings by people constitute yet another form of cross-border practice along the West Bengal-Bangladesh border, where the *dhoors* help people cross the border illegally, without a passport. Its riverine borders, are vulnerable to illegal human crossings, besides other items. Complicated procedures for passport generation and travel expenses involved in 'legal' travels drive people to cross illegally, via rivers, holding on to cattle, or in the thick of night or on a foggy winter morning – even at the risk of life. Centres and agents providing fake documents, like voter cards, Aadhar cards (showing a person's unique ID number), ration cards and passports to the 'illegal migrants' flourish all along the West Bengal border.

Cattle smuggling across this border is by far the most widespread and lucrative practice. Cattle procured from the northern and western provinces of India are stocked at strategic locations near the West Bengal border, from where they are made to cross with the help of a lineman. The export ban on cattle imposed by India is a major factor in the flourishing of its illegal version. While the demand for beef in Bangladesh is not met by its limited supply, India has a cattle surplus due to its low demand for beef. The official number of cattle seized does not reflect the scale of the trade. The increase in cattle smuggling around the times of festivities such as *Eid* stands as an example of the demand–supply imbalance between the two states concerned. The staggering profits made from cattle smuggling ensure its continuance, despite fencing and increased alertness along the border. In fact, as new technologies are employed for border control, new means of smuggling evolve simultaneously. With the increasing difficulty of walking the cattle across the border due to the hindrance caused by fencing, cattle are now being made to walk up makeshift ramps built over the fences or to swim across rivers. Instances of packaged beef (in meat form) being thrown over the fences to the other side have also been reported recently.

With the current right-wing Bhartiya Janta Party government in power in India (2014–to the present), the cattle trade has come under fresh scrutiny, but the profit it generates and its contribution to the Indian economy will ensure that cross-border cattle smuggling remains officially illegal but economically viable, both as a local livelihood opportunity and as a contributor to the Indian national economy, albeit unofficially.

Cattle traders come from far and near. Locals are hired as labourers to load the cows onto the trucks. Transactions worth hundreds of thousands (both in Indian and Bangladeshi currencies) happen each day. The auctioning of seized cattle by the Border Security Force (India's border guards) contributes to the cattle trade, since the bidders are mostly smugglers who re-smuggle the cattle at high prices.

The relation between the cattle traders and the border guards on both sides is generally dictated by the unstated rules of the trade and is, hence, mostly harmonious, for the benefit of both the traders and the border guards. The presence of border outposts in front of the cattle markets or *haats* along the border is ample proof of this unstated understanding. An operative ethics is also at work in the case of this particular transaction, in terms of the cattle traders referring to themselves as more ethical than smugglers of drugs or other 'harmful' commodities. This also explains why the cattle smugglers rarely call themselves smugglers, and prefer the more respectable 'trader' label.[11]

The wholesale cattle *haats* are a thriving economy in themselves, complete with shops catering to every need of the traders; items sold at the shops range from food, tea, toiletries, clothes to tyres and petrol and anything else a trader, having travelled from afar, might need. Local townspeople rent out rooms to these traders for overnight accommodation. There are local 'committees' supervising these illegal markets. The committees are chosen by the cattle traders from among themselves, and are responsible for supervising the overall operation. Particular sites along this border are especially convenient for cattle markets because of the hassle-free operations ensured by the border guards at these sites. The irony is well expressed by a trader: 'Other kinds of crimes have diminished significantly because the cattle businesses have improved the overall economy of the area,' he says. This indicates how the spatial specificity of the border creates its own perceptions of reality and survival concerns. Instances of violence between border guards and traders are not altogether absent, though these arise mostly when the credibility of the guards as security personnel is questioned or due to disputes over payment between the trader and border guards. But such instances of violence do not deter cattle smugglers. 'The smugglers are daring and have a don't-care attitude. Border life has made them daring,' is how one border guard puts it. They also point to how restrictions on using lethal weapons by border guards (enforced by the Indian government) encourage cattle smugglers not just to carry on smuggling but also to counter-attack the guards with lethal weapons of their own. In fact, the unrestricted use of lethal weapons by smugglers against the border guards evokes an interesting response from the border guards – that of their 'masculinity being at stake'.[12]

Besides cattle, firearms and fake currency notes (FICN) stand next in terms of lucrative smuggling items, which are smuggled either individually or along with cattle, or even among consignments of fruits, eggs, rice, vegetables and other daily necessities, which generally go unchecked by the guards. Most of the firearms used in Bangladesh are sourced from India through its border. Smugglers are often also the buyers of firearms, which they use to defend themselves against rival networks and/or border guards. Buyers also include insurgent outfits, which have confessed to being involved in cross-border cattle trade, while being actively involved in smuggling guns and ammunitions for their own political use. Smugglers of firearms have their own names for each of the varieties of firearms, which they use as code names during transaction. As and when these names are decoded by the police and the border guards, new names appear.[13]

Changes in the global or national situation affect the local trends in smuggling. Things like firearms and fake currency notes are especially under scrutiny since 2000, as the situation in India and Bangladesh regarding fundamentalist activities has changed. Also, governments' economic policies (for example, the demonetisation programme by the Indian government in 2016) affect cross-border smuggling. Smuggling of FICN increased many times over across the West Bengal border following the demonetisation programme, and has kept expanding in its scope and profitability ever since.[14] Smuggling routes also keep shifting as and when they are traced by border guards and police.[15] Other kinds of crisis, like the recent Covid-19 pandemic (since February 2020), also affected smuggling practices, both in terms of increased smuggling due to a curfew on people gathering, and also smuggling of masks due to their unavailability in the market, especially in the initial days of the pandemic.

Currency coins (known as *Rejki* in smuggling lingo) adding up to thousands of rupees also form an interesting item of smuggling, where the process involves procuring currency coins from across West Bengal and smuggling them into Bangladesh, where they are melted into metal blades. Local foundries or ferro-alloy factories along the West Bengal border also melt coins into metal sheets before smuggling them to Bangladesh. The huge profit made out of this explains why drivers of public vehicles, small-scale traders and even women homemakers in and around Kolkata have been reported to be involved in smuggling coins.[16]

Bullion smuggling, that is, gold smuggling from Bangladesh to India, in various forms, has been rampant along this border for quite some time, especially in the form of gold bars/biscuits. The involvement of clearing agents in bullion smuggling, working in the customs department at the border checkpoints, indicates the profitability of this kind of smuggling. Newer ways of bullion smuggling, like plating metallic frames of luggage with gold (which are otherwise meant to be made of aluminium), or even throwing gold bars wrapped in cloth pouches across the fence, are being deployed as age-old ways have become easily trackable by customs officials and border forces.[17] Youngsters, especially students, are increasingly being drawn into gold smuggling given the return it ensures.[18] People have been reported to be hired, as salaried employees, for gold smuggling – indicating the well-organised system of operation gold smuggling has called into place.[19]

Besides the riskier and more expansive trading in drugs, cattle, firearms or fake currencies, the people living along the West Bengal-Bangladesh border survive on smuggling items of daily necessity, from a few litres of petrol/diesel to a few kilograms of spices, vegetables and eggs, utensils, electronic items, clothing, tools, audio-visual discs, cooking ware, newspapers. The seasonal nature of agriculture, coupled with the fluctuating prices of crops on either side of the border, ensures a steady demand for such items. Newspapers are smuggled across the border, despite the availability of both locally published as well as national newspapers along the whole length of the West Bengal-Bangladesh border. Smuggling of second-hand motorbikes is on the rise, given the combination of their size and the guaranteed profit on them, compared to smuggling other lighter or heavier vehicles. A new motorbike is unaffordable, but smuggled ones (mostly stolen) are sold at a much lower price, especially to the young population.[20] The male smugglers carry female sex workers, disguised as their wives, on their pillions and drive the bike up to the border, where the vehicles are hidden among the crop fields, to be smuggled on a boat across the river to Bangladesh at an opportune moment. The riverine islands are often the transit hubs for such vehicles. Sometimes, the entire vehicle is disassembled and packed in a bag/container to be ferried across the border. India-made motorbikes fetch double their price in Bangladesh, making them a lucrative smuggling item.

The smuggling of these daily necessities highlight the rudimentary nature of smuggling along the border; it also backs up the claim made earlier in this chapter that cross-border smuggling is not necessarily linked to global smuggling networks, but forms part of the everyday survival strategies and lived experiences of the people involved. The border people learn to use the reality of the border in their best interests, irrespective of whether their activities are legal or illegal. Smuggling practices, especially of fake currency notes and cough syrup, are often seen as 'cottage industries' by the local residents, irrespective of whether they are directly involved with it or not.[21] In the absence of other legal industries or job opportunities in the border areas, smuggling practices are often the only choice available to the local population. Even if this was not the case, these practices are deeply built into the lives of the border dwellers, that they fail to (or refuse to) call the practices as smuggling.

One of my respondents gave a vivid description of not just the process of cross-border smuggling practices along this border but also the nature of relations between the smugglers and border guards. She pointed out that smuggling to them, that is the border people involved in it, is what teaching is to me – 'a profession', and is unperturbed by the fact that it is considered 'illegal' officially. She talked about the 'kindness' of some of the border guards in 'cooperating' with the people by letting them know what would be 'good time' to smuggle things out. She talked about how daily prices of vegetables and cereals decide the direction of the flow of goods, besides the exclusivity of certain luxury and electronic products on either side. The higher ranked border officials might not know about these practices, or are at least not personally involved. It is the guards patrolling the border who mostly engage in it. She talked about how a newly posted battalion initially takes a strict vigilant approach towards 'nuisance'. Gradually, familiarity results in complicity. If the poverty of the local people is an important reason for their involvement in such practices, the meagre salary of the border guards explains their involvement in these practices as well. She talked about how unfenced areas are more conducive for smuggling, unlike the hurdles posed by the fenced areas. On being asked about probable alternatives when the area was eventually fenced, she said with a grin:

> If the border is fenced someday, we will find other ways to carry on the work we are doing now. Do the fenced areas lack smuggling practices? Just as an animal finds its food under any circumstances, even we will do the same. God has given us a brain, so I am sure we will find a way. In fact, then the guards themselves will help us find other ways.[22]

Geographies *and* modus operandi

The riverine islands and protruding landmasses across the Bengal border (called *chars* and *ghoj*) are ideal locations for the transit of smuggled items because of their strategic locations. Being located between India and Bangladesh, and often not officially recognised as a part of any one state, these riverine islands, detached from the mainland and not easily visible to the guards, are used for storing smuggled items before they are taken across the border. While the detachment of the islands from the mainland poses the greatest threat to their inhabitants, leaving them as stateless, the same detachment provides a conducive milieu for smugglers, both within the inhabitants and those in transit.

Natural factors like foggy days or dark nights make surveillance more difficult for the patrolling constables. Winters pose a huge threat to the border guards because the available equipment, such as binoculars, SSTs (searchlights) or night-vision cameras fail to penetrate the dense fog. The thick cover of clothing which the people don in winter makes it easier for smugglers to hide smuggled goods. The folds of *sarees* worn by women and specially made jackets are used. Decreasing water levels in the winter months also ensure increased border crossings.

The Public Distribution System (PDS) on the West Bengal side of the border also contributes to such practices. The PDS system in India ensures the distribution of items like sugar, wheat, rice and so on to villagers at subsidised rates. Goods from PDS distribution centres, which are generally located outside the villages, are carried to the villages by salespersons. While they are required to record the quantities of items carried into the villages at the border guards' camps, the number of trips that they make is not restricted. The extra amounts that reach these border villages are smuggled to the other side.

Kinds of people involved

A careful observation of smuggling practices in this region suggests that there are clear categorisations regarding the forms and items of smuggling between men, women and even children. Women are mostly involved in smuggling lightweight items, while also 'making use' of their clothing which is mostly long drapes or sarees. Children usually accompany the female members of the families or do 'lightweight jobs' individually, while male members do the more arduous and riskier jobs.

The involvement of transgender people in cross-border smuggling in certain parts of the West Bengal-Bangladesh border cannot be overlooked in this regard. The fact that a substantial number of transgender people are involved in smuggling in certain areas of this border indicate its significance. One such respondent explains that their being 'neither male, nor female' keeps the border guards at bay, as the 'male' guards feel that 'handling *hijras*' undermines their dignity.[23] However, border guards point to humanitarian grounds for 'letting them' do what they do, since 'they do not mostly have families or people to fend for them'.

Equally significant is the involvement of physically disabled people, including disabled children, in cross-border smuggling practices. 'They make use of their disability to carry on the smuggling. They carry light things like marijuana, heroin and so on. But we leave them because of their disability, and on humanitarian grounds,' is how a border guard explains it.

Border markets and the legalisation discourse

Talks of formalisation and legalisation of border markets along the West Bengal-Bangladesh border have been on the radar for quite some time now between India and Bangladesh – indicating how the states' perception of handling cross-border practices is being manifested in its changed or reworked policies. Border officials realise that smuggling is not something that can be solved by policing. They have been suggesting 'open *haats*', local markets, along the border where people from both sides can trade legally. The use of the word 'open', interestingly, stands in contradiction to the idea of the border as a closed 'container' as envisioned by the state and as enforced through the erection of fences.

The prospect of meeting relatives and friends from across the border is also evident in the responses of the civilians with regard to these border markets, besides that of being able to trade without fear. The way the existing border *haats* flourish during festivities, such as *Durga Puja* and *Eid*, stands as proof of their prospects once they are properly organised. Many of these *haats* were in existence long before the creation of the border, but lost much of their significance after the partition. Those that still function are labelled illegal. Thus, *haats* are a natural culmination of not just the exchange of various products across the border but also of cross-border cultural ties that the border people on both sides share, besides having great potential for contributing towards the economies of both India and Bangladesh, legally.

Use of language and signs

The most interesting aspect of smuggling across the Bengal border, and cross-border smuggling at large, is the array of vocabulary and sign languages which continue to evolve as part of the evolving nature of transactions. Signs, symbols and local vocabulary devised by the smugglers are ways to bypass the presence of the authorities and border guards, and are often difficult to decode. As and when they are decoded, and smugglers become aware that this has been done, they devise still newer vocabularies and modes. Just as the techniques and signals of the border guards (devised to track and catch smugglers) are decoded by the smugglers, the smugglers in turn devise their own techniques to escape being tracked – which in turn are decoded by the guards. The absence, or rarity, of any real violence between smugglers and border guards makes the whole process look like a complicit game of chasing and hiding, rather than any effectual effort to either curb smuggling (by border guards) or consider a change to livelihood options other than smuggling (by smugglers). Both parties are aware of the others' presence, agendas and networks. Labelling one another as criminals (as do border guards in relation to the smugglers) and/or accomplices (as do smugglers regarding the guards' involvement) seems more important than any actual effects this has on the activities themselves.

Common sense, uncommon lives

It would often seem that mechanisms of statecraft, logics of economic development and scientific advancement have been used more wisely and profitably by smugglers than by the states trying to prevent smuggling. The participants are aware of the state machinery that they function within, while they also have their own hierarchies of governance and operative ethics. They are largely driven by what we know as 'common sense'.[24] 'The concept of a collective common sense', as Sophia Rosenfeld puts it, 'sometimes in alliance with the idea of the rational individual, sometimes in conflict – played a vital, if often tacit, role in the construction of democracy's popular, as opposed to constitutional, face' – vis-à-vis the state, examples of which abound across the Bengal border. On the other hand, states have interpreted common sense in their own ways, given the volatile nature of the concept – where, Pierre Bourdieu reminds us, as opposed to democracy and populism, common sense:

> has become a kind of structural or constitutive censorship. It has turned into an unspectacular instrument of domination that works constantly and silently not only to keep individuals in line but also to exclude outlying voices as either criminal or crazy and to limit the parameters of public debate.[25]

In such cases, common-sense perceptions of statehood propounded by states threaten the citizenship statuses of its people and render some of their everyday practices as illicit.

The West Bengal-Bangladesh border is an interesting study in such diverse understandings of common sense, and the dissonant exigencies of those who negotiate the border. The partition of Bengal in 1947 'breached the notions of the moral economy' of the people by restricting their movements and rupturing traditional socioeconomic links. The most long-lasting effect was on livelihood practices, which Willem van Schendel explains through his concept of scales: *scales-we-almost-lost*, indicating a pre-border web of relations that has weakened but not vanished; *state-scale*, indicating the web of relations that the state created through the creation of the border; and *border-induced scales*, indicating the web of relations created by the border itself. The various patterns of livelihood practices which we see across this border, and especially those deemed illegal by states, are indications not just of how geopolitical concerns and changed cartographies push certain activities and transactions underground. The framework also helps in making sense of how people negotiate such scales through their 'common sense', primarily founded upon survival needs but also within the larger structure of governance mechanisms.

The role of the border guards in these livelihood narratives of this border, especially in the smuggling discourses, indicate how state agents are 'drawn into' border narratives – their common sense helping them to sort out their own ways of negotiating the border. Their uniforms and other visible trappings of territorial discipline do not necessarily match the spatiality of their everyday relations or how they place themselves in the border milieu – indicating a contrast between thought and action. The 'lure of the border' makes the border guards susceptible to practices which weaken the states' security agendas and makes them as much a part of the border milieu as the civilians.

While the logic of statehood renders the state responsible for securing its borders as a marker of its sovereignty and as a container of its subjects, the ideological and material manifestation of this logic gives rise to a complex relation between the state and those who inhabit its border. In the process, the pattern of consciousness or common sense that border people are seen to develop works itself out in two phases: first, in the initial phase, in terms of negotiating the fact that the definition of the 'local' has changed: that what used to be local is now on the other side of the border; that their former next-door neighbours are now separated from them by an international border; that it is no longer possible to move around freely, and mobility will be controlled and gauged; and that citizenship status will now need to be proved every now and then. And, second, in terms of gradually coming to terms with the fact that the border is here to stay; that it is a reality in their lives and that they will now have to redesign their lives and livelihood practices around the border. Making sense and making use of the border is the culmination of this thought pattern. This explains why we have border people who talk, simultaneously, about the need to 'secure' the border from illegal transactions and movements, and about how the border brings them ample opportunities to earn illegally. The border guards, too, talk about their duties as protectors of the borders while simultaneously talking about how their lives as border guards make them participants in illegal transactions.

Taking a cue from Gramsci's thought, it would be unfair to call contradictory common senses, or the contrast between thought and action, 'self-deception'. Self-deception, as a theory for this contradictory nature of consciousness, cannot explain the actions and practices of a large mass as concerns us here. What explains this pattern of consciousness is the explanation put forward by Gramsci, where he says that such a contrast works at two levels. One is when the people are acting as an organic totality in dealing with the specific realities that they find themselves in. This conception of the world might be fuzzy but it has its own manifestations in various practices. The other level is when this same group, for reasons of submission and subordination, adopts a conception from a dominant group which it affirms verbally and believes itself to be following, especially in 'normal times, i.e. when its conduct is not independent and autonomous, but submissive and subordinate'.[26] This is why we have border civilians talking about how the border needs to be fenced, how the border guards do a commendable job of securing the border, how the border guards should 'punish' offenders if needs be, how every border inhabitant should cooperate with the state as a responsible citizen, while simultaneously talking about how the realities of the border and the challenges it poses make it an almost obvious choice for many of them to have recourse to illegal means of using the border and thus question the very security that they so passionately feel needs to be ensured. The border guards, too, simultaneously talk about their duty, as protectors of the states, to guard the borders, and about how restrictions on the use of lethal weapons make their job difficult, while simultaneously explaining how their life at the border drives them to involve themselves in illegal cross-border transactions.

Allowing cross-border transactions, both legal and illegal, within the structure of security agendas, offers states the necessary ideological justification for both controlling their borders while also accommodating the little subversions within its fold. This makes these subversions appear non-antagonistic and holds together a potentially divided society in a single whole.[27] As for the border people, this structure allows them to be part of the larger paradigm of statehood and gives them rightful claims to citizenship, while also giving them opportunities to act according to their common sense to fulfil their survival needs.

Common sense is a volatile, unrigid concept. There is no single definition of common or good sense, neither is there a consensus on whether common sense is necessarily good sense, or whether good sense is necessarily practical in nature – questions which Gramsci recurrently poses.

He saw common sense as 'the uncritical and largely unconscious way of perceiving and understanding the world that has become "common" in any given epoch'.[28] Correspondingly, he uses the phrase 'good sense' to mean the practical, but not necessarily rational or scientific attitude. With Gramsci's insights as a framework, smuggling practices across the West Bengal-Bangladesh border serve as an interesting case study of how 'good', 'common' and 'practical' senses are intertwined. Instead of being too taken up by which group – the commoners/smugglers and the border guards – makes a better claim to common, good or practical sense, it is better to observe the effects that these multidimensional plays of senses have on the various socioeconomic, cultural and political narratives which evolve across this border. If 'politics' is what binds together the two dimensions of common senses, then the objective of trying to understand such narratives should ideally consist of trying to understand the peculiarities of this politics, and whether the evolving forms of this politics, especially as manifested in the changing policies of the states, is actually a move towards achieving what Gramsci calls *politico-practical hegemony* – bringing the praxis of survival and theories of statehood together, in dialogue.

Notes

1. Simon Harvey, *Smuggling: Seven Centuries of Contraband* (London: Reaktion Books, 2016), p. 12.
2. Ibid., p. 77.
3. Eric Hobsbawm, *Bandits* (London: Weidenfeld and Nicolson, 2000), p. 45.
4. Willem van Schendel and Abraham Itty (eds), *Illicit Flows and Criminal Things: States, Borders, and the Other Side of Globalisation* (Bloomington, IN: Indiana University Press, 2005), p. 4.
5. David Ludden, 'Presidential address: Maps in the mind and the mobility of Asia', *Journal of Asian Studies* 62(4), 2003, p. 1062.
6. This work is a part of my doctoral dissertation, and a portion of this has been published in my monograph, Debdatta Chowdhury, *Identity and Experience at the India-Bangladesh Border: A Crisis of Belonging* (London: Routledge, 2018).
7. Antonio Gramsci, *Selections from the Prison Notebooks*, trans. Quentin Hoare and Geoffrey Nowell Smith (London: Elec Book, 1999).
8. Chowdhury, *Identity and Experience at the India-Bangladesh Border*, p. 45; Anupratan Mohanto, 'Oligoli te bhoot namchhe' ('Smuggling activities through secret routes'), *Anandabazar Patrika*, 9 September 2019, https://www.anandabazar.com/district/north-bengal/smugglers-become-active-in-night-in-hili-border-area-1.1043018 (accessed 12 January 2020).

9. Chowdhury, *Identity and Experience at the India-Bangladesh Border*, pp. 46–48; Jayanta Sen, 'Dal par koralei kella fotey' ('A lot to gain from smuggling drugs'), *Anandabazar Patrika*, 8 September 2019, https://www.anandabazar.com/district/north-bengal/hili-border-has-became-a-open-field-for-smugglers-1.1042612 (accessed 12 February 2020).

10. Ceaser Mondol, 'Gorupacharer route'e ekhon Yaba'r romroma: Madok corridor'e Kolkata'i praankendra' ('Kolkata at the heart of drug smuggling'), *Anandabazar Patrika*, 3 January 2019, https://www.anandabazar.com/state/yaba-found-safe-corridor-through-bengal-cattle-smuggling-route-leading-kolkata-into-main-centre-dgtl-1.926187 (accessed 15 August 2019).

11. Chowdhury, *Identity and Experience at the India-Bangladesh Border*, pp. 50–3.

12. Ibid.

13. Sujauddin Biswas, 'Kancher jinish ashchhe shabdhanei' ('Arms smuggling in full swing'), *Anandabazar Patrika*, 18 March 2019, https://www.anandabazar.com/district/nadia-murshidabad/lok-sabha-election-2019-arms-smuggling-on-the-rise-in-murshidabad-ahead-of-poll-1.967509 (accessed 3 March 2019).

14. Biman Hajra, 'Jaal note'e jerbaar police' ('Hard time for police in fake currency smuggling'), *Anandabazar Patrika*, 12 September 2019, https://www.anandabazar.com/district/nadia-murshidabad/police-at-fix-to-solve-fake-indian-currency-note-issue-1.1044241 (accessed 2 January 2020).

15. Staff Correspondent, 'Malda chhere ebar corridor shorchhe Dinajpur'e: Jaal'e teen, udhhar sare chho' lakh'er jaal note' ('6.5 lakh recovered in counterfeit note smuggling'), *Anandabazar Patrika*, 3 July 2019, https://www.anandabazar.com/state/stf-rounded-up-three-ficn-racketeers-in-kolkata-recovered-counterfeit-note-of-6-5-lakh-dgtl-1.1012587 (accessed 9 November 2019).

16. Chowdhury, *Identity and Experience at the India-Bangladesh Border*, p. 57.

17. Suprakash Mandal, 'Jyotsna'e katatar'er opor diye urey ashe chakti' ('Night smuggling in moonlight'), *Anandabazar Patrika*, 15 April 2019, https://www.anandabazar.com/state/lok-sabha-election-2019-politics-and-economy-of-nadia-border-is-under-the-influence-of-trafficking-1.979813 (accessed 2 November 2019); Staff Correspondent, 'Bharat-Bangladesh shimante udhhar pray 6 koti'r chorai sonar biscuit' ('Gold biscuits worth crores recovered in Indo-Bangla border'), *Anandabazar Patrika*, 25 May 2019, https://www.anandabazar.com/state/dri-seizes-valued-6-crores-of-smuggled-gold-dgtl-1.997170 (accessed 13 November 2019).

18. Staff Correspondent, 'Sona pachar'e tana hochhe poruader' ('Students are being involved in gold smuggling'), *Anandabazar Patrika*, 26 May 2019, https://www.anandabazar.com/state/smugglers-are-now-using-teenage-school-students-for-smuggling-gold-1.997295 (accessed 14 January 2020).

19. Sunando Ghosh, 'Beton diye rakha hochhe sona pachar'er lok' ('Salaried men appointed for gold smuggling'), *Anandabazar Patrika*, 12 September 2019, https://www.anandabazar.com/calcutta/men-recruited-for-gold-trafficking-in-bara-bazar-arrested-1.1044280 (last accessed 14 January 2020).

20. Biman Hajra, 'Raat'er dike ashun, half daam'e debo' ('Smuggled motorbikes available at half price in Farakka'), *Anandabazar Patrika*, 23 June 2019, https://www.anandabazar.com/district/nadia-murshidabad/illegal-bikes-are-selling-at-very-low-price-in-farakka-1.1008378 (accessed 7 December 2019).

21. Suprakash Mandal, 'Par hoye jaye gun, par hoy kori' ('Currency and arms smuggling before general elections'), *Anandabazar Patrika*, 16 April 2019, https://www.anandabazar.com/state/lok-sabha-election-2019-hard-security-on-election-time-does-not-able-to-stop-fake-currency-and-gun-1.980229 (accessed 5 February 2020).

22. Chowdhury, *Identity and Experience at the India-Bangladesh Border*, pp. 59–60.

23. In the Indian subcontinent, *hijras* are regarded as a 'third gender'; most *hijras* see themselves as 'neither man nor woman'. They cannot accurately be described as 'eunuchs' or hermaphrodites' or 'transsexual women'. Most *hijras* were born male or 'intersex' (with ambiguous genitalia); many will have undergone a ritual emasculation operation, which includes castration. Some other individuals who identify as *hijras* were born female. Although most *hijras* wear women's clothing and adopt female mannerisms, they generally do not attempt to pass as women. Becoming a *hijra* involves a process of initiation into a *hijra* family, or small group, under a 'Guru' (teacher/master).

24. Sophia Rosenfeld, *Common Sense: A Political History* (Cambridge, MA: Harvard University Press, 2011), p. 3.

25. Bourdieu, quoted in Robert Holton, 'Bourdieu and common sense', in Nicholas Brown and Imre Szeman (eds) *Pierre Bourdieu: Fieldwork in Culture* (Lanham, MD: Rowman and Littlefield), p. 14.

26. Gramsci, *Selections from Prison Notebooks*, p. 326–7.

27. Partha Chatterjee, *Nationalist Thought and the Colonial World: A Derivative Discourse?* (Delhi: Oxford University Press, 1986); Partha Chatterjee, *The Politics of the Governed: Reflections on Popular Politics in Most of the World* (New York: Columbia University Press, 2004).

28. Gramsci, *Selections from Prison Notebooks*, p. 322.

8

The Bus Economy:
A 90-day Gateway across
Zimbabwe-South Africa

Kennedy Chikerema

In 2015 over 10,000 people and 4,000 vehicles were processed on a daily basis at the Beitbridge border post between South Africa and Zimbabwe with the majority of travellers being Zimbabweans.[1] These large influxes, it may be argued, have not only fostered diverse cultural and social exchanges but also introduced new inventive and productive economic practices. Such inventiveness can be seen, for instance, in the use of the 90-day visitor's visa. In many instances, Zimbabweans and other foreign nationals have secured economic opportunities through this temporary visa. Having a passport at hand, the 90-day visitor's visa can be easily obtained at the ports of entry where foreigners are allowed to conduct leisure activities in South Africa. Once granted, the visa is used for trading activities which, from the authorities' perspective, is seen as smuggling. According to the Department of Home Affairs in South Africa (DHA), The 90-day visitor's visa is the third most obtained visa by Zimbabweans.[2]

Zimbabwe's anaemic economic situation has led many to venture outside the country for economic security. Zimbabwean cross-border traders, disguised as tourists or visitors, use this visa with the intention of making a short-term visit to seek economic opportunities by buying bulk goods and shipping them back to Zimbabwe in buses and taxis through irregular channels. Braving the threats of police harassment, muggings, bribery, lack of accommodation and financial support, the traders manage to conduct their business undercover.

Traders arrive in Johannesburg, usually in the early hours of the morning, at certain bus stations. Staying for only one and a half days, some traders start their shopping process, looking for good deals on goods found

at China malls, small retail spaces and wholesalers to buy bulk goods for resale, while other traders seek accommodation from the various hotels in the city close to retail spaces and bus ports. Depending on the situation, most traders store their goods in their hotel rooms or within rented storage facilities at the various bus stations where they are occasionally weighed.

The economic effects of this informal trading in Johannesburg have dramatically shaped the spatial nature of the city. Johannesburg is an economically dynamic city with numerous business opportunities and flourishing ethnic economic enclaves: Nigerians, Chinese, Zimbabweans, Ethiopians, Malawians, Zambians, Somalians, Indians and Bangladeshis. These economic enclaves have become the main venues utilised by Zimbabwean traders. Each of these foreign communities, despite their semi-legal status, has managed to secure a livelihood within the city to some degree.

In Johannesburg there are several bus stations functioning as 'ports' that cater to Zimbabwean cross-border traders. One of the busiest is the Powerhouse bus station, a privately owned station situated in Braamfontein, in the centre of the city, in what is known as an informal business district. Despite being situated on a small site, the station manages to house over 23 bus companies that operate on a schedule basis. Here, traders can also use amenities such as public showers and toilets, storage facilities, takeaways, ticket offices and waiting areas, to mention a few. On the outside of the station traders make use of the collection of small-scale retail spaces where they can buy goods at the very last minute. Carefully packaged, goods of all shapes and sizes, ranging from beds to boxes of foodstuffs are loaded into the buses with general luggage.

Long-distance buses are loaded with luggage and goods such as furniture and boxes of cooking oil from the different bus stations in Johannesburg. These buses travel to many destinations throughout sub-Saharan Africa, such as Mozambique, Angola, Malawi, and Zambia, to mention a few. These buses travel from Johannesburg to Harare or Bulawayo in Zimbabwe. They pass through many other large cities in Zimbabwe as well. The journey from Johannesburg to Bulawayo, the second largest city in Zimbabwe, is about a 12-hour journey with many intermediate stops such as at police road blocks, toll gates, the border and refreshment stops. Each of these affects the journey time, either by increasing or decreasing it. These intermediate stops at times have also become places where opportunistic markets take place on both sides of the border. For instance, at the Beitbridge checkpoint, the large number of traders crossing it who are engaged in small-scale smuggling, and the high import taxes of up to 60 per cent on goods transported from South Africa to Zimbabwe, have created an irregular income source for the immigration and customs officials. In 2017, the Zimbabwean government gave the police the power to mount police roadblocks within a 10 km radius of the checkpoints. This, in turn, placed great strain on the trade as at times, in order to get past these roadblocks, each bus had to pay the equivalent of R150.

TYPES OF GOODS TRADED		SOURCES	
NEW CLOTHING	41%	WHOLESALERS	58%
ACCESSORIES	29%	CHINA MALLS	50%
TOILETRIES	19%	FACTORIES	44%
GADGETS	19%	ORIENTAL PLAZA	31%
FURNITURE	46%	OTHER	8%
OTHER	22%	SMALL RETAILERS AND SUPERMARKETS	34%
FOOD	25%		
SECOND HAND CLOTHING	25%		

PURCHASE CHART
List of the most common goods bought and their main source within Johannesburg.

Upon arriving at Bulawayo, goods are offloaded from the bus and carried through to formal and informal retail markets in the city. The Bulawayo street vendor market, one of the busiest parts of the town, is where most of the buses arrive. From this point traders take goods to different markets throughout the city, formal and informal. Some of these markets, which are demarcated street parking lots, are right around the corner from the bus ports.

As buses arrive at or depart from the Johannesburg and Bulawayo, they encounter various circumstances, from the numerous actors and agents that make a contribution to the small-scale cross-border trade, consisting of state officials and individuals found at different points of interaction, to market conditions in different sites they enter. Different individuals, institutions and structures either contribute to or hinder the trade.

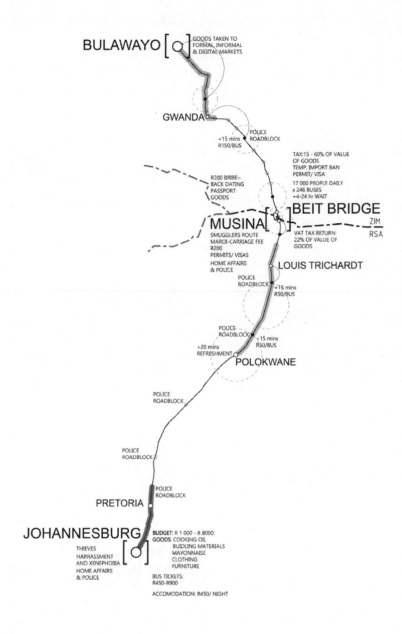

BULAWAYO   GOODS TAKEN TO
FORMAL, INFORMAL
& DIGITAL MARKETS

GWANDA

POLICE
ROADBLOCK
+15 mins
R150/BUS

TAX:15 - 60% OF VALUE
OF GOODS
TEMP. IMPORT BAN
PERMIT/ VISA

17 000 PEOPLE DAILY
x 246 BUSES
+4-24 hr WAIT

R200 BRIBE=
BACK DATING
PASSPORT
GOODS

MUSINA   BEIT BRIDGE
                                         ZIM
SMUGGLERS ROUTE   VAT TAX RETURN: RSA
MAROI-CARRIAGE FEE   22% OF VALUE OF
R200   GOODS
PERMITS/ VISAS
HOME AFFAIRS   LOUIS TRICHARDT
& POLICE

POLICE
ROADBLOCK
          +15 mins
          R50/BUS

POLICE
ROADBLOCK
          +15 mins
          R50/BUS
+20 mins
REFRESHMENT
                POLOKWANE

POLICE
ROADBLOCK

POLICE
ROADBLOCK 2

POLICE
ROADBLOCK

PRETORIA

JOHANNESBURG   BUDGET: R 1 000 - R 8000:
               GOODS: COOKING OIL
THIEVES   BUILDING MATERIALS
HARRASSMENT   MAYONNAISE
AND XENEPHOBIA   CLOTHING
HOME AFFAIRS   FURNITURE
& POLICE
               BUS TICKETS:
               R450-R900

               ACCOMODATION: R450/ NIGHT

The cross-border trader at different intermediate stops comes into contact with agents such as immigration officials, shop owners, policemen, drivers, conductors, hotel owners, vendors and so on. The interactions between different actors blur the boundary between formal and informal.

Located at the intersection of the major transport and retail hubs in this specific geography, the Powerhouse bus stations in Braamfontein and in Johannesburg, the route from Johannesburg to Bulawayo, and the markets close to the bus stations in Bulawayo are all strategic sites for the passengers with 90-day visas to operate their businesses. The combination of visa policies, the inherent legislative gaps within the Immigration Act in South Africa, travelling infrastructures and historical mobility in the region generates what can be called a *90-day gateway*. Through this gateway and in practice, cross-border traders enact a 90-day irregular special economic zone. This trading zone along the transit route contributes to the national economy. It allows cross-border traders to assert a sense of agency over their economic freedom, safety and rights for a short period of time despite the existing legal constraints.

Notes

1.   Henri-Count Evans, 'Corruption, smuggling and border jumping: The Beitbridge border post', *Fair Planet*, 24 November 2015, https://www.fairplanet.org/story/corruption-smuggling-and-border-jumping-the-beitbridge-border-post (last accessed 10 April 2021).
2.   Department of Home Affairs, White Paper on International Migration for South Africa, 2017, p. 26, https://www.gov.za/sites/default/files/gcis_document/201707/41009gon750.pdf (accessed 10 February 2022).

9

Illicit Design Sensibilities: The Material and Infrastructural Potentialities of Drug Smuggling

Craig Martin

On first sight a tabletop full of consumer goods appears to be nothing out of the ordinary. Such items are emblematic of the material cultures of mass consumerism; goods we simply take for granted. But as with the historical, social and cultural study of consumer culture, when one looks more closely at the objects in question they inevitably reveal much more. The packaging in question states: 'TPU magic water bag push up bras'. One could reflect upon societal expectations that foster a culture where such products are produced and consumed. However, in this specific case, 'magic water' takes on an even more ominous character. For the 'magic water' inserts are in fact a liquid form of the illegal narcotic methylamphetamine, amounting to a total of 190 litres.

In December 2015, Australian police and security services intercepted the consignment of £500 million worth of the drug smuggled into Australia.[1] The media reporting of the seizure showed the police press conference where these boxes of push-up bras were displayed alongside plastic bags containing pots of glue. Like the bras, the glue pots – discovered in later police raids – also contained the liquid form of the drug, this time totalling 530 litres. The intrigue in this example – and the key aspect this chapter investigates – lies in the modification and disguise of everyday commodities for the trafficking of illegal drugs across international borders. Knowledge of geography, movement, as well as practical aptitude and technical ingenuity, are common threads which link the actions of smugglers across history and geography, be they trafficking alcohol, tobacco or drugs. In many ways the straightforward definition of smuggling belies the inherent creativity in shipping illicit goods. Where smuggling is deemed 'a clandestine economic practice that we can simply define as bringing in or taking out from one jurisdiction to another without authorization' this does not capture the elaborate material and infrastructural practices one might identify with the Australian example.[2]

To better capture the practices of creative ingenuity such examples of smuggling exhibit, this chapter investigates the materialities of drug smuggling. More specifically, it addresses how artefacts and infrastructures play a crucial role in the movement of illicit drugs across national and international borders. Its primary focus is on the concealment of illicit narcotics amidst legal freight and, in addition, how smugglers adapt extant objects to disguise their use as conveyors of drugs. In doing this, I consider the importance of illicit logistical planning coupled with extensive knowledge of infrastructure and, fundamentally for the chapter – the artefactual *potential* of legal artefacts. This latter point leads on to a further core premise of the chapter: that the practices employed by smugglers of illegal narcotics (and other contraband) go beyond normative ideas of creative ingenuity; instead they are akin to a form of designerly sensibility, where the practicalities of goal-oriented 'problem solving' approaches are demonstrated. By this I refer to the idea of design in broader terms than is perhaps commonly understood. So, rather than design 'as an expert activity, aimed at the design of products for serial production using the industrial technology of the period',[3] I align it with a wider range of skills and competences geared towards addressing particular problems: socio-material understanding; complex planning; integrative thinking; practicality; and collaboration. Critical to the idea of design sensibilities developed here is Lucy Suchman's notion of configuration.[4] Design as a form configuration is concerned with how socio-technical artefacts, systems and material imaginaries are shaped and joined together to form new assemblages. Crucially, as I argue in this chapter, these competences which have traditionally been the domain of professional designers are distributed so that many other 'design protagonists' are engaged in responding to problems.[5] Of course, I do not suggest that smugglers see themselves as design protagonists, rather I use this analytic lens as a heuristic device of sorts to investigate the specific relationship between smuggling practices and the materialities of artefacts and infrastructures. I think through the practices of concealment and disguise as a type of design sensibility and how smugglers envision the materialities of artefacts and infrastructures, and, significantly, their potential beyond their intended purpose. Further to this I also argue that smugglers configure smuggling assemblages to be perceived in a certain way, that is, as normalised features of different mobility systems such as freight or passenger transport.

As with much research into illicit practices there are important caveats to highlight in relation both to the research context itself and the broader aims of investigating such cultures of illegality. Most pertinently, in discussing a variety of smuggling methods, I am only considering those that have been intercepted rather than those that have evaded seizure and thus could be seen as inherently more ingenious. In some ways this speaks to the failure one associates with many social practices but, as is common in such instances, failure can often lead to improved forms of social or technical awareness, or indeed even more sophisticated approaches to smuggling.[6] Rather than seeking information from smugglers themselves, the discussion here is framed by methods that have ultimately *failed*.[7] Suffice to say that the academic study of criminality is riven with this inherent methodological fallibility.[8] Equally, the study of drug trafficking is deeply ethical, both in relation to the harmful social effects noted already, but also the 'celebration' of ingenuity itself. There is a fine balance between a considered investigation of the methods utilised by organised criminal groups and the perennial fascination with, and gratification derived from such forms of cunning.[9] My aim here is to consider the skills and knowledges employed by drug smugglers, not simply to celebrate them but rather to raise awareness that such practices are incredibly sophisticated and, in many ways, mirror the material, technical and logistical aptitude of professional designers and planners.

Material infrastructures of drug smuggling

In her study of illicit global mobilities Gargi Bhattacharyya argues that organised crime is *dependent* on legitimated economic structures.[10] While these are alternate modes of transnational business activity, they are still financial practices nonetheless. She notes that organised crime 'has a necessarily symbiotic relationship with the formal economy and makes its profits from providing an alternative route through the interstices of "legitimate" transnational business'.[11] Smuggling can be seen as a business activity in its own right, focused on 'supply, delivery, finance, and contractual enforcement'.[12] It is entangled with the very constitution of trade flows, notwithstanding the illicit qualities of these flows. In this opening section I develop this notion of 'dependency' by suggesting that there is a reliance at play in the utilisation by drug smugglers of legal systems, artefacts and infrastructures. To begin this discussion, an outline of the different smuggling methods will help to situate the key arguments on dependency.

Smuggling is an inherently distributive practice.[13] In general terms it is formed by various forms of mobility: from small-scale smuggling by individuals, through larger-scale operations such as weapons smuggling, to the 'under-invoicing' of goods declared.[14] With narcotics smuggling a similar diversity of practices is present. This is partly due to the nature of the drugs themselves, the historical and geopolitical contexts of production, distribution and consumption,[15] as well as forms of seizure and resultant effects on previous methods of smuggling. There are also distinctions between the smuggling activities of lower-level (small quantities) and high-level (large quantities) distribution. As Caulkins et al. note, there is little evidence to suggest there are *typical* approaches to drug smuggling, an argument that is clear in relation to new trafficking methods becoming necessary following interception.[16] Any semblance of identifiable patterns of approach would of course be highly detrimental to smugglers in aiding interdiction.

However, while acutely mindful of the empirical evidence questioning common patterns of smuggling, in the specific context of the materialities and infrastructures of drug smuggling I identify two interrelated sets of approaches, illustrated by way of examples from the Sinaloa Cartel. In February 2019, Joaquin Guzmán – otherwise known as El Chapo – was found guilty of 26 drug-related charges in addition to one murder conspiracy. El Chapo was ostensibly the head of the Sinaloa Cartel, a Mexican-organised crime syndicate known primarily for narcotics trafficking into the US. The trial in New York 'has offered a detailed insight into the way the US-Mexico border has determined the structure of one of the world's most lucrative businesses'.[17] Following El Chapo's conviction, the US Attorney's Office issued a press release detailing the extent of the Sinaloa's activities.[18] The cartel trafficked drugs from Mexico to wholesale distribution centres in Atlanta, Arizona, Chicago, Los Angeles, Miami, and New York, before the drugs were shipped to buyers. To smuggle large quantities of drugs into the US took ingenious methods, some of which have attained almost mythical status, particularly the use of a large-scale catapult to fire quantities of marijuana into the US. This incident, in 2011, came after a fence had been erected between the border of Mexico and Arizona.[19] Other methods employed by the cartel were similarly sophisticated: the use of semi-submersibles and full submarines, as well as 7 tons of cocaine smuggled in a consignment of canned jalapenos.[20]

These latter two examples provide the grounds for identifying the two sets of approaches to smuggling referred to earlier. First, the cartel's use of narcosubmarines is a method utilising transport technologies *separate* from established routes. Here there is clear evidence of highly developed technical knowledge and sophisticated engineering acumen in designing and constructing these stand-alone drug trans-shipment vehicles.[21] Second, their use of the shipment of canned jalapenos as a front to hide the cocaine demonstrates the covert use of *legitimate* integrated transport infrastructure. Instead of a separate infrastructure of illicit conveyance being created, this latter case shows 'dependency' on established legal infrastructures of trans-shipment. These methods are not mutually exclusive, rather they may be combined in order to evade interdiction and seizure of the drugs. Both approaches also employ technical knowledge associated with the configurative sensibilities of socio-material artefacts and infrastructures I discuss later, but in this chapter the main focus is on the latter, that is, the use of legitimate infrastructure: I suggest this approach demonstrates an even more sophisticated understanding of problem-solving, specifically how smugglers have adopted and adapted established functions of legitimate artefacts and the material connectivity of physical infrastructures. Although the creation of discreet trans-shipment vehicles such as narcosubmarines or the use of low-key airstrips is clearly concerned with engineering, design, and planning, the case I develop is that appropriating the interconnective potential of licit artefacts and infrastructures is even more akin to the way in which the complex ill-defined problems of design are dealt with.[22]

The focus here on harnessing legitimate transportation networks and supply chains raises a plethora of potential examples: the use of land and sea transport routes; adaptation of existing commercial vessels such as fishing boats;[23] the use of postal or parcel networks; commercial flights; the concealment of drugs in legal freight shipments; or, perhaps most infamously, the use of drug couriers, more commonly known as 'drug mules'.[24] This is something of a catch-all term, identifying individuals who knowingly attempt to smuggle illegal drugs using primarily international air travel (but also ships) as their main method of cross-border transportation. However, there are important distinctions to make: mules also include 'body-packers', those who have secreted drugs about themselves by ingesting them internally in their stomachs or inserting them into the rectum or vagina in prepared condoms or the fingers of latex gloves.[25] The dangers of this are self-evident.[26] The term 'mules' also refers to couriers who strap drugs to their bodies using either adhesive tape or specially designed vests or girdles, as well as those (wittingly and unwittingly) carrying drugs in adapted luggage or other travel goods, such as tourist souvenirs or toiletries. Fundamental to the methods adopted by mules, or more pointedly the smuggling organisations employing or bribing the mules, is the act of *concealment*.

Concealment of drugs upon and within the body is a clear example of how legal forms of mobility infrastructures are appropriated by smugglers. But one of the obvious distinctions between this approach and other forms of concealment in legal shipment routes is that of scale. Where individual couriers might be able to conceal small amounts of narcotics this is very limited when compared with the use of global freight distribution channels, where illegal narcotics are concealed among legitimate cargo shipments. This was shown with the Sinaloa Cartel's concealment of cocaine amidst tins of jalapenos: such examples abound and are far too numerous to list in detail here. However, it is necessary to demonstrate the differences in scale. One such case includes the seizure in March 2018 of more than US $1.5 million worth of heroin at the Pharr-Reynosa International Bridge on the US-Mexico border – here the heroin was concealed amidst a consignment of tomatoes.[27] An even larger consignment of cocaine was seized at the Port of Baltimore in June 2019 when a shipping container loaded with beach chairs was intercepted and port authorities discovered the largest ever haul of narcotics found at the port with 151 kg of cocaine worth $10 million hidden in black sports bags among the chairs.[28] This shipment had originated in China and travelled to Baltimore through Panama destined for Maryland, highlighting the interconnectedness of cargo mobilities and the resultant infiltration of these networks by smugglers. In Melbourne, Australia, a still-larger amount of methamphetamine worth US $840 million (AU $1.197 billion) was seized by Australian Border Force officials in June 2019. The 1.6 tonnes of the drug were discovered hidden inside a shipment of stereo speakers from Bangkok.[29] Concealment is one of the most widely adopted methods used by smugglers and, while the use of freight trans-shipments is common, other forms of concealment are also in evidence, in even more 'innocent' seeming goods. Once more in Australia, in June 2019 a smaller consignment of methamphetamine, this time weighing 3 kg and worth US $695,000 (AU $1 million), was discovered hidden inside comic books.[30] The leader of the criminal gang had travelled regularly to southern California, where the narcotics were then sent via courier distribution services to Queensland hidden inside the comic books.

Mindful of the distinct geographical, political and security contexts of these various examples, there is still much to be learnt from the range of cases, particularly in terms of the ingenuity and planning required for concealing the illegal substances. In the next section I make the case that these illegal practices exemplify a form of illicit design sensibility. As briefly noted in the introduction to this chapter, I define this as a sensibility towards the material potentiality of quotidian artefacts such as the freight containers and, even more critically, their embeddedness in global freight infrastructures.

The configuration of illicit design sensibilities

Pet transportation crates are rather rudimentary objects. They are commonly constructed from cheap plywood with wire mesh cut-outs for windows. Simple door hinges, a latch, and carry handles are other regular features. Like the examples briefly described in the previous section pet transportation crates are a relatively familiar feature of air travel. However, in the case I discuss in this section the nature of these seemingly simple transportation boxes is radically transformed. Under the floor of three such transportation crates, packets of high-purity heroin worth US $1.45 million were found at the Animal Reception Centre at Heathrow Airport in the United Kingdom. National Crime Agency officers discovered that the crates in which cats had been transported had been modified to produce false bottoms, with a cavity created to secrete the packets of heroin inside.[31]

The pet transportation business was run by Scott Parker (a dual British/ South African national) facilitating clients to transport domestic pets abroad. In fact, the company was a front for drug trafficking and Reception Centre workers discovered the heroin in June 2014. One of the investigating officers provides an insightful statement: 'Parker thought he would avoid our attention.'[32] The day-to-day operation of the business was intended to obscure the illicit activities, to literally avoid the attention of security authorities under the impression this was a legitimate commercial enterprise with the transportation crates simply part of the organisational infrastructure of the company. Masquerading as a legitimate transport company is a form of disguise in itself, an action intended to conceal its actual purposes, as are the materialities of the boxes themselves.

This example demonstrates acute awareness of the illicit potential of the structural nature of commercial enterprises through the idea of the company 'front', but crucial for this example is the focus of the company on logistics and cross-border mobilities, as well as the potentially subversive power of the transportation crates and their associated infrastructures. In many ways the transportation of illegal narcotics in this guise is akin to the complex organisational challenges of licit logistics and supply chain management. For Decker and Townsend Chapman, the structure of the drug smuggling enterprises they studied in the US is, to a certain extent, linked to licit commercial organisations.[33] They detail how such organisations consist of various 'offices', echoing the point by Caulkins et al. that their own study-group of incarcerated smugglers believed they were engaged in business activity per se.[34] Such 'offices' are formed of supply-side operations focused on production; offices of finance and transportation; a distribution office in the US; as well as independent transporters, brokers and other contacts. To transpose these illicit enterprises onto legitimate organisational structures may appear too far-fetched, however for the case I pursue here they both deal with comparable logistical hurdles: they are ultimately concerned with rigorous spatio-temporal planning. As a result, the structural organisation of narcotics smuggling highlights the centrality of transportation, distribution and mobility to these illicit enterprises.

While this could quite readily be designated as a form of 'illicit logistics'[35] or 'subversive mobilities',[36] in this section I pursue the interrelated notion of 'illicit design sensibilities'. I do so in order to highlight the levels of creative ingenuity that smugglers can be said to employ over and above a purely logistical approach to the conveyance of drugs, particularly the importance of how specific assemblages are configured to be *perceived* in certain ways. By terming this 'illicit design sensibilities' the intention is to foreground the configurative power that professional designers possess over and above the purely ingenious, arguing that a cognate sensibility is evident in the configuration of smuggling assemblages. I use 'design' as an analytic device to also provoke discussion of the ownership of design competences. While the more recent turn to designerly ways of thinking within management settings alludes to this,[37] I suggest that the sophisticated socio-technical nature of smuggling demonstrates how the competences of complex planning, socio-material knowledge, integrative thinking, and practical insight are central to illicit practices. In doing so

I question the framing of design as invariably benevolent and pose the argument that smugglers are also utilising the configurative power one more readily associates with professional design competences.[38]

Glenn Parsons, in his book *The Philosophy of Design*, identifies a variety of modalities of design competences, including the fundamental importance of its problem-centred approaches. As he puts it, 'design is the intentional solution of a problem, by the creation of plans for a new sort of thing, where the plans would not be immediately seen, by a reasonable person, as an inadequate solution'.[39] Although this may appear rather reductive it nonetheless foregrounds a genealogy of design driven by problem-solving activities above all else. The legacy of design as a problem-solving activity resides within a well-established tradition of functionalism, most commonly associated with the work of Hebert Simon in his 1969 book *The Sciences of the Artificial*. Simon's now-classic definition of design, 'everyone designs who devises courses of action aimed at changing existing situations into preferred ones', assigns design a specific function: that of addressing particular problems or 'situations' and, importantly, providing new, constructive articulations of better situations or 'solutions'.[40] The intellectual and disciplinary contexts of such a claim are important: Simon was disdainful of what he saw as the 'intellectually soft, intuitive, informal, and cooky-booky' attitude of previous attempts to identify design's epistemology.[41] The basic premise of Simon's work was an increase in the analytic rigour of approach; he was dedicated to 'forms of logic that would lead to efficient methods of problem-solving'.[42]

However, such descriptions of the design process as singularly problem-focused are rather limited in scope, as they do not adequately address the complexities of the working methods and realities of design practices, nor the nuances of the ontology of problems themselves, particularly how they are inherently ill-defined. Rather than a distinct science of design then, work on design's disciplinary specificity posited how it differs from other cognate areas such as art or craft practices, as well as the natural and human sciences.[43] For Archer, design is 'the collected experience of the material culture, and the collected body of experience, skill and understanding embodied in the arts of planning, inventing, making and doing'.[44] Its ultimate power resides in practical knowledge based upon 'sensibility, invention, validation and implementation'.[45] Beyond this, designers operate at a general level by contextualising their approaches in relation to the wider framework in which they are working, be that materials, forms, histories or methodologies.[46] The importance of framing is also attuned to Schön's argument that designers – like other professional practition-ers – bring pre-existing knowledges, skills and experience to different situations.[47] They deal with the problem by attending to the *opportuni-ties* created by the problem itself, first by identifying different facets of the problem before framing 'the context in which we will attend to them'.[48] Decisively, there is an interactive process at work whereby the problem and the designer are in dialogue, the situation of the problem 'talking back' to the designer.[49] So, while design is still concerned with fulfilling specific tasks it is not solely bound by the problem-solution paradigm, rather a space where the complexity of the problem is worked with. Indeed, Cross in his consideration of 'design intelligence' notes how designers do not treat problems as a given, they engage in their broader contexts.[50] They do so by recognising how problems are dialogical, not only between the problem and the designer, but through multidisciplinary collabora-tive practices. Crucially, Cross also notes how designers operate across multiple scales, from the manipulation of small-scale material properties through to the shaping of large-scale systemic processes.

The shaping of this complex array of systemic, material and infrastruc-tural entities has a direct correspondence to Lucy Suchman's articulation of how design as a socio-technical system is concerned with *configuration* – of joining together imaginaries and materialities.[51] It creates a shape or, as she puts it, a 'figure [...] to assign shape [...] to designate what is to be made noticeable and consequential'.[52] The role of the designer might be seen as joining together, suturing disparate assembled elements at different scales. Like Cross's design intelligence, this could be the material constitu-tion of form and the relational dynamics that facilitate the interaction of discrete units. Using the work of Madeline Akrich, Suchman then outlines how configuration is concerned with the 'distribution of competences',[53] where the responsibilities for specific skills, knowledges and competences are distributed among multiple actors, in much the same way that Cross again identifies the collaborative approaches of designers. Even more importantly for the discussions in this chapter, design-as-configuration provides a critical perspective on *who* has the ownership of, or indeed the right to the ownership of design competences. That is, do designers alone possess the material, semiotic or technical competences to resolve particular problem situations? Given the methodological and political manifestations of participatory design,[54] the genealogies of improvisation and adhocism,[55] the role of design thinking in business settings, as well as the more recent turn to the diffusion of design for social innovation, the answer to this is clear. Design competences – the ability to conceive the complexity of a problem; awareness of material and technical constraints; knowledge of planning; integrative and systemic understanding – are distributed across a wide range of contexts and actors, both professionals and non-professionals.

How then might these various notions of the configurative nature of design sensibilities and the ownership of competences relate to drug smuggling practices described in the previous section? As with nearly all forms of smuggling (narcotics, other contraband, human smuggling) one of the key 'problems' is overcoming the securitisation and policing of borders as the material manifestation of the legislative force of the nation state and international law. The examples cited earlier in the chapter signal the border as the primary mechanism of the state to impede cross-border movement of illicit substances (and people). However, borders also produce opportunities for smugglers: they do so particularly through the infrastructural and international trade apparatuses intended to produce supposedly frictionless mobility, containerisation being the paradigmatic example.[56] In the cases noted in this chapter we see something similar. The pet transportation business utilised the infrastructural mechanisms of shipping animals across international borders.

In the same way that designers are said to have a dialogical interrelationship with problems – where the problem 'talks back' – there is an intimacy between the specific security constitution of the different bordering strategies and the tactics required to evade interdiction. The tactical tools of drug smugglers develop out of an understanding of the situated contexts of national borders, be that the policing of the Mexico-US or Australian borders, or the cross-border mobilities of animals. In the case of the Sinaloa Cartel, the use of a shipment of tinned jalapenos to conceal 7 tons of cocaine was a result of their recognition of the everyday cross-border movements of these specific consumer goods; in the same way, the concealment of methylamphetamine worth £500 million shipped into Australia in 2015 was again attempted through an understanding of the trans-shipment routes of common commodities. To return to Schön's argument, the problems encountered by designers create opportunities for resolving them. My suggestion here is that the ubiquity and regularity of the commodities being transported across international borders create opportunities for smugglers to conceal narcotics in shipments of the goods or pets moving across these borders. There is a recognition of potential as well as the opportunity of dependency on these distributive networks.

The idea of an illicit design sensibility speaks to exactly this notion of the opportunities afforded by borders and the mobilities of various actors across them. Where the disguise of the methylamphetamine as liquid gel inserts is in many ways a classic definition of creative ingenuity (primarily concerned with the inventiveness of construction and the contrivance of making something), there is much more than mere contrivance in the smuggling of such large quantities of liquid meth into Australia. This is where I identify the move from illicit ingenuity to illicit design sensibilities through the power of configuring new assemblages. Although the practical aptitude of repurposing the original gel inserts and filling them with methylamphetamine is in many ways 'ingenious', I argue that such material inventiveness is part of a wider configurative capability, where the overall 'shape' of the problem was addressed in a much more holistic and systemic manner through an understanding of the flows of commodities across the border. Likewise, the pet transportation smuggling enterprise was effectively configured through the creation of the shell company itself; its place alongside other companies operating in the area of pet transportation; the material paraphernalia of the transport boxes, which form the core business of the company; and the embeddedness of the transportation crates in the mobilities of animals. Both these contexts, the disguise of the liquid methylamphetamine as the gel inserts and the spaces of concealment in the pet transportation crates are concerned with how these commodities were *designed* to be perceived – as part of the wider assemblage of licit goods trans-shipped into Australia and the UK. It is the awareness of both the material potential of the commodities themselves, coupled with the infrastructural capacity of the transnational freight networks that marks such a case out as akin to the configurative power described by Suchman, as well as the sensibilities that Cross defines as a distinctly designerly form of intelligence. So, just as the previous section briefly considered Bhattacharyya's idea of the 'symbiotic reliance' of licit and illicit enterprise, so illicit design sensibilities in the context of these instances of drug smuggling point to the idea of dependency on the infrastructural power of transnational freight networks: that is, an identification of the most common objects, symbols and actors that form the specific contexts of transnational freight transportation and animal mobilities. Appreciating the complexity of how particular situations are configured is paramount to professional design approaches as well as illicit attitudes to specific problems, as are planning competences, logistical dexterity and practical aptitude.

Conclusions

Of course, in attempting to smuggle the large quantities of methylamphet-amine into Australia the smugglers were clearly not thinking of this as a form of design, rather this was straightforwardly a practical means of over-coming the policing of the border. What I claim here is a *parallel sensibility* between traditional forms of design intelligence, sensibilities and com-petences, and the illicit practices of smugglers. Just as the more general ownership of competences does not belong solely to professional fields, so it is with design and its abilities to deal with complex problems and sit-uations. Somewhat ironically, in making the case for the value of design, Bruce Archer and Nigel Cross highlight how its domain of concrete, material knowledge through making and doing should be encompassed in everyday scenarios outside of professional settings. For the ill-defined problems that designers deal with 'are like the problems or issues or deci-sions that people are more usually faced with in everyday life'.[57]

The primary intention of this chapter has been to explore the mate-rialities and infrastructures of drug smuggling practices. They provide the means to capitalise on the situatedness of objects in the trans-ship-ment of commodities as well as the power of the infrastructures of global mobilities. In arguing this, one of the aims has also been to foreground the creative way in which smugglers utilise, co-opt and adapt artefacts as clandestine conduits. I suggested that smugglers exhibit a profoundly sophisticated understanding of the potentiality of artefacts and their materiality, be that in seeing the potential of artist's glue pots, a shipment of canned jalapenos, or pet transportation crates. The practicalities of envisioning this potential offer even more insight into the value of design sensibilities than average professional design problems, which are often comparably mundane in their remit. Although I suggest that the ingenuity of smugglers is evident in such approaches to the materiality of artefacts, the configurative power of this, coupled with systemic and infrastructural knowledge and planning, moves beyond the level of ingenuity. One of the most important points raised in the chapter is that the configurative sensi-bility of drug smugglers in understanding the complexity of transportation routes, supply chains, security constraints and border practices, is more than just ingenuity: it is akin to the sensibilities of professional design in its utilisation of planning competences, systemic awareness, and material affinity. Indeed, Buchanan's argument that design is ultimately concerned with the integration of understanding, communication and action is particularly evident when we consider the ways in which smugglers draw together and configure a wide range of actors in producing smuggling assemblages.[58] Likewise, parallel to Manzini's manifesto for diffuse design, a similar approach can be identified with smuggling, whereby *existing* materials, systems and practices are adapted and repurposed. Designers and smugglers alike are agile: they deal with problem situations by thinking on their feet, adapting to the singularities of particular issues and settings. Through a number of key assertions I ultimately come to the conclusion that one of the primary mechanisms employed by drug smugglers is configuring assemblages of artefacts and embedding them in transportation infrastructures so they are designed to be perceived in a specific or fixed way – as legitimate entities that are embedded within and fit neatly into legal infrastructures and mobilities. This does not always work – as the intercepted examples demonstrate – but in gaining access to what has been seized we are privy to some of these mechanisms.

Notes

1. *The Guardian*, 'Australian police seize huge haul of meth hidden in gel bra inserts', 15 February 2016, https://www.theguardian.com/australia-news/2016/feb/15/australian-police-seize-estimated-1bn-worth-of-methamphetamine (accessed 16 February 2016).
2. Peter Andreas, *Smuggler Nation: How Illicit Trade Made America* (Oxford: Oxford University Press, 2013), p. x.
3. Ezio Manzini, *Design, When Everybody Designs* (Cambridge, MA: MIT Press, 2015), p. 53.
4. Lucy Suchman, 'Configuration', in Celia Lury, and Nina Wakeford (eds) *Inventive Methods: The Happening of the Social* (London: Routledge, 2012), pp. 48–60.
5. Manzini, *Design, When Everybody Designs*, p. 4.
6. Charles Perrow, *Normal Accidents: Living with High-risk Technologies* (New York: Basic Books, 1984).
7. Scott H. Decker and Margaret Townsend Chapman, *Drug Smugglers on Drug Smuggling: Lessons from the Inside* (Philadelphia, PA: Temple University Press, 2008).
8. Mangai Natarajan, 'Understanding the structure of a drug trafficking organization: A conversational analysis', *Crime Prevention Studies* 11, 2000, pp. 273–98.
9. Gerald Mars, *Cheats at Work: An Anthropology of Workplace Crime* (London: Unwin, 1983).

10. Gargi Bhattacharyya, *Traffick: The Illicit Movement of People and Things* (London: Pluto Press, 2005).
11. Ibid., p. 63.
12. Kathryn Meyer and Terry Parssinen, *Webs of Smoke: Smugglers, Warlords, Spies, and the History of the International Drug Trade* (Lanham, MD: Rowman and Littlefield, 1998), p. 2.
13. Jorge I. Dominguez, 'Smuggling', *Foreign Policy*20, 1975, p. 92.
14. Carolyn Nordstrom, *Global Outlaws: Crime, Money and Power in the Contemporary World* (Berkeley, CA: University of California Press, 2007), pp. 119–20.
15. The majority of the contemporary examples of smuggling practices cited in this chapter denote flows of narcotics from the Global South to the Global North, or from east to west. The histories of smuggling and the broader trade in narcotics differ somewhat, not least the eighteenth- and nineteenth-century imperialist-mercantilist export of Indian-grown opium by the British into mainland China, leading to widespread addiction. See Simon Harvey, *Smuggling: Seven Centuries of Contraband* (London: Reaktion Books, 2016), pp. 151–63.
16. Jonathan P. Caulkins, Honora Burnett and Edward Leslie, 'How illegal drugs enter an island country: Insights from interviews with incarcerated smugglers', *Global Crime* 10(1–2), 2009, p. 69.
17. Jessica Loudis, 'Border traffic', *London Review of Books* 41(3), 2019, p. 8.
18. Department of Justice, 'Joaquin "El Chapo" Guzman, Sinaloa Cartel leader, convicted of running a continuing criminal enterprise and other drug-related charges', press release, 2019, https://www.justice.gov/opa/pr/joaquin-el-chapo-guzman-sinaloa-cartel-leader-convicted-running-continuing-criminal (accessed 14 February 2019).
19. Loudis, 'Border traffic'.
20. Department of Justice, 'Joaquin "El Chapo" Guzman'.
21. Javier Guerrero C., *Narcosubmarines: Outlaw Innovation and Maritime Interdiction in the War on Drugs* (Basingstoke: Palgrave Pivot, 2019).
22. Manuel Castells, *The Information Age: Economy, Society and Culture*, vol. III: *End of Millennium*, 2nd edn, with new Preface (Chichester: Wiley-Blackwell, 2010), p. 199.
23. Decker and Townsend Chapman, *Drug Smugglers on Drug Smuggling*, p. 71.
24. Jennifer Fleetwood, *Drug Mules: Women in the International Cocaine Trade* (Basingstoke: Palgrave Macmillan, 2014).
25. Ameripol, *Situational Analysis of Drug Trafficking – A Police Point of View: Bolivia, Brazil, Colombia, Ecuador Panama and Peru* (Bogotá: Ameripol Executive Secretariat, 2013), p. 37; Fleetwood, *Drug Mules*, p. 141.
26. James R. Gill and Stuart M. Graham, 'Ten years of "body packers" in New York City: 50 deaths', *Journal of Forensic Science* 47(4), 2002, pp. 843–6.
27. Fares Sabawi, 'Border patrol: More than $1.5 million in heroin found in tomato shipment', 2 April 2018, https://www.mysanantonio.com/

news/local/crime/article/More-than-1-5-million-in-heroin-found-in-tomato-12799993.php#photo-15328409 (accessed 4 April 2018).

28. US Customs and Border Protection, 'Federal authorities, local partners seize 333 pounds of cocaine in shipping container', 25 June 2019, https://www.cbp.gov/newsroom/local-media-release/federal-authorities-local-partners-seize-333-pounds-cocaine-shipping (accessed 27 June 2019).

29. Guillaume Goudreau, 'Record 1.6 tonnes of methamphetamine discovered in music speakers by Australian border officers', 7 June 2019, https://www.illicit-trade.com/2019/06/record-1-6-tonnes-of-methamphetamine-discovered-in-music-speakers-by-australian-border-officers/ (accessed 8 June 2019).

30. Guillaume Goudreau, 'Australian police smash gang that smuggled methamphetamine from US to Queensland in comic books', 12 June 2019, https://www.illicit-trade.com/2019/06/australian-police-smash-gang-that-smuggled-methamphetamine-from-us-to-queensland-in-comic-books/ (accessed 14 June 2019).

31. Ian Evans, '"Pet relocation" smuggler gets seven years in the UK', *Saturday Star*, 20 June 2015, p. 4.

32. Cited in ibid.

33. Decker and Townsend Chapman, *Drug Smugglers on Drug Smuggling*, p. 36.

34. Caulkins et al., 'How illegal drugs enter an island country', p. 68.

35. Gautam Basu, 'The role of transnational smuggling operations in illicit supply chains', *Journal of Transportation Security* 6(3), 2013, pp. 315–28; Nicky Gregson and Mike Crang, 'Illicit economies: Customary illegality, moral economies and circulation', *Transactions of the Institute of British Geographers* 42(2), 2017, pp. 206–19.

36. Erik Cohen, Scott A. Cohen and Xiang (Robert) Li, 'Subversive mobilities', *Applied Mobilities* 2(2), 2017, pp. 115–33.

37. Tim Brown, 'Design thinking', *Harvard Business Review*, June 2008, pp. 84–92; Lucy Kimbell, 'Rethinking design thinking: Part 1', *Design and Culture* 3(3), 2011, pp. 285–306; Lucy Kimbell, 'Rethinking design thinking: Part 2', *Design and Culture* 4(2), 2012, pp.129–48; Cameron Tonkinwise, 'A taste for practices: Unrepressing style in design thinking', *Design Studies* 32(6), 2011, pp. 533–45.

38. On the malevolent power of design see Mahmoud Keshavarz, *The Design Politics of the Passport: Materiality, Immobility, and Dissent* (London: Bloomsbury Academic, 2019); Craig Martin, *Deviant Design: The Ad Hoc, the Illicit, the Controversial* (London: Bloomsbury Academic, forthcoming).

39. Glenn Parsons, *The Philosophy of Design* (Cambridge: Polity Press, 2016), p. 11.

40. Herbert Simon, *The Sciences of the Artificial*, 3rd edn (Cambridge, MA: MIT Press, 1996), p. 111.

41. Ibid., p. 112.

42. Victor Margolin, *The Politics of the Artificial: Essays on Design and Design Studies* (Chicago: University of Chicago Press, 2002), p. 236.

43. Bruce Archer, 'Design as a discipline', *Design Studies* 1(1), 1979, pp. 17–20; Nigel Cross, 'Designerly ways of knowing', *Design Studies* 3(4), 1982, pp. 221–7; Nigel Cross, 'Designerly ways of knowing: Design discipline versus design science', *Design Issues* 17(3), 2001, pp. 49–55; Nigel Cross, *Design Thinking* (London: Bloomsbury Academic, 2011); Lucy Suchman, 'Theorizing the contemporary: Design', *Fieldsights*, 29 March 2018, https://culanth.org/fieldsights/design (accessed 13 August 2019).

44. Cited in Cross, 'Designerly ways of knowing', 1982, p. 221.

45. Archer, 'Design as a discipline', p. 20.

46. Richard Buchanan, 'Wicked problems in design thinking', *Design Issues* 8(2), 1992, p. 17.

47. On framing see Kees Dorst, *Frame Innovation: Create New Thinking by Design* (Cambridge, MA: MIT Press, 2015).

48. Donald Schön, *The Reflective Practitioner: How Professionals Think in Action* (New York: Basic Books/Harper Collins, 2008), p. 52.

49. Cross, *Design Thinking*, p. 23.

50. Ibid., p. 136.

51. Suchman, 'Configuration', p. 48.

52. Ibid., p. 49.

53. Ibid., p. 56.

54. Erling Bjögvinsson, Pelle Ehn, and Per-Anders Hillgren, 'Design things and design thinking: Contemporary participatory design challenges', *Design Issues* 28(3), 2012, pp. 101–16.

55. Charles Jencks, and Nathan Silver, *Adhocism: The Case for Improvisation*, expanded and updated edn (Cambridge, MA: MIT Press, 2013).

56. Craig Martin, 'Shipping container mobilities, seamless compatibility, and the global surface of logistical integration', *Environment and Planning A* 45(5), 2013, pp. 1021–36.

57. Cross, 'Designerly ways of knowing', 1982, p. 225.

58. Buchanan, 'Wicked problems in design thinking', p. 6.

10

A Partial Offering:
In and Out of Smuggling

Simon Harvey

> We clamor for the right to opacity for everyone.
>
> (Édouard Glissant, *Poetics of Relation*)

What is offered up to us when we look, from afar, at smuggling and its most visible contraband – people? Some kind of fact is presented to us through news media that gives an impression of inundation. Like never before, we are able to see migrant people arriving on beaches in southern Spain, Sicily, the Greek islands or elsewhere. Available imagery has shifted from patchy, grainy, black and white night-time CCTV pictures to mass-circulation television camera footage, under a glaring sun, that feeds into rolling news, or else mobile phone shots that quickly go viral. The rhetoric around these circulations is both sensationalist and paranoid. Part of the fear is that the frame binding this transparent image of arrival will break. Hence these migrants are held, in more than one sense of the word. The anxiety is not just that so-called 'fortress Europe' will be breached, but also that the visibility of the contraband – the scrutiny focused on these people – will dissolve and that they will split up and go underground. Transparency, a feted ideal in social democratic politics, and something that in its purest form can have no outside, nothing outside of the frame, will, in this case, have failed. In some ways this is an allegory of Foucault's 'space of surveillance' which, we are told, we should all resist, but how?

One answer might be to see like the smuggler – both for the migrant within the frame and for those of us spectating from outside of it. In this regard, I will focus on the potentiality of both the partial visibilities of smuggling and the partial offerings that smugglers make, before, briefly, borrowing some of its effectiveness to consider how it might offer potential for ways that we can work across disciplines, within the academy.

First, though, we should perhaps look a little more closely at how transparency works in relation to contraband circulations.

Transparency and smuggling

Is it so bad to make things visible? According to critic of transparency, philosopher and critical theorist Byung-Chul Han, part of the problem is what he calls the 'iconic compulsion to become a picture', that 'everything must become visible'.[1] We are suspected of something if we are beyond the frame. Being in the frame is to be, as Han puts it, operational but: 'subordinate to a calculable, steerable and controllable process'.[2] Heidegger expressed this in terms of both picture and framing. Picture, for him, meant:

> that which sounds in the colloquial expression to be 'in the picture' about something ... 'To put oneself in the picture' about something means: to place the being itself before one ... to keep it permanently before one.[3]

He considered framing (*Ge-stell*) to be a means of control through keeping an image stable and fast in front of you, excluding any other inhabitation of the scene. Heidegger could have been talking about transparency and who controls it. Francophone poet, novelist and literary critic Édouard Glissant also privileged opacity over transparency which, in reality, even beyond the frame, offers only a privileged few apparently clear sight and the right to get the measure of and understand the other.[4]

A critique of transparency is eloquently put by each of these theorists. How do we relate it to smuggling on the ground? How might we perceive smuggling beyond the binary of total secrecy – the traditional way of imagining smuggling – and this relatively new framework of transparency? Can one, as either participant or observer, 'put oneself in the picture' of the smuggling event at the same time that one strives to break its framing or to be only partially there? Approaches to working with smuggling vary, involving more or less immersion, and even if, like myself, we only have limited exposure to the field of this clandestine practice, there is still much that we can learn through thinking and trying to see like a smuggler. There are many ways of engaging with or against its framing, thinking of it less as a still and more as transition, circulation or mobility.

It must surely be possible to enter this other frame, to see like a smuggler, or at least to reframe the picture. That perennial outsider, Jean Genet gives us a lucid example of seeing like a smuggler in *The Thief's Journal* (1949, translated into English in 1964). As he hides in the grass waiting for his moment to cross the border, illegally, into Czechoslovakia, Genet imagines not only a way across, but a way on into the nation: 'I would penetrate less into a country than to the interior of an image [...] apprehend directly the essence of the nation I was entering.'[5] It is a path onwards, an option not immediately apparent for today's migrants with their restricted horizons. For Genet, though, it is opportunity that is framed.

For the most part, we are not privileged to have this clear smuggling sightline, for it to represent such opportunity to us. Far from becoming the active smuggler we remain passive; contraband emerges around us. It is not that we can't see it coming; smuggling can be very visible. For example, during the latter part of the twentieth century, and up until 2004, it was sometimes hard to miss the convoys of overladen trucks transporting contraband across the 100 km or so from ports on the Guajira Peninsula shore in northern Colombia to the entrepôt town of Maicao. At these smuggler ports, Portete and Nuevo, boxes of illicit merchandise, mainly electronic goods, liquor and fashionable clothes, would be piled high on the quays. It was possible to film them, as Colombian television crews occasionally did, and to talk to the smugglers. It was an opportunity to reframe this usually secretive activity.

Figure 10.1   Wayuu woman talking about smuggling, Guajira Peninsula, Colombia

Source: Still from the film *Contraband Desert* (by Simon Harvey, 2005).

But these images weren't firmly framed – accumulation here appearing more like the deluge that threatens to break the frame. However, they might also be caught, in another way, in Han's theory of transparency. He moves on to another form of it that is perhaps more relevant for the imaging of contemporary smuggling. It is still a framing but a much looser one, necessary because media representation is now less about a single, framed, still image than a flood of imagery. This is a characteristic of the new transparency, and quite apposite for depicting smuggling as inundation. Maintaining attention, not control, is now the key, and as such the frame becomes multiple like those in a rolling subliminal narrative, less like a still that lingers in the mind. It echoes a more general trend: in all areas we accumulate knowledge through a deluge of information that gives us a sense of being 'present' and, in another sense, kept in the picture (in that, for instance, we can google up any fact, at virtually any time). However, there is no longer any distance to think, even to frame a thought. With regard to building up an historical consciousness of it, there is little in the way of events or persons to use as evidence (any more than when it was an invisible activity). Indeed, representation of smuggling becomes like Jean Baudrillard's world of proliferating simulacra: a 'universe emptied of event'.[6] The few real anchors that provide specific references to places and people soon blur into one. It even becomes difficult to keep the border in focus. Han puts it this way:

> The compulsion for transparency dismantles all borders and thresholds. Space becomes transparent when it is smoothed, leveled [sic] and emptied out. Transparent space is semantically impoverished.[7]

These media images, be they of people or goods, washing up on the shore, leave us with a simplistic idea of smuggling and its contrabands. Do they really offer us a way of working with it? It was scarcely any easier before smuggling was brought into a surveillance space, before it was flattened out. Back then, it often seemed a little too black and white, and at other times overly colourful.

This latter perception isn't anything particularly new, and it perhaps owes something to the simplification of smuggling through its romanticisation over the centuries. Even in the twentieth century there was a tendency to picture smuggling worlds in terms of light and dark, with none of the grey tones which, away from media spotlight, we now associate with it. Consider this following romanticised viewpoint that makes a strong distinction between the self-image of the smuggler and that of authority – two varying depictions or framings. It comes from Henry de Monfreid, hashish smuggler on the Red Sea in the early part of the twentieth century:

> To me that other world, its confused objectives, its preoccupations, its stifling proximities, its 'honourable callings' that permitted so many interpretations, seemed purposeless. My world, the clean world of the sea, was to the governor a secret garden, remote, shadowy, poisonous.[8]

A little like Genet, Monfreid's perspective is clear. He is able to seize some kind of clarity and agency within a framing that would have his world as always shadowy. But surely these windows onto specific smuggling lives are rare exceptions in the twentieth century in which contrabanding either went underground or became hyper-visual to the extent that one doesn't really see it all, despite its transparency. It is perhaps part of what video artist and activist Ursula Biemann is getting at with her interweaving of these two different registers of clandestine mobility in her series of engagements with the differing, partial or totalising, visibilities of smuggling. For example, in *Remote Sensing* (2003) and *Sahara Chronicle* (2006–9), she shows the capture of smuggling through distant, all-seeing aerial and satellite surveillance technologies, but then counters it with interviews with smugglers and workers at the site of smuggling.[9] On the ground, her camera puts together stories that have been fractured by the prevailing visual narrative and are excluded from its framework. She reintroduces a sense of event and gives voice to those that she encounters involved in smuggling. It is a subaltern voice.

Running contrary to this capture, Biemann's interviews offer something else. It is actually echoed within some of the television news footage in Colombia, where the abstract image of accumulation of boxes of contraband is displaced by something more real: a Wayuu[10] woman talks about her work around smuggling. She is permitted to have a voice and can speak from the site of smuggling, from the event. She doesn't celebrate the work, but at the same time speaks of it providing a living where none other would be possible.

Although some involved in smuggling are permitted to speak here, it is still the case that they are often participating in it out of desperation. Participants are frequently exploited and, far from the clean world of romantics like Monfreid, their reality remains gritty and their horizons limited. On-the-ground experience of smuggling is, to a certain extent, reframed (but still framed) as a passive, commandeered experience. What it does do is move us beyond the recent relentless, event-free noise of smuggling that can flatten out and silence the critical discourse around it. Transparent scrutiny of smuggling can't achieve this. But should we not be looking to unframe rather than simply reframe the scene? Could it be that in order to see like a smuggler, to discern something affirmative in its strategies of circumvention and improvisation, even to imagine a kind of ethics in its creation of loosely bound communities, we should turn our attention towards that which is partially seen and partially offered?

Partial visibilities

In order to see how effective smugglers can be, one has only to look at informal economies, particularly grey markets.[11] Moisés Naím, author of a book about these other circulations and how they have affected us all, *Illicit: How Smugglers, Traffickers and Copycats are Hijacking the Global Economy*,[12] suggests that these informal activities are often like black holes, sucking in all light. Conversely, others have taken inspiration from certain other aspects, not least the partial visibility, of these illicit but not always entirely illegal activities, suggesting that we can glean some inspiration from them. Cultural theorists and activists Helge Mooshammer and Peter Mörtenböck appear in the latter category, most comprehensively with their research project (also a book and atlas) *Informal Market Worlds*.[13]

How do grey markets escape being frozen under the scrutiny of surveillance? Elsewhere I have written about the range of different forms that grey markets take,[14] resulting in a kind of typology of them, but isn't this just another kind of framing? In my own defence I might say that they are neither easily framed nor categorised, and so their shape shifts and the functions of each slips into that of the formal markets around them. They slide between frames, even forming hybrid markets. Illicit goods are only a part of the offering and these often lie in among legitimate merchandise. The ratio of one to the other often changes. Sometimes an entire market mutates from one form to another. For instance, when I visited Ciudad del Este in eastern Paraguay in 1990 it was little more than a town of wooden stalls along mud roads, but, with its growth as a centre for the dispersal of contraband electronics, *galerias* (malls – glassy and brazen) appeared, which then also sold non-contraband goods. Still, hawkers, *sac-oleiros*, from São Paolo would haul bagloads of these cheap goods across

Figure 10.2 'Legalize your contraband', Maicao, Guajira Peninsula, Colombia
Source: Still from the film *Contraband Desert* (by Simon Harvey 2005).

Friendship Bridge, straddling the border, to the town of Foz do Iguaçu on
the Brazilian side. The goods were often cheap; contraband in the sense of
invoiced beneath their actual monetary value so as to stay within the $300
export value limit. From Foz they would be taken on scheduled smuggler
buses (Tuesday from São Paolo, back Wednesday) to the larger Brazilian
city. There is a sense of return here in that this *galeria*-bought, second-gen-
eration contraband, which once upon a time could only be acquired on
the street, is now sold in São Paolo on the streets again, in particular on
Rua 25 de Março.

Many smugglers have carried contrabands that have had immense
import and they haven't always hidden all that they do; we haven't always
lived in a transparent world. They were able to keep a low profile, smuggling maintaining partial appearances. An example is Anglo-German
Rudolf Ackermann, based in Mexico for four years from 1825 onwards,
who supplied 'dangerous' books around Latin America at a time when the
Spanish empire was being assailed from all quarters. In among ordinary
books he secreted proscribed ones. They were hardly smuggled, simply
quietly shipped in through ports that had lower profiles beside their prestigious neighbours, for instance Santa Marta rather than Cartagena in

New Granada (now in Colombia) and Tampico rather than Veracruz in New Spain (now in Mexico). Exactly how influential these books were, is anybody's guess, but when he supplied two portable lithograph printing presses to Bolivarian rebels it had great impact. But does smuggling have to make an impact in this singular way to be of interest to us? After all, part of the effectiveness of grey markets is that their merchandise continues in circulation elsewhere, perhaps, as Arjun Appadurai describes the travels of goods, coming in and out of commodity status.[15]

It is this partial visibility, its avoidance of capture in a freeze frame of transparency, that could offer us a way into its flows, from which we might learn from its efficiencies. One reason why informal economies and grey markets have been fertile ground for thinking through alternative subjectivities and means of organising community is because not only are they irregularly organised they are also loosely framed. They don't fit into immutable and discrete categories. Mobility is key.

Attempts are made, of course, usually ineffectually, to demonstrate control over such unsanctioned mobilities. Helge Mooshammer tells us how certain informal markets are designated as 'notorious' by the office of the US Trade Representative (USTR), putting them in a legal category of 'known to all'.[16] It is pure rhetoric though, because they are only ever partially and occasionally known to anybody. RCN (Colombian television) news has shown not only the flood of contraband into the Guajira, a peripheral borderland, but also customs officers carrying out a show destruction event in which hundreds of bottles of liquor are smashed for the cameras. Mooshammer points to similar 'ceremonies' that are carried out by the Thai Department of Intellectual Property. Thousands of confiscated fake goods, worth several hundred million dollars are destroyed. But grey markets themselves are events in the sense that they come and go and transmute, more powerful than these demonstrations of apparent control which are merely token.

Mooshammer and Mörtenböck identify tremendous flexibility in the informal economy. Formal markets cannot command the supply networks of informal ones and so the latter are more attuned to actual needs of the population. They also have more complex circuits of usage and recycling. The grey market, found as it often is in large cities, overcomes separation of periphery and centre. Where the formal and informal are interwoven, or have something of a symbiotic relationship, then creativity is redistributed.[17] Others, such as Robert Neuwirth, in his book *Stealth of Nations: The Global Rise of the Informal Economy*,[18] have noted the creative potential of the so-called *debrouillards* of the informal sector – its motivated, self-organised, self-reliant, efficient and adaptable participants. Not only are smuggling circulations effective because they are partially visible, they are also smart in not offering up everything for scrutiny.

Partial offerings

In the aforementioned entrepôt town of Maicao on the Guajira Peninsula, some way south of the contraband ports, on the main east–west highway, one can 'legalise' the contraband. Why not certify the goods yourself if the main channels are monopolistic and often corrupt? In other words, pay a small tax, well-short of the government's demands, although within its expectations, and the goods enter a 'legal' framework. This is illicitness in action (not illegality) – the grey area of smuggling – but this is another discussion. Suffice to say here, that this is a partial offering.

There are some colourful examples in history of partial offerings by smugglers into the context or framework of a more official cause. The Lafitte brothers, Jean and Pierre, chased out of New Orleans for contrabanding and overly keen privateering, were recruited back to fight the British and save the city during the War of 1812. Smugglers from Deal and Folkestone on the south coast of England continued to smuggle to France during the Napoleonic wars, while still claiming that they were essentially patriotic, albeit on their own terms. Religion, in the context of colonialism, also has its examples. In *Idols behind Altars* (1929), Anita Brenner, an expatriate American scholar of Mexican art, describes indigenous practices of hiding images of pre-Colombian gods in the most holy parts of Roman Catholic churches as a response to being forced to convert. Yoruba gods were similarly merged, syncretically, in the only superficially Christian Afro-Caribbean religion called Santería. It allowed for participation without belonging.

A shift now to the potential for acting like a smuggler in other contexts closer to us (for me, visual cultural practices), carrying with us this idea of a partial offering that disrupts transparency. Raqs Media Collective is an artist/activist group founded in Delhi in 1992.[19] They have participated in many important art exhibitions over the past 25 years or so, including Documenta (2001) in Kassel and the Venice Biennale (2003 and 2005). They are well-known and respected participants in contemporary cultural circuits, many of which fall within the framework of the so-called 'art market'. As such, their work is there to be seen; staged and framed in that context. Although it is also a kind of collaboration, it operates more like what contemporary art theorist Pamela M. Lee calls a 'pseudo collective'.[20] It eschews the form of a more recognisable collective that might, for instance, have publicity and noisy protest action at the heart of its activism, perhaps gathering around a highly visible banner. Raqs' artworks offer us only partial evidence in their evocation of things like forced migration. In the work *Lost New Shoes* (2005), we are left with just a pile of smart trainers whose owners have had to leave quickly. There is a latency in much of their work that contradicts the group's high profile in the art world. Lee calls the work a 'restive kind of presence, neither wholly there nor completely absent but trafficking in some in-between and uncharted space'.[21] Much of the work goes under the radar, like contraband.

There is another dimension to their practice that is called Sarai,[22] a new-media and publishing initiative existing since 1998. It is a collaboration with film and urban studies theorists Ravi Vasudevan and Ravi Sundaram and is housed in the basement of the Centre for the Study of Developing Societies (CSDS, established in 1963), a large town house located in a leafy suburb of New Delhi. Unlike Raqs, it avoids conventional circuits of exhibition and display entirely, and its participatory events take place either outside of art spaces or online, cohering through quite unflashy things like source coding. Otherwise, it is just a space for research and dialogue. Even more than Raqs' work, Sarai is a partial, or incomplete offering.

Another form of partial offering takes the form of participation without belonging. It is a subjective position at the heart of almost all of Jacques Derrida's work. We are given, in many of his texts or advice on textual reading (which in our context now might be the framing of smuggling), the clue that there is often a contraband in what is framed before us and even though we see it, and recognise it, we don't get all of it, only a partial offering:

> in the process of this recognition, something else happens in the form of a contraband [*en contre-bande*]. People must be able to recognize it and at the same time recognize that they are dealing with something they can't identify, something they don't know.[23]

Contraband recurs in several of Derrida's books including *Glas* (1974) and *A Taste for the Secret* (1997), but it is in the essay 'The Law of Genre' (1980) that he uses this specific term 'participation without belonging' to refer to the situation of texts outside of genre at the same time that they participate in it. I came across it first in another essay 'Passions: An Oblique Offering' from 1992, in which he expresses an absolute right not to answer in a request for him to respond to a book of essays about him. Of course, he responds by not answering at great length.

A little more belonging, apparently, is the work of Albert Camus, who Édouard Glissant suggests is one of the (in part) outsider authors that learners of pure French go to, not because his writing is transparently understandable despite its otherness, but because it is of a type that has 'the least threatening opacity'.[24] However, as with Derrida, it can only be a partial offering and Glissant goes on to state that using Camus' literature as an exemplar is a misreading of his work which is complex and offers something relatively palatable to us at the same time that it recedes into, or insists upon its latent opacity. As Glissant puts it, Camus' work can '… both confide and withdraw at the same time'.[25]

Whether or not we find Camus' work straightforward, albeit harbouring contrabands, Derrida's is certainly not so, and we are almost encouraged to lose ourselves in the textuality of his philosophy. But what has this particular deconstructivist concept of participation without belonging got to do with smuggling and, in particular, smuggling into southern Europe?

Derrida was always an outsider, participating but also always, as philosopher J. Hillis Miller puts it, 'refraining'.[26] He was Jewish but not of Judaism, from Algeria but not Algerian, legally French but never really French. He four times participated in unofficial academies (he was never asked to become a professor at any of the classical centres of philosophical study in France). Interestingly, it was when on a trip to Prague to participate in one of these unofficial forums, the Jan Hus Association in 1981, that he was framed (in the sense of falsely accused) and later acquitted, for drug smuggling. He never lasted long in these extra-official pursuits, but for a time he always wanted to be, partially at least, in the frame but, crucially, on his own terms.

Participation without belonging produces a smuggler subjectivity, and partial offerings into other frameworks are a necessary way of re-jigging that frame. Just as smuggled migrants must become like smugglers in order to move on from their framing on the beaches, to withdraw from their visibility in newsfeeds that give us an illusion of the transparent 'Truth' of migration, so too we should perhaps participate but be wary of belonging too much. For the refugee, there has to be an alternative to moving on only to a series of seemingly endless detentions, reduced, as Agamben states, to 'bare life'.[27] Glissant's concept of opacity offers hope in this regard: it is 'impossible to reduce anyone, no matter who, to a truth he would not have generated on his own. That is, within the opacity of his time and place.'[28] At risk of placing too much emphasis on the potentiality of smuggling beyond its reality on rough seas and densely surveyed beaches, we could extend the thinking around it to include contraband actions within academia, where it might have its own 'truth', albeit an opaque one involving partial offerings.[29]

Interdisciplinary work, if it is to go beyond a kind of diplomacy between university departments, could benefit from being thought of as a milieu ripe for smuggling: there are, after all, borders, checks and validations to be overcome. Flow of knowledge can be difficult: other academic disciplines loom before us like completed pictures, everything there and present, each object of knowledge extant, immanent to that discipline and only available to be unveiled by us if we follow correct and visible protocols.[30] We are expected to lay bare our offerings, to open ourselves up to free trade in already defined knowledge. Often these channels fail us: they don't allow for ongoing circulations of strange or latent knowledge, for other ways of doing things – semi-licit practices. In response to this, adopting the modality of the smuggler can make us agile and adaptive, tactically effective in the trading of our cultural capital. Ideas must be permitted to travel freely and, where they are obstructed or reduced to the language of dominant channels of circulation, contraband tactics might come into play. Everybody should have the right to be in and out of sight, and site, and to open up new routes between them. In her essay '"Smuggling" – An embodied criticality', visual cultures theorist Irit Rogoff suggests 'unbounding' (unframing) categories (of knowledge) that preclude access to what we do not yet know, thereby also allowing inhabitation of new subjectivities. Furthermore, meaning production should become less of a leap from one frame to another and more about emergence of knowledge – a little like contraband items seeping into and being traded in smugglers' markets in cities around the world. Not so much to see like a smuggler, rather to think like one.[31]

Both in the field and within the academy, between disciplines, we must sometimes receive others' knowledge in oblique ways. This way we escape the flatness, the banality, of always transparent exchange. One might speculate that it is better not to declare all in order just to assimilate; instead, sometimes, to offer only partially, on one's own terms and at times of one's own choosing.[32] Sometimes we might belong, at others less so. We might want to behave like a smuggler, although once we do we should not be expected to be always like this. We might go in and out of a contraband modality, just as smugglers are sometimes also fishermen or truck drivers or, like Ackermann, simply booksellers.

The consideration of smuggling's partial visibilities and partial offerings in this speculative chapter leaves many areas untouched and several questions unanswered, among them: Is it always transgressive[33] (might it often, instead, simply replicate conditions of control, offering another legality)? Can its romantic reputation survive its renowned violence and exploitation? And, an extension of this last, can we conceive an ethics of smuggling when it is so often driven by selfishness and the profit motive?

Quite a bit has been written about the importance of improvised ways of creating community through relations inherent in alternative gatherings like grey markets,[34] but one should also note that they can quickly fall apart. In 2004, the Wayuu community of workers involved in smuggling in the Guajira Peninsula was decimated by an attack by right-wing paramilitaries at one of the smuggler ports. It seemed to end activity there and is a reminder of the potential violence present at such apparently harmless smuggling sites. The framing of migrants on the beaches commits another kind of violence, one of removing their horizons.

There is, however, a possibility of an ethical perspective on smuggling and it begins with the necessity of examining our own relation to it, not least considering how, historically and contemporaneously, we have relied upon it.[35] It is important to challenge its framing, almost always, as an external threat. We might also attempt to put ourselves in the shoes of the migrant and ask what is at stake in the smuggling experience beyond the necessity of survival and reaching some kind of destination? Some of its ethical potential perhaps derives from what happens on arrival: not surrendering all to another system – withholding something; speaking for oneself; retaining some autonomy in finding one's own niche, place or site (not just a designated one such as a transit or refugee camp); and holding onto one's juridical subjectivity rather than acquiescing to a state of bare life. It might entail struggling for the means to produce human rights as much as fighting to be given them. In smuggling terms, one should retain choice of when and where to declare. In sum, only a partial offering (into the frame), and on one's own terms.

It is easy for this to seem a little remote, and so, drawing upon partial visibilities and returning with only partial offerings – a smuggler modality – is perhaps important for all of us. Glissant calls for a 'right to opacity for everyone'.[36] Although written in a context of Caribbean, Antillean identity expressed through language and literature, Glissant's call nevertheless resonates more broadly with this ethical dimension to smuggling, indeed also giving it a political twist. For him, it is not transparency that is 'based on a Right' (transparency here stands for full knowledge and clear epistemological practice),[37] rather opacity becomes one. In political and pragmatic terms, he even considers opacity as the 'basis for a Legitimacy'.[38] In other words, the partial declarations of smugglers might be only an exaggeration of how we organise society anyway: through opaque rather than transparent means.

The open-endedness of informal migrational or contrabanding practices – relays of participants and goods, often only connected through loose transactional, barely social ties – is another issue. It poses further questions about smuggling: for instance, does smuggling fragment community rather than, according to the romantic story of the smuggler, bring people together? But this open-endedness also offers possibility and this is to do with moving on and passing on. It is vital for know-how to be handed on, for all of us stranded in one way or another to become a smuggler, for the migrant to adopt some of the tactics of the smuggler – in order to move on. The contraband must become smuggler, and, for our part, we should move beyond thinking of the former as passive and the latter as active.

This chapter has explored the possibility of thinking smuggling as concept beside literal smuggling on the ground. I have been preoccupied with this for some time now,[39] and I remain convinced that there should be space, in academic thinking and practice, for smugglers to pass on to us their smart, although partial knowledge.

Notes

1. Byung-Chul Han, *The Transparency Society* (Stanford, CA: Stanford University Press, 2015), p. 13.
2. Ibid., p. 1.
3. Martin Heidegger, *Off the Beaten Track*, trans. Julian Young and Kenneth Haynes (Cambridge: Cambridge University Press, 2002), p. 67.
4. See Édouard Glissant, *Poetics of Relation* (Ann Arbor, MI: University of Michigan Press, 1997 [1990]).
5. Jean Genet, *The Thief's Journal* (London: Faber and Faber, 1973 [1949]), p. 213.
6. Jean Baudrillard, *Fatal Strategies* (Los Angeles, CA: Semiotext[e], 2008 [1983]), quoted in Han, *The Transparency Society*, p. 2.

7. Han, *The Transparency Society*, p. 31.

8. Henry de Monfreid with Ida Treat, *Pearls, Arms and Hashish – Pages from the Life of a Red Sea Navigator* (London: Gollancz, 1930), pp. 105–6.

9. Much of Biemann's other work also deals with informal economies, for instance *Contained Mobility* (2004) and *Black Sea Files* (2005).

10. Wayuu are the indigenous people of the peninsula and have been involved in smuggling for centuries, albeit that at certain times, right from the beginning of the Spanish empire in the late sixteenth century, it has been perceived, particularly at local level, only as petty contrabanding (of everyday goods). Wayuu involvement in this alternative to official Seville-sanctioned trade, which was channelled through major centres in South America, steadily grew in conjunction with settlers who, during the seventeenth century, contrabanded out of need for scarce goods, not all of them luxuries. It became a much larger opportunity for Wayuu during the eighteenth century and the Bourbon state began to frame it more as smuggling as we know it (for instance in Britain before and after the Napoleonic Wars). Wayuu have been involved in smuggling ever since, although this pattern of continually reframing it as more or less illegal/illicit has persisted, certainly into the latter part of the twentieth century.

11. Grey markets do not sell illegal goods like cocaine or guns. The merchandise is not illegal in itself and it might even have been brought across a border legally (although not always), but it would not be authorised by the manufacturer or official distributor to be sold in the new country. It might also be fake.

12. Moisés Naím, *Illicit: How Smugglers, Traffickers and Copycats are Hijacking the Global Economy* (New York: Random House, 2005).

13. Helge Mooshammer and Peter Mörtenböck, *Informal Market Worlds* (Rotterdam: NAI010 uitgevers, 2015).

14. See Simon Harvey, *Smuggling: Seven Centuries of Contraband* (London, Reaktion, 2016), Chapter 16.

15. See Arjun Appadurai, 'Introduction: Commodities and the politics of value', in Arjun Appadurai (ed.) *The Social Life of Things: Commodities in Cultural Perspective* (Cambridge: Cambridge University Press, 1986).

16. Helge Mooshammer, 'Other markets', in Helge Mooshammer and Peter Mörtenböck (eds) *Visual Cultures as Opportunity* (Berlin: Sternberg Press, 2016), pp. 12–13.

17. Ibid., p. 22.

18. Robert Neuwirth, *Stealth of Nations: The Global Rise of the Informal Economy* (New York: Pantheon Books, 2011).

19. Raqs (more commonly meaning 'rarely asked questions') is composed of Monica Narula, Jeebesh Bagchi and Shuddhabrata Sengupta.

20. See Pamela M. Lee, *Forgetting the Art World* (Cambridge, MA: MIT Press, 2012), pp. 147–84.

21. Ibid., p. 177.

22. Sarai are the rest houses found along trade routes, built during Mughal times.

23. Peter Brunette and David Wills, 'The spatial arts: An interview with Jacques Derrida', *Deconstruction and the Visual Arts: Art, Media, Architecture* (Cambridge: Cambridge University Press, 1993), pp. 28–9.

24. Glissant, *Poetics of Relation*, p. 116.

25. Ibid., p. 116.

26. J. Hillis Miller, 'Don't count me in: Derrida's refraining', *Textual Practice* 21(2), 2007, pp. 279–94.

27. See Giorgio Agamben, *Homo Sacer: Sovereign Power and Bare Life*, trans. Daniel Heller-Roazen (Stanford, CA: Stanford University Press, 1998).

28. Glissant, *Poetics of Relation*, p. 194.

29. Of course, there are limitations to the analogy of contraband within academia and actual smuggling – after all the desperation of the refugee and the guile of the smuggler are not at all the same as the frustration of the academic and their attempts at trafficking knowledge into/from other university departments.

30. There are times when academic exchange can be merely a matter of formality, simply about recognition. Thinking about this reminded me of a moment, paradoxically outside of the halls of research, when, in 2002, I was poking around taking pictures in the informal market streets of Maicao. I was framing, in a way, the contraband and the smugglers. I was asked what I was doing, who I was. I mumbled something like: I was an art historian, doing research. It sufficed. I had offered an identity, it was like a visa, but it actually only had power in its absurdity. Ironically, this is often still how these things work in the academy – we present ourselves to each other, full of competences, but still a little opaque in our transparency.

31. Irit Rogoff, '"Smuggling – An embodied criticality", 2006, https://xeno-praxis.net/readings/rogoff_smuggling.pdf (accessed January 2019).

32. That is, participating within the collective work of the discourse, but not belonging fully. So often projects stall in bureaucracy, in so-called 'audit culture', another kind of move towards transparency.

33. Indeed, it is important to note that it isn't always helpful to talk of different sides here, just as in conceptualisations of state action we should not assume that the state is monolithic, always down on smuggling, which is then posited as transgressive and counter to it. Perhaps, in order to see like a smuggler, one must have customs, to a degree, inside of oneself.

34. See, for instance Janet Roitman, 'Productivity in the margins of the state: The reconstitution of state power in the Chad Basin', in Veena Das and Deborah Poole (eds) *Anthropology in the Margins of the State* (Santa Fe, NM: SAR Press, 2004), pp. 191–224. Also Mooshammer and Mörtenböck, *Informal Market Worlds*.

35. My book, Harvey, *Smuggling: Seven Centuries of Contraband*, takes this as its primary focus.
36. Glissant, *Poetics of Relation*, p. 194.
37. Ibid., p. 111.
38. Ibid., p. 194.
39. See Simon Harvey, *Smuggling in Theories and Practices of Contemporary Visual Culture*, PhD thesis, Goldsmiths, London University, 2005.

Afterword: Seeing Freedom

Nandita Sharma

Riffing on James C. Scott's classic, *Seeing Like a State: How Certain Schemes to Improve the Human Condition Have Failed*, the chapters in this volume challenge us to view our world from the perspective of 'smugglers' as well as the smuggled.[1] This shift in perspective requires us to acknowledge that the very term 'smuggler' is a state category. It is the name given to people transgressing state laws governing the mobility of things, people, and practices, a name that carries enormous, negative consequences, up to and including the loss of one's life. 'Smuggling', then, inherently runs up against states and the power they exert over their claimed territories, and everything and everyone in them. 'Smuggling' also offends today's international legal regime, which makes national sovereignty, with its respect for national restrictions on political membership, sacrosanct. Talking about and acting against 'smugglers' therefore represents a view taken from the vantage of state power, one that normalises states' restrictions on free movement.

'Seeing like a smuggler' offers us an opportunity to return the state's gaze. 'Smuggler' is not an identity accepted by those so classified. Our contemporary order of nation-states has failed those who rely on smuggled goods or who are themselves smuggled. In this postcolonial world where the national form of state power rules, seeing like a smuggler further allows us to side-line what Michel-Rolph Trouillot calls the 'spatialization effect' of state power. We are able to imagine ourselves as something more than 'citizens' of one or another nation-state and as 'belonging' only in the territory defined by their political borders. As Carlos, a resident on the Mexican side of the Mexico/Guatemala border who 'smuggles' corn puts it in Rebecca Galemba's chapter, 'The [geopolitical border] line belongs to the government.... The path belongs to the communities ...'

The marking of national borders, of course, did not create the phenomena states call 'smuggling'. Some smugglers today rely on infrastructures and routes developed long before national borders existed. In addition, since all national borders have severed long-established relationships between people and things now divided by the geopolitical border, many activities now criminalised as 'smuggling' are nothing more than a continuation of similar activity taking place in the same area for centuries. The nation-states that criminalise it are far newer. Far from changing people's practices, then, anti-smuggling laws only work to criminalise interactions taking place across – and against – state lines. As Debdatta Chowdhury points out in Chapter 7, even as international borders breached people's long-standing moral economy by restricting the movement of people and things across the border, people have, as they must, adapted by reorganising their lives to take the border into account. This includes engaging in criminalised activities of smuggling.

This important collection adopts a 'borders from below' approach to show that the activities of 'smugglers' are usually not the spectacular sort that end up on the front pages of tabloids but, much more often, an everyday part of people's lives, necessitated, of course, by the multiple prohibitions enacted by the nation-states they encounter. People who do the work of 'smuggling' often understand themselves as traders, workers, solidarity activists, business people, and more. The fact that some of these contradict one another (i.e. business person and worker) reveals that while states attempt to totalise the people captured by its category of 'smuggler', those captured by this category are far from being uniform. For some – perhaps most – smuggling is a critical subsistence activity, while for a select few it is part of larger business ventures, ones that usually traverse the state line between legal and illegal operations. Seeing like a smuggler, then, does not offer us a singular view of the world. That being said, seeing like a smuggler *does* give us a vantage point that states would rather we ignore: that in today's world 'the border has to be crossed', as Aliyeh Ataei reminds us in Chapter 3.

This collection further examines the *social relations* of smuggling: those that produce the need for smugglers as well as the social relations between smugglers and the smuggled. Indeed, the chapters relate how the boundaries between smugglers and smuggled can blur. Simon Harvey (Chapter 10), for instance, shows us that sometimes, 'smuggled migrants must become like smugglers in order to move on … [and] to withdraw from their visibility in newsfeeds …'

It can certainly be said that smugglers both compensate for and reflect gross inequalities in our world. In direct contravention to nation-states increased fortification of their borders against the world's poor, smugglers move those people (and things) that states decree ought not to be moved (or at least not be moved by smugglers). Smugglers thus provide an alternate route against the immobilisation strategies of states. Smugglers have specific knowledge about border controls that are useful to people exercising their freedom to move against all odds. They know how states, labour markets, and borders work. Smugglers also teach the smuggled how to 'pass' as the people whose identities they adopt (e.g. a devoted Muslim performing the Hajj). In Chapter 5, Amin Parsa states what many subjugated people know, that 'unofficial economic interactions of various actors ... sustain lives more effectively than official laws'.

Indeed, many people living in places dependent on smuggling do not see it as a criminal activity but, instead, as key to their survival. Ataei documents the bonds developed through smuggling. She discusses three separate incidents in which people moved from Afghanistan into Iran by Mohammad Osman Yusefzai refused to testify against him after Iranian border police arrested him as a 'human trafficker'. Ataei recognises that both the smuggled and the smuggler understood that Yusefzai's job was to 'make people's lives better'. No wonder then that, as Tekalign Ayalew Mengiste (Chapter 1) shows that, in everyday life contexts, 'smugglers attract more community support than the state in communities living along migration routes'.

When we stop seeing like a state and instead see smuggling from the perspective of those engaged in it (at one end or the other), we see that, often, there are strong social ties between smugglers, migrants, and others within and across national borders. In stark contrast to the atomising practices of official border controls, 'smuggling', as Tekalign notes, can be 'a socially and culturally embedded collective practice', one that 'becomes a collective enterprise'. Smugglers and the smuggled alike are forced to navigate dangerous situations, including moving through war-torn areas and across borders of nation-states at war. For many people, today's smugglers, like those in the past, are life-savers. Just think of the conductors of the Underground Railroad moving enslaved people to their freedom in the United States, the most well-known being Harriet Tubman, who was also castigated by slavers as a 'criminal'.

While nation-states shine a cop's bright light on the movements of those things, people, and other living beings made into contraband (as enslaved people were also regarded), they try to keep us in the dark about the political work done by national borders. The secret of border controls that smuggling reveals is that they do not work. And, that they are not meant to work in the way that states claim they want them to. Border controls don't stop movement. They regulate that movement by declaring whose movements are 'legal' and whose are 'illegal'. Increasingly, as nation-states cut off most, if not all, lawful means of gaining access to their territories, the forseeable result is that a growing number of people in our world are forced to live – and work – as 'illegals'. As Parsa notes, those who are illegalised are systematically 'excluded from meaningful political participation and economic prosperity'. This makes them cheaper to employ and subjects them to the arbitrary power of not only states and their deportation regimes but to all manner of people willing to exploit their illegalised status.

In this sense, then, the criminalisation of smuggling operates to further *nationalise the capitalist wage*. While people made illegal find their labour power cheapened, those with the status of national citizen are granted a 'citizenship premium' in the form of higher wages and other entitlements available only through the regime of national citizenship. Seeing like a smuggler, then, tells us that capitalism is reliant on states to create categories of people who fall outside of the law. The law thus becomes a key technology of labour discipline and social division. What smuggling shows us, then, is that the nation-state is not a hermetically sealed container made of its citizens. It is a place where citizens and non-citizens live together in a state of apartheid. Illegality becomes a way for states to organise the extraction of more value from the smuggled and to try and render them politically mute. This, at least in the long-run, works for none of the workers. Instead, greater competition within capitalist markets, especially labour markets, is the result. It is essential, therefore, that we see smuggling and state laws against it as part of the class struggle. Indeed, many smugglers can be seen as 'social bandits'.[2]

Of course, the work that national borders do to create and reproduce ruling relations is no secret to states or to capital. It is precisely because nation-states and global capital rely on the separation of people by nationalism in order to insulate themselves from radical political dissent, that restrictions on free movement into national territories exist. What is most unfortunate, however, is that such facts are not seen by those clamouring for ever more sanctions on smugglers in the name of protecting 'human rights'. Adopting the view of nation-states, such efforts wrongly hold smugglers accountable for the very real harms done by state laws and by the mechanisms of capitalist markets.

It is true that smugglers try to conceal from the law the people and/or things they are smuggling (indeed, people rely on such concealment!). But laws against smuggling also conceal something: the fact that states and capital are responsible for the harms ascribed to smugglers. Anti-smuggling laws and discourses thus work to depoliticise the foundations of the global system of ruling relations. In particular, a focus on smuggling obscures the complicity of nation-states in acts that produce destruction, destitution, and death. This is perhaps nowhere more evident than in the galling discourse of 'anti-smuggling' and/or 'anti-trafficking' deployed by nation-states against the 'most visible contraband', which as Harvey notes, is people.

Extreme state violence has been unleashed in the name of 'stopping smugglers' from moving people into nation-states that would deny them official permission to enter. Instead of addressing the conditions causing distress for people on the move – be it the conditions they encountered where they live(d), on their journey, or at their destination – nation-states are targeting the people who have the wherewithal to help them move. To take one example, the European Union's (EU) 'Operation Sophia', a military operation begun in 2015 had, by 2019 (quite gleefully it has to be said), destroyed over 550 boats used to move people across the Mediterranean into the EU in the name of 'protecting' migrants.

Phase two of the operation sent EU states' war ships and military helicopters to board, search, seize and divert vessels on the high seas suspected of being used to 'smuggle' or 'traffick' people. With a straight face, UK Defence Secretary, Michael Fallon, upon announcing the sending of warships to prevent people from moving, stated: 'we will not stand by and let this smuggling trade escalate; we will confront this criminal activity which risks the lives of innocent people every day'.[3] Par for the course, he made no mention of how he would ensure that people could move without the aid of smugglers.

During this same period, the member states of the EU centralised their border control policies via Frontex, the European Border and Coast Guard Agency. Their priority was to increase surveillance of and erect further obstacles to people trying to move. At the same time, EU member states enacted measures to criminalise *non-state* search-and-rescue operations, such as those of solidarity movements. The predictable – and clearly calculated – result was the loss of more lives. Since 2015, the Central Mediterranean Route (CMR) has become the deadliest waterway for migrants in the world.[4] This is nothing short of an organised abandonment of people on the move and it is intensifying still. An April 2020 news report found that 'the Greek government has secretly expelled more than

1,000 refugees from Europe's borders in recent months, sailing many of them to the edge of Greek territorial waters and then abandoning them in inflatable and sometimes overburdened life rafts'.[5] Cunningly, the use by nation-states of the rhetoric of 'combatting smugglers' allows them to masquerade as *the* entity designed to protect life, even as they enact policies that knowingly result in much misery, hardship, and a mounting death toll. Perversely, the figure of the 'smuggler' allows nation-states to present themselves as rescuers rather than as the entity *refusing* to rescue people. Going after 'smugglers', nation-states are killing those who rely on them (and sometimes smugglers too).

Rather than accept the standard state explanation for smuggling – that it is a sign of the 'depravity of smugglers', 'weak governance', a 'lack of control' over the border, 'the absence of state agents', or a 'culture of contraband' – smuggling is a sign of the *existence* of the law. As the chapters in this important volume clearly show, the two co-evolve. Smuggling is the law's shadow. For example, as Nichola Khan shows us (Chapter 2): 'Smuggling anywhere emerges symbiotically and relationally with regard to market restrictions, tax conditions and economic geography.' Immigration controls, high import taxes, and global wage and currency differentials all result in the need for smuggling. Recognising the symbiosis of the law and smuggling allows us to escape the totalising gaze of the state and, instead to see both smugglers and smuggled as filling in the gaps created by a social system designed to fail most people.

Such a positionality, Chowdhury, argues, makes it possible to ask whether smugglers can be seen as subalterns. Certainly smugglers and the smuggled are unable to speak but are, instead, spoken for by states and by those sanctioned by states to speak (e.g. 'good citizens', non-governmental organisations and so on).[6] In dominant narratives, it is impossible for smugglers or the smuggled to tell the truth that states, far from creating the order that serves as the pretext for their existence, create disorder, at least for most people on our planet.

In the process of 'combatting smuggling', the very foundation of nation-state power – separating people into the dichotomous state categories of Citizen and Migrant – is maintained, and normalised. As Galemba (Chapter 4) well understands, this dichotomisation 'serves to divide humanity into those who deserve rights, are legitimate business actors, and "legal" border crossers while conjuring the mirror image of the criminal or deviant who becomes relegated to the realm of the unnatural to be subjected to criminalisation and stigma'. In this regard, we can see the discourse of smuggling and the national border controls that criminalise it as part of the colonial legacy of 'thingification'.[7] Through anti-smuggling laws, both smugglers and the smuggled are objectified and reified as *figures*, not real people caught up in the very ruling relations nation-states and global capital organise. As such, they are rendered as legitimate targets for the most extreme forms of state violence. Seeing like a smuggler opens up the possibility for this truth to be heard and acted against.

It is, at the same time, crucial that we not mistake smuggling as *ending* violence in people's lives or *ending* the inequalities and injustices they face. The work that smugglers do, after all, is to bring the entire process together: the smuggled, the border control structures, the clandestine routes, the timing, the contacts, the shelters, the local officials, the employers. Smugglers' knowledge of these are commodities for sale to people who must find a way to pay for the smugglers' goods and services. As Ataei puts it, both the smuggler and those who erect the border infrastructure separating national territories 'earn a living from the border'.

Smuggling, then, while often transgressive is not always (or even usually) revolutionary. Indeed, for some smugglers, abuse is part of the business strategy. As Galemba notes, then, the logics of smuggling are 'not necessarily in opposition to, or external to state logics, even if smugglers defy state regulations by subverting border controls'. We can see this in the global geopolitical context of international sanctions when, for example, smugglers known as *kolbar* (those who move goods carried on their backs) in the borderlands of Iran and Iraq, transport goods that are legally prohibited by US-led sanctions against Iran. This benefits the Iranian government, which sees smuggling as a way to ease the intended devastation of US-led sanctions, even as Iran criminalises (and, not infrequently, kills) those moving the goods, with the knowledge that people will continue to engage in such backbreaking and dangerous activities rather than starve.

We can see also this in its minutiae when, for instance, we see smugglers bribe state officials to look the other way. What is the difference between smugglers and such officials (who, as Galemba notes, not only demand bribes but also pocket state taxes collected at official border-crossings)? Their engagement in illicit markets does not disrupt their (or others) dependency on capitalist markets for survival. Indeed, as anyone reliant on smugglers knows, illicitness inflates costs and thus profits. Harvey thus asks, 'can we conceive an ethics of smuggling when it is so often driven by selfishness and the profit motive?'

Perhaps, but only if we insist on a decommodification of smuggling and a decriminalisation of social justice. Nation-states (and those preceding them) have shown that they can absorb the profit-based activities of smugglers. However, no nation-state can survive challenges to its foundational tenet: the idea that the political community is equivalent to the 'nation' and the related belief that 'good citizens' obey nation-state laws. When people act across – and especially when they act against – nation-state borders and challenge the differences made between Citizen and Migrant in service of greater profits and control to capital, both the political power of nation-states and the material basis of global capital is threatened. This is why those who are motivated to move people across borders by their desire to extend solidarity – and not for profit – are, along with smugglers and the smuggled, criminalised.

One of the most intriguing insights offered by this excellent collection, therefore, is the way that its editors, Mahmoud Keshavarz and Shahram Khosravi, frame the project. Namely, that smuggling 'is not merely an economic service but demands us to engage with the question of borders ethically and politically'. The ethical stance we must take is to repoliticise that which nation-states' anti-smuggling efforts are meant to conceal: smuggling is not an 'external threat' but a structural feature of the international order. Perhaps then it is time to also see like the *smuggled* and demand the elimination of national borders.

Smuggling (including being smuggled) are ways to survive the active abandonment that most people experience from the ruling relations of postcolonialism. Seeing like a smuggler – and, even more, so the smuggled – shows us that what we should be opposing is not smuggling per se but the criminalisation of mobility and the commodification of life. This book makes an important contribution towards this aim.

Thus, while there now exists a large body of activist and scholarly work criticising the anti-trafficking efforts of international governing bodies (e.g. the United Nations), nation-states (and sub-state governments), as well as non-governmental organisations, this volume offers a sustained critique of anti-smuggling. It contributes to our understanding that anti-smuggling is not the legitimate half of the international protocols (and national laws) against smuggling and trafficking. Instead, anti-smuggling measures are also revealed as central to the production of the very outcomes that the rich, powerful, and famous condemn. Seeing like a smuggler pierces this fog of war and lets us see that our freedom rests on our rejecting the state and class rule.

Notes

1. James C. Scott, *Seeing Like a State* (New Haven, CT: Yale University Press, 2008).
2. Eric J. Hobsbawm, *Primitive Rebels: Studies in Archaic Forms of Social Movement in the 19th and 20th Centuries* (Manchester: Manchester University Press, 1971).
3. Rebecca Perring, 'British warship brought in to DESTROY people smuggler boats run by 30,000 gang members', *Express*, 16 September 2015, https://www.express.co.uk/news/uk/605686/People-smuggling-trafficking-migrant-crisis-British-warship-Mediterranean-sea (accessed 23 May 2021).
4. International Organization for Migration (IOM), 'Missing Migrants Project', n.d., https://missingmigrants.iom.int/region/mediterranean (accessed 23 May 2021).
5. Patrick Kingsley and Karam Shoumali, 'Taking hard line, Greece turns back migrants by abandoning them at sea', *New York Times*, 14 August 2020, https://www.nytimes.com/2020/08/14/world/europe/greece-migrants-abandoning-sea.html (accessed 23 May 2021).
6. Gayatri Chakravorty Spivak, 'Can the subaltern speak?', in Patrick Williams and Laura Chrisman (eds) *Colonial Discourse and Postcolonial Theory: A Reader* (New York: Columbia University Press, 1994).
7. Aimé Césaire, *Discourse on Colonialism*, trans. Joan Pinkham (New York: Monthly Review Press, 1972 [1955]).

Bibliography

Books, articles, and book chapters

Abbink, Jon, 'Transformations of Islam and communal relations in Wollo, Ethiopia', in René Otayek and Benjamin F. Soares (eds) *Islam and Muslim Politics in Africa* (New York: Palgrave Macmillan, 2017), pp. 65–83.

Achilli, Luigi, 'The "good" smuggler: The ethics and morals of human smuggling among Syrians', *Annals of the American Academy of Political and Social Science* 676, 2018, pp. 77–96.

Adey, Peter, 'Surveillance at the airport: Surveilling mobility/mobilising surveillance', *Environment and Planning A: Economy and Space* 36(8), 2004, pp. 1365–80.

Adugna Fekadu, Priya Deshingkar and Tekalign Ayalew Mengiste, *Brokers, Migrants and the State: Berri Kefach 'Door Openers' in Ethiopian Clandestine Migration to South Africa* (University of Sussex School of Global Studies, Migrating Out of Poverty Research Consortium, Working Paper 56, 2019).

Agamben, Giorgio, *Homo Sacer: Sovereign Power and Bare Life*, trans. Daniel Heller-Roazen (Stanford, CA: Stanford University Press, 1998).

Ameripol, *Situational Analysis of Drug Trafficking – A Police Point of View: Bolivia, Brazil, Colombia, Ecuador Panama and Peru* (Bogotá: Ameripol Executive Secretariat, 2013).

Amiri, Dawood, *Confession of a People-Smuggler* (Melbourne: Scribe, 2014).

Andreas, Peter, 'Smuggling wars: Law enforcement and law evasion in a changing world', in Tom Farer (ed.) *Transnational Crime in the Americas* (New York: Routledge, 1999), pp. 85–98.

Andreas, Peter, *Smuggler Nation: How Illicit Trade Made America* (Oxford: Oxford University Press, 2013).

Appadurai, Arjun, 'Introduction: Commodities and the politics of value', in Arjun Appadurai (ed.) *The Social Life of Things: Commodities in Cultural Perspective* (Cambridge: Cambridge University Press, 1986).

Archer, Bruce, 'Design as a discipline', *Design Studies* 1(1), 1979, pp. 17–20.

Aretxaga, Begoña, 'Maddening states', *Annual Review of Anthropology* 32(1), 2003, pp. 393–410.

Asociación Nacional de Instituciones Financieras, *Marihuana, legalización o represión* (Bogotá, DC, Colombia: ANIF, 1979).

Basu, Gautam, 'The role of transnational smuggling operations in illicit supply chains', *Journal of Transportation Security* 6(3), 2013, pp. 315–28.

Baudrillard, Jean, *Fatal Strategies* (Los Angeles, CA: Semiotext[e], 2008 [1983]).

Benjamin, Walter, *Illuminations* (New York: Schocken Books, 1969).

Bey, Hakim, *TAZ: The Temporary Autonomous Zone, Ontological Anarchy, Poetic Terrorism* (New York: Autonomedia, 2003).

Bhattacharyya, Gargi, *Traffick: The Illicit Movement of People and Things* (London: Pluto Press, 2005).

Bjögvinsson, Erling, Pelle Ehn and Per-Anders Hillgren, 'Design things and design thinking: Contemporary participatory design challenges', *Design Issues* 28(3), 2012, pp.101–16.

Bocarejo, Diana, 'Thinking with (il)legality: The ethics of living with bonanzas', *Current Anthropology* 59(S18), 2018, pp. 48–59.

Britto, Lina, *Marijuana Boom: The Rise and Fall of Colombia's First Drug Paradise* (Oakland, CA: University of California Press, 2020).

Brown, Tim, 'Design thinking', *Harvard Business Review*, June 2008, pp. 84–92.

Brunette, Peter and David Wills, 'The spatial arts: An interview with Jacques Derrida', in Peter Brunette and David Wills (eds) *Deconstruction and the Visual Arts: Art, Media, Architecture* (Cambridge: Cambridge University Press, 1993).

Buchanan, Richard, 'Wicked problems in design thinking', *Design Issues* 8(2), 1992, pp. 5–21.

Buckley, Charles, *An Anecdotal History of Old Times in Singapore* (Singapore: Fraser & Neave, 1902).

Castells, Manuel, *The Information Age: Economy, Society and Culture*, vol. III: *End of Millennium*, 2nd edn with new Preface (Chichester: Wiley-Blackwell, 2010).

Caulkins, Jonathan P., Honora Burnett and Edward Leslie, 'How illegal drugs enter an island country: Insights from interviews with incarcerated smugglers', *Global Crime* 10(1–2), 2009, pp. 66–93.

Celikkol, Ayse, *Romances of Free Trade: British Literature, Laissez-faire, and the Global Nineteenth Century* (New York: Oxford University Press, 2011).

Césaire, Aimé, *Discourse on Colonialism*, trans. Joan Pinkham (New York: Monthly Review Press, 1972 [1955]).

Chatterjee, Partha, *Nationalist Thought and the Colonial World: A Derivative Discourse?* (Delhi: Oxford University Press, 1986).

Chatterjee, Partha, *The Politics of the Governed: Reflections on Popular Politics in Most of the World* (New York: Columbia University Press, 2004).

Chowdhury, Debdatta, *Identity and Experience at the India-Bangladesh Border: The Crisis of Belonging* (London: Routledge, 2018).

Cohen, Erik, Scott A. Cohen and Xiang (Robert) Li, 'Subversive mobilities', *Applied Mobilities* 2(2), 2017, pp. 115–33.

Coutin, Susan Bibler, 'Being en route', *American Anthropologist* 107(2), 2005, pp. 195–206.

Crawford, John, 'Crawford's mission to Siam and Hue', *The Quarterly Review*, 110, 1826.

Cronin, Stephanie, 'Noble robbers, avengers and entrepreneurs', in Stephanie Cronin (ed.) *Crime, Poverty and Survival in the Middle East and North Africa: The 'Dangerous Classes' since 1800* (London: I.B. Tauris, 2020), pp. 81–104.

Cross, Nigel, 'Designerly ways of knowing: Design discipline versus design science', *Design Issues* 17(3), 2001, pp. 49–55.

Cross, Nigel, *Design Thinking* (London: Bloomsbury Academic, 2011).

Crummey, Donald (ed.) *Banditry, Rebellion and Social Protest in Africa* (London: James Currey, 1986).

Das, Veena and Deborah Poole (eds) *Anthropology in the Margins of the State* (Santa Fe, NM: School of American Research Press, 2004).

Daza Villar, Vladimir, *La Guajira, el tortuoso camino a la legalidad* (Bogotá, Dirección Nacional de Estupefacientes – Oficina contra la Droga y el Delito de Naciones Unidas, 2003), pp. 16–37.

de Leon, Jason, *Land of Open Graves: Living and Dying on the Migrant Trail* (Oakland, CA: University of California Press, 2015).

de Monfreid, Henry, with Ida Treat, *Pearls, Arms and Hashish – Pages from the Life of a Red Sea Navigator* (London: Gollancz, 1930).

de Regt, Marina and Medareshaw Tafesse, 'Deported before experiencing the good sides of migration: Ethiopians returning from Saudi Arabia', *African and Black Diaspora: An International Journal* 9(2), 2016, pp. 228–42.

Decker, Scott H. and Margaret Townsend Chapman, *Drug Smugglers on Drug Smuggling Lessons from the Inside* (Philadelphia, PA: Temple University Press, 2008).

Dominguez, Jorge I. 'Smuggling', *Foreign Policy* 20, 1975, p. 92.

Donnan, Hastings and Thomas M. Wilson (eds) *Borders: Frontiers of Identity, Nation, and State* (Oxford: Berg Press, 1999).

Dorst, Kees, *Frame Innovation: Create New Thinking by Design* (Cambridge, MA: MIT Press, 2015).

Dua, Jatin, *Captured at Sea* (Oakland, CA: University of California Press, 2019).

Errington, Frederick, Tatsuro Fujikura and Deborah Gewertz, *The Noodle Narratives: The Global Rise of an Industrial Food into the Twenty-first Century* (Berkeley: University of California Press, 2013).

Farooqi, Amar, *Smuggling as Subversion: Colonialism, Indian Merchants, and the Politics of Opium, 1790–1843* (Lanham, MD: Lexington Books, 2005).

Ferguson, James and Akhil Gupta, 'Spatializing states: Toward an ethnography of neoliberal governmentality', *American Ethnologist* 29(4), 2002, pp. 981–1002.

Fleetwood, Jennifer, *Drug Mules: Women in the International Cocaine Trade* (Basingstoke: Palgrave Macmillan, 2014).

Flynn, Donna, 'We are the border: Identity, exchange, and state along the Bénin-Nigeria border', *American Ethnologist* 24(2), 1997, pp. 311–30.

Foucault, Michel, *Discipline and Punish: The Birth of the Prison*, trans. Alan Sheridan (New York: Vintage Books, Random House, 2nd edn, 1995).

Galemba, Rebecca B., '"Corn is food, not contraband": The right to "free trade" at the Mexico–Guatemala border', *American Ethnologist* 39(4), 2012a, pp. 716–34.

Galemba, Rebecca B., 'Remapping the border: Taxation, territory, and (trans) national identity at the Mexico-Guatemala border', *Environment and Planning D: Society and Space* 30(5), 2012b, pp. 822–41.

Galemba, Rebecca B., *Contraband Corridor: Making a Living at the Mexico-Guatemala Border* (Stanford, CA: Stanford University Press, 2018).

Galemba, Rebecca B., 'Report: Coyotes from the same wolf', *NACLA Report on the Americas* 51(1), 2019, pp. 49–54.

Gallien, Max, *Smugglers and States: Illegal Trade in the Political Settlements of North Africa* (PhD thesis, London School of Economics and Political Science, 2020).

Genet, Jean, *The Thief's Journal* (London: Faber and Faber, 1973 [1949]).

Gilbert, Nigel, 'Emergence in social simulation', in Nigel Gilbert and R. Conte (eds) *Artificial Societies: The Computer Simulation of Social Life* (London: Routledge, 2006), pp. 144–56.

Gill James R. and Stuart M. Graham, 'Ten years of "body packers" in New York City: 50 deaths', *Journal of Forensic Science* 47(4), 2002, pp. 843–6.

Glissant, Édouard, *Poetics of Relation* (Ann Arbor, MI: University of Michigan Press, 1997 [1990]).

González-Plazas, Santiago, *Pasado y presente del contrabando en La Guajira: Aproximaciones al fenómeno de ilegalidad en la región* (Bogotá, DC, Colombia: Editorial Universidad del Rosario, 2008).

Gootenberg, Paul, 'Talking like a state: Drugs, borders, and the language of control', in Willem van Schendel and Abraham Itty (eds) *Illicit Flows and Criminal Things States, Borders, and the Other Side of Globalization* (Bloomington, IN: Indiana University Press, 2005), pp. 101–27.

Gootenberg, Paul, 'Cocaine's long march north, 1900–2010', *Latin American Politics and Society* 54(1), 2021, pp. 159–80.

Gramsci, Antonio, *Selections from the Prison Notebooks*, trans. Quentin Hoare and Geoffrey Nowell Smith (London: Elec Book, 1999).

Gregson, Nicky and Mike Crang, 'Illicit economies: Customary illegality, moral economies and circulation', *Transactions of the Institute of British Geographers* 42(2), 2017, pp. 206–19.

Guerrero-C, Javier, *Narcosubmarines: Outlaw Innovation and Maritime Interdiction in the War on Drugs* (Basingstoke: Palgrave Macmillan, 2019).

Hall, Stuart, 'Encoding, decoding', in Simon During (ed.) *The Cultural Studies Reader*, 2nd edn (New York: Routledge, 1993).

Han, Byung-Chul, *The Transparency Society* (Stanford, CA: Stanford University Press, 2015).

Hart, David, *Banditry in Islam: Case Studies in Morocco, Algeria and the Pakistan North West Frontier* (Wisbech: Middle East and North African Studies Press, 1987).

Hartman, Saidiya, *Wayward Lives, Beautiful Experiments: Intimate Histories of Social Upheaval* (New York: W.W. Norton, 2019).

Harvey, Simon, *Smuggling in Theories and Practices of Contemporary Visual Culture*, PhD thesis (Goldsmiths: London University, 2005).

Harvey, Simon, *Smuggling: Seven Centuries of Contraband* (London, Reaktion, 2016).

Hay, Douglas, Peter Linebaugh, John G. Rule, E.P. Thompson, and Cal Winslow (eds) *Albion's Fatal Tree: Crime and Society in Eighteenth-century England* (London: Allen Lane, 1979).

Heidegger, Martin, *Off the Beaten Track*, trans. Julian Young and Kenneth Haynes (Cambridge: Cambridge University Press, 2002).

Hernández Castillo, R. Aída, *Histories and Stories from Chiapas: Border Identities in Southern Mexico* (Austin, TX: University of Texas Press, 2001).

Heyman, Josiah McC. and Alan Smart, 'States and illegal practices: An overview', in Josiah McC. Heyman (ed.) *States and Illegal Practices* (Oxford: Berg Press, 1999), pp. 1–24.

Hobsbawm, Eric, *Bandits* (London: Weidenfeld and Nicolson, 2000 [1969]).

Hobsbawm, Eric, *Primitive Rebels: Studies in Archaic Forms of Social Movement in the 19th and 20th Centuries* (Manchester: Manchester University Press, 1971).

Holston, James, *Insurgent Citizenship – Disjunctions of Democracy and Modernity in Brazil,* (Berkeley: University Presses of California, 2009).

Hudson, Ray, 'Conceptualizing economies and their geographies: Spaces, flows and circuits', *Progress in Human Geography* 28(4), 2004, pp. 447–71.

Hudson, Ray, 'Economic geographies of the (il)legal and the (il)licit', in Tim Hall and Vincenzo Scalia (eds) *A Research Agenda for Global Crime* (Northampton: Edward Elgar Publishing, 2019), pp. 11–27.

James, C.L.R., *The Black Jacobins: Toussaint L'Ouverture and the San Domingo Revolution* (London: Penguin, 2001 [1938]).

James, G.P.R., *The Smuggler: A Tale* (Leipzig: Bernhard Tauchnitz, 1845).

Jencks, Charles and Nathan Silver, *Adhocism: The Case for Improvisation*, expanded and updated edn (Cambridge, MA: MIT Press, 2013).

Judd, Mary, 'Is harmony possible in a multiracial society? The case of Singapore', in Rik Pinxten and Ellen Preckler (eds), *Racism in Metropolitan Areas* (New York: Berghahn Books, 2005), pp. 107–11.

Kefale, Asnake and Zerihun Mohammad, *Ethiopian Labour Migration to the Gulf and South Africa* (Addis Ababa: Forum for Social Studies (FSS), 2015).

Kenney, Michael, *From Pablo to Osama: Trafficking and Terrorist Networks, Government Bureaucracies, and Competitive Adaptation* (University Park, PA: Penn State University Press, 2007).

Keshavarz, Mahmoud, *The Design Politics of the Passport: Materiality, Immobility, and Dissent* (London: Bloomsbury Academic, 2019).

Khosravi, Shahram, *'Illegal' Traveller: An Auto-ethnography of Borders* (Basingstoke: Palgrave Macmillan, 2010).

Khosravi, Shahram, 'What do we see if we look at the border from the other side?', *Social Anthropology* 27(3), 2019, pp. 409–24.

Kimbell, Lucy, 'Rethinking design thinking: Part 1', *Design and Culture* 3(3), 2011, pp. 285–306.

Kimbell, Lucy, 'Rethinking design thinking: Part 2', *Design and Culture* 4(2), 2012, pp. 129–48.

Kleinman, Arthur, *What Really Matters: Living a Moral Life Amidst Uncertainty and Danger* (Oxford: Oxford University Press, 2006).

Kloppenburg, Sanneke, 'Mapping the contours of mobilities regimes: Air travel and drug smuggling between the Caribbean and the Netherlands', *Mobilities* 8(1), 2013, pp. 52–69.

Knafo, Samuel, *The Making of Modern Finance: Liberal Governance and the Gold Standard* (Abingdon: Routledge, 2013).

Lambek, Michael, *The Ethical Condition: Essays on Action, Person and Value* (Chicago: University of Chicago Press, 2015).

Laurent, Muriel, *Contrabando en Colombia en el siglo XIX: Prácticas y discursos de resistencia y reproducción* (Bogotá, DC: Universidad de los Andes Facultad de Ciencias Sociales-Ces, 2008).

Laurent, Muriel, 'Contrabandistas y aduaneros en la costa Caribe en el periodo federal', in José Polo Acuña and Sergio Paolo Solano D. (eds) *Historia social del Caribe colombiano: Territorios, indígenas, trabajadores, cultura, memoria e historia* (Medellín: Cartagena. 2011).

Law, John, and John Urry, 'Enacting the social', *Economy and Society* 33(3), 2004, pp. 390–410.

Lee, Pamela M., *Forgetting the Art World* (Cambridge, MA: MIT Press, 2012).

Linebaugh, Peter and Marcus Rediker, *The Many-headed Hydra: Sailors, Slaves, Commoners, and the Hidden History of the Revolutionary Atlantic* (Boston, MA: Beacon Press, 2000).

Loudis, Jessica, 'Border traffic', *London Review of Books* 41(3), 2019, p. 8.

Ludden, David, 'Presidential address: Maps in the mind and the mobility of Asia', *Journal of Asian Studies* 62(4), 2003, pp. 1057–78.

Maher, Stephanie, 'Out of West Africa: Human smuggling as a social enterprise', *Annals of the American Academy of Political and Social Science* 676(1), 2018, pp. 36–56.

Malkki, Liisa H., 'Refugees and exile: From 'Refugee Studies' to the national order of things', *Annual Review of Anthropology* 24(1), 1995, pp. 495–523.

Manzini, Ezio, *Design, When Everybody Designs* (Cambridge, MA: MIT Press, 2015).

Margolin, Victor, *The Politics of the Artificial: Essays on Design and Design Studies* (Chicago: University of Chicago Press, 2002).

Mars, Gerald, *Cheats at Work: An Anthropology of Workplace Crime* (London: Unwin, 1983).

Martin, Craig 'Desperate mobilities: Logistics, security and the extra-logistical knowledge of appropriation', *Geopolitics* 17(2), 2012, pp. 355–76.

Martin, Craig, 'Shipping container mobilities, seamless compatibility, and the global surface of logistical integration', *Environment and Planning A* 45(5), 2013, pp. 1021–36.

Martin, Craig, 'Smuggling mobilities: Parasitic relations, and the aporetic openness of the shipping container', in John Urry, Thomas Birtchnell and

Satya Savitzky (eds) *Cargomobilities: Moving Materials in a Global Age* (New York: Routledge, 2015), pp. 65–86.

Martin, Craig, 'The socio-material cultures of global crime: Artefacts and infrastructures in the context of drug smuggling', in Tim Hall and Vicenzo Scalia (eds) *A Research Agenda for Global Crime* (Northampton, MA: Edward Elgar Publishing, 2019), pp. 147–59.

Martin, Craig, *Deviant Design: The Ad Hoc, the Illicit, the Controversial* (London: Bloomsbury Academic, forthcoming).

Mathew, Nisha, 'At the crossroads of empire and nation-state: Partition, gold smuggling, and port cities in the western Indian Ocean', *Modern Asian Studies* 54(3), 2020, pp. 898–929.

Mbembe, Achille and Janet Roitman, 'Figures of the subject in times of crisis', *Public Culture* 7(2), 1995, pp. 323–52.

McNair, John Frederick Adolphus, *Prisoners Their Own Warders* (London: A. Constable and Co., 1899).

Melissaris, Emmanuel and Mariano Croce, 'A pluralism of legal pluralisms', *Oxford Handbooks Online* (2017).

Mercado, Yoleida, Seili Quintero and Yenis Sierra, 'Riohacha en tiempos de marimba', PhD thesis, Universidad de la Guajira, Riohacha, 2000.

Meyer, Kathryn and Terry Parssinen, *Webs of Smoke: Smugglers, Warlords, Spies, and the History of the International Drug Trade* (Lanham, MD: Rowman and Littlefield, 1998).

Miller, J. Hillis, 'Don't count me in: Derrida's refraining', *Textual Practice* 21(2), 2007, pp. 279–94.

Mintz, Sidney, *Sweetness and Power: The Place of Sugar in Modern History* (New York: Penguin, 1986).

Mitchell, Timothy, 'The limits of the state: Beyond statist approaches and their critics', *American Political Science Review* 85(1), 1991, pp. 77–96.

Monod, Paul, 'Dangerous merchandise: Smuggling, Jacobitism, and commercial culture in southeast England, 1690–1760', *Journal of British Studies* 30(2), 1991, pp. 150–82.

Mooshammer, Helge and Peter Mörtenböck, *Visual Cultures as Opportunity* (Berlin: Sternberg Press, 2016).

Mörtenböck, Peter, Helge Mooshammer, Teddy Cruz and Fonna Forman (eds) *Informal Market Worlds Reader: The Architecture of Economic Pressure* (The Netherlands: NAI010 Publishers, 2015).

Mountz, Alison, 'Human smuggling, the transnational imaginary, and everyday geographies of the nation-state', *Antipode* 35(3), 2003, pp. 622–44.

Naím, Moisés , *Illicit: How Smugglers, Traffickers and Copycats are Hijacking the Global Economy* (New York: Random House, 2005).

Natarajan, Mangai, 'Understanding the structure of a drug trafficking organization: A conversational analysis', *Crime Prevention Studies* 11, 2000, pp. 273–98.

Neuwirth, Robert, *Stealth of Nations: The Global Rise of the Informal Economy* (New York: Pantheon Books, 2011).

Nordstrom, Carolyn, *Global Outlaws: Crime, Money, and Power in the Contemporary World* (Berkeley, CA: University of California Press, 2007).

Parsons, Glenn, *The Philosophy of Design* (Cambridge: Polity Press, 2016).

Perrow, Charles, *Normal Accidents: Living with High-risk Technologies* (New York: Basic Books, 1984).

Plarier, Antonin, 'Rural banditry in colonial Algeria', in Stephanie Cronin (ed.) *Crime, Poverty and Survival in the Middle East and North Africa: The 'Dangerous Classes' since 1800* (London: I.B. Tauris, 2020), pp. 105–16.

Restrepo, Andrés López and Álvaro Camacho Guizado, 'From smugglers to warlords: Twentieth-century Colombian drug traffickers', *Canadian Journal of Latin American and Caribbean Studies* 28(55–6), 2003, pp. 249–75.

Richardson, J.A., *The Geology and Mineral Resources of the Neighbourhood of Raub Pahang* (Kuala Lumpur: Geological Survey Department Federated Malay States, 1939).

Roitman, Janet, 'Productivity in the margins of the state: The reconstitution of state power in the Chad Basin', in Veena Das and Deborah Poole (eds) *Anthropology in the Margins of the State*(Santa Fe, NM: SAR Press, 2004), pp.191–224.

Roitman, Janet, 'The ethics of illegality in the Chad Basin', in Jean Comaroff and John L. Comaroff (eds) *Law and Disorder in the Postcolony* (Chicago: University of Chicago Press, 2006), pp. 247–72.

Rosenfeld, Sophia, *Common Sense: A Political History* (Cambridge, MA: Harvard University Press, 2011).

Rumford, Chris, 'Towards a multiperspectival study of borders', *Geopolitics* 17(4), 2012, pp. 887–902.

Sáenz Rovner, Eduardo, 'Entre Carlos Lehder y los vaqueros de la cocaína. La consolidación de las redes de narcotraficantes colombianos en Miami en los años 70', *Cuadernos de Economía* 30(54), 2011, pp.105–26.

Sáenz Rovner, Eduardo, 'Colombians and the drug-trafficking networks in New York in the 1970s', *Innovar* 24(53), 2014, pp. 223–34.

Sanchez, Gabriella and Luigi Achilli, *Critical Insights on Irregular Migration Facilitation: Global Perspectives* (Florence: European University Institute, Robert Schuman Centre for Advanced Studies, 2019).

Scheele, Judith, *Smugglers and Saints of the Sahara: Regional Connectivity in the Twentieth Century* (New York: Cambridge University Press, 2015).

Schenk, Catherine, 'The global gold market and the international monetary system', in Sandra Bott (ed.) *The Global Gold Market and the International Monetary System from the late 19th Century to the Present* (New York: Palgrave Macmillan, 2013), pp. 17–38.

Schön, Donald, *The Reflective Practitioner: How Professionals Think in Action* (New York: Basic Books/Harper Collins, 2008).

Scott, James C., *Seeing Like a State: How Certain Schemes to Improve the Human Condition have Failed* (New Haven: Yale University Press, 1998).

Sheller, Mimi, 'Air mobilities on the US–Caribbean border: Open skies and closed gates', *Communication Review* 13(4), 2010, pp. 269–88.

Simon, Herbert, *The Sciences of the Artificial*, 3rd edn (Cambridge, MA: MIT Press, 1996).

Slota, Stephen C. and Geoffrey C. Bowker, 'How infrastructures matter', in Ulrike Felt, Fouché Rayvon, Clark A. Miller and Laurel Smith-Doe (eds) *The Handbook of Science and Technology Studies* (Cambridge, MA: MIT Press, 2016), pp. 529–54.

Smith, Joshua M., *Borderland Smuggling: Patriots, Loyalists, and Illicit Trade in the Northeast 1783–1820* (Gainesville, FL: University Press of Florida, 2006).

Soleimani, Kamal and Ahmad Mohammadpour, 'Life and labor on the internal colonial edge: Political economy of kolberi in Rojhelat', *British Journal of Sociology* 71(4), 2020, pp. 741–60.

Spivak, Gayatri Chakravorty, 'Can the subaltern speak?', in Patrick Williams and Laura Chrisman (eds) *Colonial Discourse and Postcolonial Theory: A Reader* (New York: Columbia University Press, 1994).

Suchman, Lucy, 'Configuration', in Celia Lury and Nina Wakeford (eds) *Inventive Methods: The Happening of the Social* (London: Routledge, 2012), pp. 48–60.

Suchman, Lucy, 'Theorizing the contemporary: Design', *Fieldsights*, 29 March 2018, https://culanth.org/fieldsights/design (accessed 13 August 2019).

Tarlo, Emma, *Entanglement: The Secret Lives of Hair* (London: Oneworld, 2016).

Taussig, Michael, *The Magic of the State* (New York: Routledge, 1997).

Tekalign Mengiste Ayalew, *Struggle for Mobility: Risk, Hope and Community of Knowledge in Eritrean and Ethiopian Migration Pathways towards Sweden*, PhD thesis, Stockholm University, 2017.

Thompson, E.P., *The Making of the English Working Class* (New York: Pantheon Press, 1976).

Thoumi, Francisco E., 'Legitimidad, lavado de activos y divisas, drogas ilegales y corrupción en Colombia', *Ensayo y Error* 1(1), 1996, pp. 22–45.

Thoumi, Francisco E., 'Illegal drugs in Colombia: From illegal economic boom to social crisis', in Menno Vellinga (ed.) *The Political Economy of the Drug Industry: Latin America and the International System* (Gainesville, FL: University Press of Florida, 2004), pp. 70–84.

Thoumi, Francisco E., 'The Colombian competitive advantage in illegal drugs: The role of policies and intitutional changes', *Journal of Drug Issues* 35(1), 2005, pp. 7–26.

Tonkinwise, Cameron, 'A taste for practices: Unrepressing style in design thinking', *Design Studies* 32(6), 2011, pp. 533–45.

Trocki, Carl, *Opium and Empire: Chinese Society in Colonial Singapore, 1800–1910* (Ithaca, NY: Cornell University Press, 1990).

Trouillot, Michel Rolph, 'The anthropology of the state in the age of globalization: Close encounters of the deceptive kind', *Current Anthropology* 42(1), 2001, pp. 125–38.

van de Bunt, Henk, Dina Siegel and Damián Zaitch, 'The social embeddedness of organized crime', in Paoli Letizia (ed.) *The Oxford Handbook of Organized Crime* (Oxford: Oxford University Press, 2014), pp. 321–39.

van Schendel, Willem and Abraham Itty (eds) *Illicit Flows and Criminal Things: States, Borders, and the Other Side of Globalisation* (Bloomington, IN: Indiana University Press, 2005).

Vásquez Cardoso, S., *La Guajira, 1980–1935*. Honours thesis, Universidad de los Andes, 1983.

Veitch, Scott, *Law and Irresponsibility: On the Legitimation of Human Suffering* (Abingdon: Routledge–Cavendish, 2007).

Walters, William, 'Migration, vehicles, and politics: Three theses on viapolitics', *European Journal of Social Theory* 18 (4), 2015, pp. 469–88.

Williams, Patricia J., *The Alchemy of Race and Rights: Diary of a Law Professor* (Cambridge, MA: Harvard University Press, 1992).

Woodiwiss, Michael, *Double Crossed: The Failure of Organized Crime Control* (Chicago: University of Chicago Press, 2017).

Xenakis, Sappho, 'Trouble with the outlaws: Bandits, the state, and political legitimacy in Greece over the *longue durée*', *Journal of Historical Sociology* 34(3), 2021, pp. 504– 16.

Zewdu, Girmachew Adugna, 'Ethiopian female domestic labour migration to the Middle East: Patterns, trends, and drivers', *African and Black Diaspora: An International Journal* 11(1), 2018, pp. 6–19.

Newspapers, magazines and online references

Biswas, Sujauddin (2019) 'Kancher jinish ashchhe shabdhanei' ('Arms smuggling in full swing'), *Anandabazar Patrika*, 18 March 2019, https://www.anandabazar.com/district/nadia-murshidabad/lok-sabha-election-2019-arms-smuggling-on-the-rise-in-murshidabad-ahead-of-poll-1.967509 (accessed 3 March 2019).

Borna News (2019) 'Hichgah doost nadashtim kollbar bashim/Toseh nayaftegi ma ra be inja resandeh ast', 1 October 2019, https://www.borna.news/fa/tiny/news-904659 (accessed January 2021).

Business Times, 'Smuggling threatens India's economy', 16 July 1984.

Colombo, Sergio and Andrea Prada Bianchi, 'For Kurdish smugglers, Iran sanctions are starting to bite', *Foreign Policy*, 24 February 2019, https://foreignpolicy.com/2019/02/24/for-kurdish-smugglers-iran-sanctions-are-starting-to-bite/ (accessed 8 November 2020).

de la Hoz, Francisco (2018) 'Incautan avioneta que era transportada en un camión por La Alta Guajira', *El Heraldo*, 6 January 2018, https://www.elheraldo.co/la-guajira/incautan-avioneta-que-era-transportada-en-un-camion-por-la-alta-guajira-444120 (accessed 23 May 2021).

Department of Justice (2019) 'Joaquin "El Chapo" Guzman, Sinaloa Cartel leader, convicted of running a continuing criminal enterprise and other drug-related charges', press release, https://www.justice.gov/opa/pr/

joaquin-el-chapo-guzman-sinaloa-cartel-leader-convicted-running-contin-uing-criminal (accessed 14 February 2019).

DHA (Department of Home Affairs), White Paper on International Migration for South Africa, July 2017, http://www.dha.gov.za/WhitePaperonInterna-tionalMigration-20170602.pdf (accessed 10 March 2020).

Evans, Henri-Count, 'Corruption, smuggling and border jumping: The Beitbridge border post', *Fair Planet*, 24 November 2015, https://www.fairplanet.org/story/corruption-smuggling-and-border-jumping-the-beitbridge-border-post/ (accessed 10 April 2021).

Evans, Ian (2015) 'Pet relocation smuggler gets seven years in the UK', *Saturday Star*, 20 June 2015, p. 4.

Ghosh, Sunando, 'Beton diye rakha hochhe sona pachar'er lok' ('Salaried men appointed for gold smuggling'), *Anandabazar Patrika*, 12 September 2019, https://www.anandabazar.com/calcutta/men-recruited-for-gold-traffick-ing-in-bara-bazar-arrested-1.1044280 (accessed 14 January 2020).

Goudreau, Guillaume, 'Record 1.6 tonnes of methamphetamine discovered in music speakers by Australian border officers', 7 June 2019, https://www.illicit-trade.com/2019/06/record-1-6-tonnes-of-methamphetamine-discovered-in-music-speakers-by-australian-border-officers/ (accessed 8 June 2019).

Goudreau, Guillaume, 'Australian police smash gang that smuggled metham-phetamine from US to Queensland in comic books', 12 June 2019, https://www.illicit-trade.com/2019/06/australian-police-smash-gang-that-smug-gled-methamphetamine-from-us-to-queensland-in-comic-books/ (accessed 14 June 2019).

Guardian (2016) 'Australian police seize huge haul of meth hidden in gel brain inserts', 15 February 2016, https://www.theguardian.com/australia-news/2016/feb/15/australian-police-seize-estimated-1bn-worth-of-methamphetamine (accessed 23 May 2021).

Hajra, Biman, 'Jaal note'e jerbaar police' ('Hard time for police in fake currency smuggling'), *Anandabazar Patrika*, 12 September 2019, https://www.anandabazar.com/district/nadia-murshidabad/police-at-fix-to-solve-fake-indian-currency-note-issue-1.1044241 (accessed 2 January 2020).

Hajra, Biman, 'Raat'er dike ashun, half daam'e debo' ('Smuggled motorbikes available at half price in Farakka'), *Anandabazar Patrika*, 23 June 2019, https://www.anandabazar.com/district/nadia-murshidabad/illegal-bikes-are-selling-at-very-low-price-in-farakka-1.1008378 (accessed 7 December 2019).

Hamshahri Online, 'Kodam ostanha balatarin va kodam ostanha kamtarin nerkh bikari ra darand?', 5 April 2020, https://hamshahrionline.ir/x6fw7 (accessed 8 November 2020).

Hamshahri Online, 'Chand revayat az koshteshodan 4 hamvatan marzneshin', 9 September 2020, http://hamshahrionline.ir/x6G5c (accessed 5 December 2021).

Hataw and Loez, 'Between Iran and Iraq: Kolbars do not bend', *Nawext*, 17 January 2020, https://www.nawext.com/post/view/between-iran-and-iraq-kolbars-do-not-bend (accessed November 2020).

Hedwards, Bodean, 'The Buddhist people smuggler', https://allegralaboratory. net/hedwards-the-buddhist-people-smuggler/ (accessed 26 April 2021).

International Organization for Migration (IOM), 'Missing Migrants Project', https://missingmigrants.iom.int/region/mediterranean (accessed 23 May 2021).

IRNA (Islamic Republic of Iran News Agency), https://plus.irna.ir/ news/83897923/ (accessed 8 November 2020).

Islamic Republic of Iran Government, Ministers Cabinet Administrative Regulation, 'Organising Trade in Informal and Temporary Border Markets', 2017, http://qavanin.ir/Law/PrintText/227175 (accessed 8 November 2020).

Islamic Republic of Iran Government, Ministers Cabinet Administrative Directive, 'Amendment to Article 1 of Directive concerning 41 items essential for border inhabitants', 2018, http://www.epe.ir/News/19894 (accessed 8 November 2020).

Keshavarz, Mahmoud and Shahram Khosravi, 'The magic of borders', *e-flux Architecture*, 2020, https://www.e-flux.com/architecture/at-the-border/ 325755/the-magic-of-borders/ (accessed 26 April 2021).

Kingsley, Patrick and Karam Shoumali, 'Taking hard line, Greece turns back migrants by abandoning them at sea', *New York Times*, 14 August 2020, https://www.nytimes.com/2020/08/14/world/europe/greece-migrants-abandoning-sea.html (accessed 23 May 2021).

Mandal, Suprakash, 'Jyotsna'e katatar'er opor diye urey ashe chakti' ('Night smuggling in moonlight'), *Anandabazar Patrika*, 15 April 2019, https://www. anandabazar.com/state/lok-sabha-election-2019-politics-and-economy-of-nadia-border-is-under-the-influence-of-trafficking-1.979813 (accessed 2 November 2019).

Mandal, Suprakash, 'Par hoye jaye gun, par hoy kori' ('Currency and arms smuggling before general elections'), *Anandabazar Patrika*, 16 April 2019, https://www.anandabazar.com/state/lok-sabha-election-2019-hard-security-on-election-time-does-not-able-to-stop-fake-currency-and-gun-1.980229 (accessed 5 February 2020).

Mathew, Nisha, 'God, gold and invisible routes to a cosmopolitan society in Malabar', Feature story, ARI News, September 2017, pp. 7–8.

Mohanto, Anupratan, 'Oligoli te bhoot namchhe' ('Smuggling activities through secret routes'), *Anandabazar Patrika*, 9 September 2019, https:// www.anandabazar.com/district/north-bengal/smugglers-become-active-in-night-in-hili-border-area-1.1043018 (accessed 12 January 2020).

Mondol, Ceaser, 'Gorupacharer route'e ekhon Yaba'r romroma: Madok corridor'e Kolkata'i praankendra' ('Kolkata at the heart of drug smuggling'), *Anandabazar Patrika*, 3 January 2019, https://www.anandabazar.com/state/ yaba-found-safe-corridor-through-bengal-cattle-smuggling-route-leading-kolkata-into-main-centre-dgtl-1.926187 (accessed 15 August 2019).

Mukherjee, Andy, 'Indians' love for gold puts govt in a spot', *Straits Times*, 24 April 2012.

Mukherjee, Krittivas, 'India's gold smugglers back in business', *Straits Times*, 15 August 2013.

Ortega, R., 'Al mar once mil kilos de marihuana' *Diario del Norte*, 1977, p. 5.

Perring, Rebecca, 'British warship brought in to DESTROY people smuggler boats run by 30,000 gang members', 16 September 2015, *Express*, https://www.express.co.uk/news/uk/605686/People-smuggling-trafficking-migrant-crisis-British-warship-Mediterranean-sea (accessed 23 May 2021).

Rogoff, Irit, 'Smuggling: An embodied criticality', 2006, eipcp.net/dlfiles/rogoff-smuggling (accessed January 2019).

Sabawi, Fares, 'Border patrol: More than $1.5 million in heroin found in tomato shipment', https://www.mysanantonio.com/news/local/crime/article/More-than-1-5-million-in-heroin-found-in-tomato-12799993.php#photo-15328409 (accessed 4 April 2018).

Semana, 'El fugitivo', 14 September 2003, http://www.semana.com/nacion/articulo/el-fugitivo/60642-3 (accessed 10 May 2021).

Sen, Jayanta, 'Dal par koralei kella fotey' ('A lot to gain from smuggling drugs'), *Anandabazar Patrika*, 8 September 2019, https://www.anandabazar.com/district/north-bengal/hili-border-has-became-a-open-field-for-smugglers-1.1042612 (accessed 12 February 2020).

Simon, Janek and Max Cegielski (2017) 'Polish-Indian shop', https://artmuseum.pl/en/wystawy/sklep-polsko-indyjski (accessed 17 October 2018).

Staff Correspondent, 'Malda chhere ebar corridor shorchhe Dinajpur'e: Jaal'e teen, udhhar sare chho' lakh'er jaal note' ('6.5 lakh recovered in counterfeit note smuggling'), *Anandabazar Patrika*, 3 July 2019, https://www.anandabazar.com/state/stf-rounded-up-three-ficn-racketeers-in-kolkata-recovered-counterfeit-note-of-6-5-lakh-dgtl-1.1012587 (accessed 9 November 2019).

Staff Correspondent, 'Bharat-Bangladesh shimante udhhar pray 6 koti'r chorai sonar biscuit' ('Gold biscuits worth crores recovered in Indo-Bangla border'), *Anandabazar Patrika*, 25 May 2019, https://www.anandabazar.com/state/dri-seizes-valued-6-crores-of-smuggled-gold-dgtl-1.997170 (accessed 13 November 2019).

Staff Correspondent, 'Sona pachar'e tana hochhe poruader' ('Students are being involved in gold smuggling'), *Anandabazar Patrika*, 26 May 2019, https://www.anandabazar.com/state/smugglers-are-now-using-teenage-school-students-for-smuggling-gold-1.997295 (accessed 14 January 2020).

Straits Times, 'Business boom for gold smuggling in Asia', 9 September 1984.

Straits Times, Indian couriers in gold trade', 14 October 1993.

US Customs and Border Protection (2019) 'Federal authorities, local partners seize 333 pounds of cocaine in shipping container', https://www.cbp.gov/newsroom/local-media-release/federal-authorities-local-partners-seize-333-pounds-cocaine-shipping (accessed 27 June 2019).

Notes on Contributors

Aliyeh Ataei is an Afghanistani-Iranian novelist and screenwriter. She has a Master's degree in theatre from Tehran University. Ataei lives in Tehran and writes for several domestic and international magazines and newspapers. Referred to as 'the writer of the borders', she has received several awards for her works, such as the Mehregan Adab award (one of the most prestigious and noble private literature awards in Iran) for her novel *Kafourpoosh* in 2015. Several of her short stories have been translated and published in English and French. Her recent books are a short story collection, *Cheshm-e Sag* (2019), and a book of essays, *Kor Sorkhi* (2021), both published in Terhan.

Lucie Bacon is a geographer at Migrinter (University of Poitiers) and Telemme (Aix-Marseille University). She is currently working on a PhD thesis entitled *La fabrique du parcours migratoire: La route des Balkans au prisme de la parole des migrants* (The Parcours factory: The Balkan route through the prism of migrants' words). Her work includes critical thinking on the way institutional mapping of migration phenomena masks the diverse range of experience, subjectivity and representation of migrants themselves. She works towards and advocates for cartographic representation that conveys the depth and complexity of migrants' journeys and migration routes.

Kennedy Chikerema is a graduate of the University of Johannesburg's Graduate School of Architecture, where he became keenly interested in the exploration of economic, social, and political aspects that shape modern African cities. His main interest is mobility of people and goods. Through mapping, photography, cross-sectional and axonometric drawing techniques Chikerema demonstrates an understanding of the cross-border trade. His work has been shown at the Venice Biennale in Italy in 2018 and was selected for the 10th Annual International Forum of Urbanism Conference in Hong Kong in 2017. He has also published various other contributions, including to *Architectural Ethnographies*.

Debdatta Chowdhury is an Assistant Professor in Gender Studies at the Centre for Studies in Social Sciences, Calcutta. She earned her doctoral degree from the University of Westminster London (2014), for which she looked at border narratives across the West Bengal-Bangladesh border. Her monograph, titled *Identity and Experience at the India-Bangladesh Border: The Crisis of Belonging*, has been published by Routledge (2018). Her areas of interest include border studies, especially in the context of South Asian borders. She also teaches and researches gender issues, especially at the intersection of caste, ethnicity, and human geography. 'Marginal citizenship' forms the larger thematic in her research concerns.

Rebecca B. Galemba is an Associate Professor at the Josef Korbel School of International Studies and Co-Director of the DU Center for Immigration and Policy Research at the University of Denver. Her research interests include border studies, migration, Latin America, immigration and labour, and informal and illicit economies. Her book, *Contraband Corridor: Making a Living at the Mexico-Guatemala Border*, was published by Stanford University Press in December 2017. The Spanish translation, *La Cadena: Vida y negocio en el límite entre México y Guatemala*, was published by UNAM-CIMSUR in 2021. Her work also appears in anthropological and interdisciplinary journals, including *American Ethnologist*, the *Journal of Ethnic and Migration Studies*, the *Journal of Environment and Planning D: Society and Space*, the *Anthropology of Work Review*, *Political and Legal Anthropology Review*, the *Journal of Latin American and Caribbean Anthropology*, *International Migration Review*, and the *European Journal on Criminal Policy & Research*.

Javier Guerrero-C is a Colombian sociologist. He holds a Master's by Research and a PhD in Science and Technology Studies from the University of Edinburgh (UK). He is currently a lecturer at the Instituto Tecnológico Metropolitano in Medellín, Colombia and postdoctoral researcher at the Centro de Estudios de Seguridad y Drogas (CESED) de la Universidad de los Andes. His research interests focus on the interplay between outlaw innovation, technology and security in the war on drugs.

Simon Harvey is a visual cultures theorist and writer. His research interests include: smuggling and visual culture; new geographies of art practice; counter cartographies; concepts and practices of rhythm; and art and public space. He is the author of *Smuggling: Seven Centuries of Contraband* published by Reaktion Books (2016).

Mahmoud Keshavarz is a Senior Lecturer in Design Studies at the University of Gothenburg and a Research Associate at the Engaging Vulnerability Research Program, Uppsala University, where he holds a Docent in Cultural Anthropology. His work examines intersections between design, anthropology and border politics, and addresses the violent yet imaginative capacities of materialities of (im)mobility. Keshavarz is the author of *The Design Politics of the Passport: Materiality, Immobility, and Dissent* (2019), Co-Editor-in-Chief of the journal *Design and Culture*, as well as a founding member of Decolonizing Design collective and the Critical Border Studies network.

Nichola Khan is Reader in Anthropology and Psychology, and Director of the Centre for Spatial, Environmental and Cultural Politics at the University of Brighton. Her research centres on themes of war, violence, migration, and legacies of British colonialism and empire. She has published numerous articles and four books: *Mohajir Militancy in Pakistan* (Routledge, 2010); *Cityscapes of Violence in Karachi* (Oxford University Press, 2017); *Mental Disorder: Anthropological Insights* (University of Toronto Press, 2017); and *Arc of the Journeyman: Afghan Migrants in England* (University of Minnesota Press, 2020). Currently she is working on a fifth book entitled *The Breath of Empire: Respiratory Legacies and Transgenerational Trauma in Anglo-Chinese Relations*, which builds on research conducted on the Covid-19 pandemic and empire during a Visiting Scholarship at Harvard Medical School. She has also conducted research on migrant health in Europe, and works primarily with anthropological, psychosocial, and literary approaches.

Shahram Khosravi is Professor of Social Anthropology at Stockholm University. His research interests include anthropology of Iran, forced displacement, border studies, and time. Khosravi is the author of several books such as: *The Illegal Traveller: An Auto-ethnography of Borders* (2010); *After Deportation: Ethnographic Perspectives* (2017); and *Waiting: A Project in Conversation* (2021). He has been an active writer in the international press and has also written fiction. He is also cofounder of Critical Border Studies, a network for interaction between scholars, artists and activists.

Craig Martin is Reader in Design Studies at the University of Edinburgh. He is a cultural geographer and design theorist whose research examines the ethics and social complexity of design, including the dissolution of traditional boundaries between good and bad design, as well as licit and illicit forms of social action. He is the author of *Shipping Container* (2016), part of the Object Lessons series by Bloomsbury Academic. *Deviant Design:*

The Ad Hoc, the Illicit, the Controversial, his next book, is forthcoming with Bloomsbury Academic.

Amin Parsa is a Senior Lecturer at the Sociology of Law Department at Lund University in Sweden. Parsa holds a PhD in public international law from Lund University. His research portfolio falls at the intersection of law and technology, the politics of international law and human rights law, the laws of armed conflict, international migration and refugee law as well as media and technology studies.

Nandita Sharma is Professor of sociology at the University of Hawaii at Manoa. She is an activist/scholar who works in No Borders movements and those struggling for a planetary commons. She is, most recently, the author of *Home Rule: National Sovereignty and the Separation of Natives and Migrants* (Duke University Press, 2020).

Tekalign Ayalew Mengiste is Assistant Professor of Social Anthropology in the College of Social Sciences at Addis Ababa University and an affiliated researcher at the Department of Social Anthropology, Stockholm University. His research interests include mobility, the migration industry, transnationalism, and human smuggling. He has published peer-reviewed journal articles and book chapters. His recent publications are 'Refugee protections from below: Smuggling in the Eritrea-Ethiopia context', *ANNALS* (2018), and 'Intensifications of border governance and defiant migration trajectories in Ethiopia', *Geopolitics* (2021).

Index